Russian Cinema

1

1

2012

Inside Film Series

More information can be found at:
www.booksites.net/mclean

RUSSIAN CINEMA

David Gillespie

An imprint of **Pearson Education**

Harlow, England • London • New York • Boston • San Francisco • Toronto
Sydney • Tokyo • Singapore • Hong Kong • Seoul • Taipei • New Delhi
Cape Town • Madrid • Mexico City • Amsterdam • Munich • Paris • Milan

Pearson Education Limited
Edinburgh Gate
Harlow
Essex CM20 2JE
England

and Associated Companies throughout the world

Visit us on the World Wide Web at:
www.pearsoneduc.com

First published 2003
© Pearson Education Limited 2003

ISBN 0 582 43790 3

British Library Cataloguing-in-Publication Data
A catalogue record for this book can be obtained from the British Library

Library of Congress Cataloging-in-Publication Data
   Gillespie, David C.
     Russian cinema / David Gillespie.
       p.   cm. – (Inside film)
     Includes bibliographical references and index.
     ISBN 0-582-43790-3 (pbk.)
       1. Motion pictures–Soviet Union–History.   2. Motion pictures–Russia
   (Federation)–History.   I. Title.   II. Series.
   PN1993.5.R9 G48 2002
   791.43'0947–dc21   2002022859

10   9   8   7   6   5   4   3   2   1
07   06   05   04   03   02

Typeset in 10/13pt Giovanni Book by 35
Printed in China
EPC/01

CONTENTS

PREFACE

This book is not intended as a historical or sociological survey of the Russian film industry or its development. Such studies exist both in English and Russian and exceptional examples can be found in the Bibliography or Further Reading (Taylor, Lawton, Youngblood, Faraday and others). Rather, my intention is to subject Russian film, from its early years to the last years of the twentieth century, to an examination of what I see as its major genres. Historical and political factors are discussed only to the extent to which they impinge on the production and reception of films. Also, although some chapters are arranged chronologically, I do not intend solely to show how genres developed and evolved over the decades, but rather to show the cultural dynamics and aesthetic values that have been major contributing factors to the development and status of Russian cinema.

This, then, is a study of the aesthetics of Russian film examined as cinematic texts, based on the premise that cinema in Russia has always been regarded by its major practitioners as an art form, a continuation of the cultural traditions of nineteenth-century literature and art. The politicians who mostly controlled cinema were also, of course, aware of the potential cinema had for education and political enlightenment (propaganda, for want of another word) and encouraged, coaxed or coerced film-makers into serving the state, although it must be said that most of them were perfectly willing to accede. If an audience can be entertained, it can be educated that much easier.

The book is structured through chapters that explore the different genres of Russian film, although influences and overlaps with films from non-Russian countries of the former Soviet Union are also discussed where relevant (for example, those by the Georgian Tengiz Abuladze and the Georgian–Armenian Sergo Paradzhanov). The aesthetic (i.e. sight and sound) framework is established in the first chapter, then subsequent chapters discuss the role of the literary tradition and adaptation; comedy and the function of laughter and humour; history and the 'destiny' of Russia; women in film (as represented and as representing); shifting ideologies in film; the Russian war film and the changing perception of confrontation and struggle; aspects of private life (personal relationships, youth, town and country living). Inevitably, some films cut across various genres, but cross-referencing has been kept to a minimum for reasons of cohesion. Also, it may surprise some that certain films are omitted from what would seem to be their 'generic' section and discussed elsewhere (the literary adaptations of Nikita Mikhalkov, for instance, are included in terms of their 'ideology'), but I have generally tried to bring out what I perceive to be the most salient aspects of any given film.

The final chapter departs from generic analysis and is devoted to the work of Andrei Tarkovskii, the most important Russian film-maker of the post-Stalin period and possibly the whole of the twentieth century. Tarkovskii embodies the *auteur* principle like no other in Russian film, exploring reality and history through personal memory, perception and experience. An afterword is reserved for films that were *not* made in Soviet times, where 'non-existence' can equally define the nature of cinema as sanctioned 'existence'.

In the course of the work on this book, I have benefited from the comments, advice and practical help of various friends and colleagues. Among them are Wendy Everett, Brian Neve and Ernie Hampson of the University of Bath, Birgit Beumers of the University of Bristol, Steve Hutchings, Peter Barta and Graham Roberts of the University of Surrey and Frank Beardow of the University of Sunderland. Special thanks go to Alex Ballinger of The McLean Press for his unfailing support and enthusiasm. There are over 300 films under discussion; any inaccuracies or misrepresentations remain, of course, the result of my own inattention.

I use the Library of Congress system for the transliteration of Russian names and words. For the sake of simplicity, I have chosen to be consistent: thus Tarkovskii, Paradzhanov, Gorkii and other spellings that may initially seem unfamiliar. However, I have also used commonly preferred spellings of some familiar names: Yeltsin, Chechnya, Yalta. The soft sign has been removed from Russian names (usually indicated in Roman script by ': thus Pyrev, Eldar, Mosfilm and so on) and I have anglicised the Cyrillic 'ks' to 'x' (Alexandrov, Alexei, etc.).

A special word of thanks must go to Natasha and the Annas, for their patience, forbearance and active support throughout the months and years of this project.

Parts of this book have been presented as papers at conferences at the University of Sunderland (literary adaptations, May 2000), the University of Nottingham (laughter and comedy, July 2000), the University of Bangor (history, January 2001), and Oxford Brookes University (the post-Soviet comedy, November 2001). I am most grateful to all colleagues whose comments and suggestions have helped influence its final form.

The book is dedicated to my mother.

LIST OF PHOTOGRAPHS

The sight and sound of Russian film
1. Petr Masokha in *Earth* (Alexander Dovzhenko, 1930) **p.4**

The literary space
2. Valentina Iakunina, Olga Mashnaia and Iana Poplavskaia in *Vassa* (Gleb Panfilov, 1983) **p.14**
3. Vladimir Mashkov and Ingeborga Dapkunaite in *Katia Izmailova* (Valerii Todorovskii, 1994) **p.24**
4. Oleg Menshikov and Sergei Bodrov Jr. in *Prisoner of the Mountains* (Sergei Bodrov Sr., 1996) **p.26**

The Russian film comedy
5. Porfirii Podobed in *Mr West in the Land of the Bolsheviks* (Lev Kuleshov, 1924) **p.38**
6. Rural talent on its way to fame in Moscow in *Volga-Volga* (Grigorii Alexandrov, 1938) **p.41**

The course and curse of history
7. Nonna Mordiukova about to exercise revolutionary justice in *The Commissar* (Alexander Askoldov, 1967) **p.69**
8. Julia Ormond, Richard Harris, Alexei Petrenko and Oleg Menshikov in *The Barber of Siberia* (Nikita Mikhalkov, 1999) **p.76**
9. Mariia Kuznetsova and Leonid Mozgovoi in *Taurus* (Alexander Sokurov, 2000) **p.78**

Women and Russian film
10. Alexander Chistiakov and Vera Baranovskaia in *Mother* (Vsevolod Pudovkin, 1926) **p.85**
11. Renata Litvinova in *Three Stories* (Kira Muratova, 1996) **p.95**

Film and ideology
12. Vitia Kartashov leads collectivisation in *Bezhin Meadow* (Sergei Eisenstein, 1935–7) **p.108**

The Russian war film

Private life and public morality

Autobiography, memory and identity: the films of Andrei Tarkovskii

We are grateful to the following for permission to reproduce copyright material:

Artificial Eye Film Company Ltd for *The Commissar, Farewell, Mirror, Nostalgia* and *The Sacrifice*; Contemporary Films Ltd for *Mother* and *Vassa*; Lenfilm for *Taurus*; Metro Tartan Distribution Ltd for *Prisoner of the Mountains*; Mosfilm for *Bezhin Meadow, The Fall of Berlin, Volga-Volga* and *The White Sun of the Desert*; NTV for *Three Stories*; STV for *The Barber of Siberia* and *Brother*.

All pictures kindly provided by the British Film Institute, The Kobal Collection, David Gillespie and Vitaly Yerenkov. Special thanks go to Vitaly Yerenkov from Kino Kino! and Birgit Beumers for their invaluable assistance in providing images and securing copyright permissions.

Whilst every effort has been made to trace the owners of copyright material, in a few cases this has proved impossible and we would be grateful to hear from anyone with information which would enable us to do so.

CHAPTER ONE

The sight and sound of Russian film

When are we to have music, the Text?

(Barthes, 1977, p. 77)

Cinema has become the dominant art form of the twentieth century and beyond, in Russia as almost everywhere else in the world. Cinema exerts its powerful influence through the twin powers of sight and sound, providing pleasure and stimulation through these most direct of senses. However, Russian cinema has not evolved in a vacuum and the major motifs and values of the 'classical age' of the nineteenth century have very much informed the images and themes developed by Soviet film-makers and which persist to this day.

Russian and European cinema

What is a national cinema? What makes Russian cinema 'national'? What is distinct about Russian cinema and what cultural specifics inform its development? The task of this book is to address these questions and to affirm the aesthetic identity of Russian cinema within the totality of Russian and Soviet cultural discourse. Certain Russian aesthetic values, especially developed in its artistic and literary culture, have been passed down to cinema and have influenced the content and style of a film, so that in dialogical terms film culture has influenced or changed the appreciation of what can be widely termed Russian 'art'.

In the chaos and disruption of post-Soviet Russia, the cinema industry has barely managed to exist, deprived of the state funding it once enjoyed and forced to look to private, occasionally shady, sponsors for resources. As a result, the number of films produced has sharply decreased. Yet those that are made – and some to great international acclaim – reflect a vision of Russia and explore the national experience and collective identity in a manner and style very different even from the cinema of Gorbachev's glasnost a decade earlier. We are used to defining a 'European' cinema as one offering a cultural bulwark against the ever-increasing power of Hollywood, but is Russian cinema, for decades cut off from mainstream discourses, part of the European tradition? Recent attempts to define European cinema have concentrated on Europeans' sense of their own cultural identity and feeling of nationhood:

> *The national question is, of course, more acutely felt by some film-makers than by others, but it is nevertheless a constant of European cinema and it finds a range of expressions. One is the reworking or re-appropriation of genres felt to be typically American, as seen in the Italian spaghetti western, the French crime film or polar, or the German road movie. Another is the attempt to repossess the national history, a particularly acute problem in relation to Germany or Russia.*
>
> *(Forbes and Street, 2000, pp. 40–1)*

Russian cinema can certainly be seen to be part of the European cinematic context in this respect. At the same time it has its own individual identity and ethos, factors driven and informed both by the experience of the last 100 years, but also by perceived 'Russian' cultural values passed down primarily by its literature.

What is striking to the foreign observer of Russian cinema is just how much of it is influenced not so much by currents and ideas from other cinema cultures – given the enforced isolation of most of the Soviet period this lack of penetration is understandable – but rather how many themes are as relevant today as they were over 100 years ago. Russian directors today, just as in the 1920s, see their brief as primarily to educate, not to entertain, and in their aspiration to address the burning issues of the day they resemble their nineteenth-century literary brethren. Many directors and producers in pre-revolutionary cinema saw themselves not only as providing entertainment – they also sought respectability by adapting the literary classics and making films on historical themes.[1] Many of the directors of the 'golden age' (approximately 1924–30) very deliberately set film up as the 'high' art of the Revolution, a highly intellectual medium through which political ideals could be expressed with maximum (i.e. visual) effect. But the Russian artistic heritage passed on not only its own self-importance, but also ideas of historical destiny, the fate of the individual and its great moral questions. Also, it encouraged a feeling for Russia as a country, an almost palpable sense of what Russia looks, feels and smells like, not simply a backdrop for various dramas. Here the role of the landscape, the natural contours of Russia, is highly relevant.

Landscape: art and literature

In his ground-breaking work on art, the natural world and cultural memory, the historian and broadcaster Simon Schama traces the profound fascination held through the centuries by scholars, artists and statesmen for nature's basic components, in particular wood, water and rock. Moreover, this fascination has often been translated into aesthetic ideals or even political manifestos:

> [. . .] It is clear that inherited landscape myths and memories share two characteristics: their surprising endurance through the centuries and the power to shape institutions that we still live with. National identity, to take just the most obvious example, would lose much of its ferocious enchantment without the mystique of a particular landscape tradition: its topography mapped, elaborated, and enriched as a homeland. [. . .] The famous eulogy of the 'sceptred isle', which Shakespeare puts in the mouth of the dying John of Gaunt, invokes cliff-girt insularity as patriotic identity, whereas the heroic destiny of the New World is identified as continental expansiveness in the landscape lyrics of 'America the Beautiful'.
>
> (Schama, 1995, p. 15)

Landscape art is not only visually striking, but also appeals to deeper, emotional notions of home and being. Landscape art constructs certain inescapable cultural concepts:

> Landscape in art tells us, or asks us to think about, where we belong. Important issues of identity and orientation are inseparable from the reading of meanings and the eliciting of pleasure from landscape. The connection between such fundamental issues and our perception of the natural world is a key reason for the proliferation of images of landscape over the last 500 years in the West, and particularly over the last 250 years.
>
> (Andrews, 1999, p. 8)

Landscape in any national cinematic culture is therefore of enormous value, the first point of contact between viewer and director. We know that some of the early pioneers of Soviet film took a great interest in art. Lev Kuleshov's father had dabbled in art and he himself says of his own teenage years:

3

More than anything else the rich, luxuriant, festive and often monumental art of the stage painters Korovin and Golovin imprinted itself on my soul. And I decided to become a theatrical painter. [. . .] Art – the theatre and painting – thrilled me comprehensively and imperiously.

(Kuleshov and Khokhlova, 1975, pp. 16–17)

Kuleshov studied painting privately and his tastes were eclectic, including Gauguin, Van Gogh, Picasso, Toulouse-Lautrec, Renoir, Cézanne, Serov, Vrebel, Korovin and Surikov (Kuleshov and Khokhlova, 1975, p. 20). In other words, Kuleshov entered cinema not through any background in the theatre, as was more common, but through his exposure to art. Alexander Dovzhenko was another who worked in art before entering the cinema. His classic film *Earth* (1930) teems with images of mystical natural beauty and man's place within it and in his writings he picked out the landscapes of Isaak Levitan as being 'artistic, but with their sublime qualities distinct from the ten thousand mediocre things which seemed on the surface similar' (Dovzhenko, 1967, p. 234).[2]

Furthermore, Russian art has a famous landscape tradition, especially in the nineteenth century, but one that transferred into images of natural beauty

Petr Masokha in Earth *(Alexander Dovzhenko, 1930)*

4

concepts of home, identity and patriotism. Soviet critics emphasised the critical realist painting of the Itinerants ('Peredvizhniki') in the late nineteenth and early twentieth centuries, with their emphasis on real people and events and perceived social injustice. The paintings of Repin, Iaroshenko, Makovskii, Maksimov and others produce harsh and vivid images of suffering and dejection and were hailed as being 'progressive' and 'democratic'. However, landscape painting can be seen as a corrective, a move from the harsh social realities towards a more aesthetic, even poetic mainstream. The work and ideas of nineteenth-century landscape artists, such as Levitan, Kuindzhi, Klodt, Shishkin and Kiselev are among the best in the landscape tradition; they convey peace, the harmony of nature and man and the epic greatness of the Russian land, a land where sky and earth meet and both stretch into the distance and eternity. Nature is seemingly alive, trees and grass rustling in the breeze, rivers as the great arteries of Russia.

The great writers of the nineteenth century, such as Pushkin, Lermontov, Tolstoi, Fet, Tiutchev and Turgenev, also expressed their fascination with Russia's natural landscape, as well as that of the outlying reaches of the then Russian empire. Lyrical poems could find contentment in the deep forests or dewy meadows of Mother Russia. Other more adventurous souls would find excitement and awe in the majesty of the Caucasian mountains, the place where European Russia ends and the great unknown of Asia begins. As the century ends, nature comes under threat as Chekhov's cherry orchard is cut down and the urge to modernise takes over.

Landscape and film

There is ample cinematic evidence, from the 1920s to the post-Soviet period, to affirm that Russian and Soviet directors imbued natural images with the symbolic significance explored by their cultural ancestors. [3] Dovzhenko's sky canvases of the 1920s speak of majesty and grandeur and of the essential unity of nature and man. A decade or two later, the bright, summer vistas of rural Russia, with sun-baked fields and gently winding rivers viewed from above, paraded before us in 'optimistic' comedies, speak of the greatness of Russia and its true blossoming under the benevolent eye of Iosif Stalin. Alexandrov's *Volga-Volga* (1938) can be seen as a cinematic extension of Levitan's Volga, for here, in Stalin's Russia, the Volga leads inexorably to the centre of power, Moscow, where true achievement can be attained and recognised.

A more revisionist slant on the river-as-history theme could be possible only after the death of Stalin. Mikhail Kalatozov's *Loyal Friends* (1954) sees three old friends rediscover their childhood values and friendship via a raft trip down the Iauza river. In the 1970s and early 1980s rural Russia became idealised as the repository of values seen as being lost in the drive toward modernity. Books as well as films were directed at what Kathleen Parthé calls 'time backward': the reverse flow whereby the passing of time and the ebbing away of old values signify the death of a way of life deeply connected with the natural world (Parthé, 1992, pp. 48–63).

What is interesting about the role of cultural memory in the development of Russian art, and in particular film, is that the move away from nature – urbanisation, collectivisation – has been viewed negatively, as the loss of true Russia, its age-old value systems and its very identity. Constructivism was hailed as the perfect blending of man and technology, the control and utilisation of space, for the machine age that beckoned in the 1920s, but 'time, forward!' became the somewhat forlorn and discredited slogan from the 1960s onwards. Progress, in the form of electricity, unites the country, closes down the otherwise indomitable expanse of Russia, but it is resisted by the anti-rational, anti-modern forces in Russia in the latter half of the twentieth century.

The natural expanse, contours and topography of Russia thus offer a cultural space for the articulation of myths and ideologies. Landscape becomes ideological. Russian film-makers, like its writers, work within traditions established by their cultural antecedents, most notably in the nineteenth century, and can even reproduce these same images directly.[4]

The sound of music

With the coming of sound some of the most innovative Soviet directors (Eisenstein and Pudovkin, for instance) developed ideas to make sound and music more than simply a backdrop to the narrative of a film. The exalted perception of film art can be exemplified by its heavy reliance on classical music from the early years of sound onwards and both Dmitrii Shostakovich and Sergei Prokofev wrote much film music in the 1930s and 1940s. Shostakovich worked for Grigorii Kozintsev from the 1920s, with *New Babylon* (1929), through to *Hamlet* (1964) and *King Lear* (1971). He provided the score for the 'Maxim Trilogy', directed by Kozintsev and Trauberg between 1934 and 1938, Mikhail Chiaureli's *The Fall of Berlin* (1949) and Alexandrov's *The Meeting on the Elbe* the same year. The music of Sergei Prokofev, in particular, offers not only heightened background, but is also part of filmic narrative in these and succeeding years, aiding thematic development and characterisation. (The collaboration of Prokofev and Eisenstein will be examined in Chapter Four.) The use of music, and not only Prokofev's, in films of the 1930s was all the more innovative in that it became part of the diegesis, whether it be songs sung by the working class (as in the 'Maxim

Trilogy' for instance) or lyrical ballads (*Lieutenant Kizhe*, 1934). The composer Alfred Shnittke wrote music for dozens of films in the 1970s, providing scores that he would later rework into symphonies (Klimov's 1975 film *Agony* is perhaps his most famous contribution) and receiving a regular income at a time when his innovative and iconoclastic use of rhythm and harmony was disowned by a conservative musical establishment.

The early years of music in Soviet cinema were dominated by the Stalinist musical, otherwise known as the 'musical comedy', especially those directed by Grigorii Alexandrov and Ivan Pyrev, and these will be discussed in detail in Chapter Three. Russian film has also been fascinated with popular music, the music of the people, since the earliest years of sound. Furthermore, popular music has been consistently foregrounded, assisting the construction of narrative and meaning and so, like landscape, is invested with a cultural and ideological value. In Western, and especially Anglo-American, cinemas music and popular song are highly effective in conveying nostalgia and loss. This is particularly true in autobiographical films where the viewer can recognise a particular tune or melody that will be rich in association or arouse memories of times past (Everett, 2000).

Russia is probably unique within European film cultures in foregrounding popular song. The songs and guitar accompaniment that punctuate the 'Maxim Trilogy' of Kozintsev and Trauberg are memorable and performed with gusto (especially by Mikhail Zharov), but they also serve an ideological purpose. They affirm the legitimacy of working-class culture and help reclaim the Revolution for the Russian proletariat. The audience, therefore, not only sees the workers' cause triumphant, but hears it being celebrated.

Folk themes, guitar and balalaika music in particular, characterise films of the 1960s and 1970s that exercised an emotional and patriotic pull, especially films about village life. Traditional motifs mark Nikolai Moskalenko's *Russian Field* (1971) from the outset. Set against a narrative about emotional dramas in the countryside and a foreign threat to invade the Soviet Union, there are seemingly endless shots of the Russian countryside, a never-ending panorama of rivers, fields, trees and sky, the natural contours of the land underscored by its geopolitical importance. These shots of Mother Russia are invariably accompanied by angelic chorals or balalaika strings. The patriotic theme (the screenplay was written by arch-conservative Mikhail Alexeev) is thus expressed threefold: by the visual splendour of the rural landscape, the flag-waving heroics of the Soviet military and a pseudo-folkloric soundtrack.

Folk music, sanitised or otherwise, is used to different effect by Vasilii Shukshin. His 1969 film *Your Son and Brother* opens with romantic orchestral strings accompanying shots of a river in spring, ice floes heralding the release of nature from the icy grip of a long winter. Folk music follows shots of women, birds and the natural world in a hymn to the unity of man and nature. These first few minutes are filmed as slice-of-life documentary, before any dialogue or narrative development: real life, or at least as the director wishes us to see it.

Shukshin's film celebrates the Russian man's natural link with his land, his home and his roots. The diegetic use of folk music, accordion, humorous *chastushki* (folk ditties, usually suggestive) and dancing help construct a picture of the essential simplicity and honesty of life in rural Russia, a place where girls wear white that is sharply at odds with the impersonality and frayed relationships of city life (characterized by a jazz cacophony). Water flows, life goes on and orchestral strings play.

Shukshin continues to construct this rural idyll in his later films. *Happy Go Lucky* (1972) begins with soft balalaika strings and a shot of the actor–director Shukshin filmed against rolling fields, a scythe in his hand as in the Russia of old. This is a world outside time, where even horses are preferred to cars as transport. Accordion, folk song and dance are all set against a backdrop of fields, river and sky in a celebration of the vastness of Russia. Shukshin's most famous film, *Red Guelder Rose*, which opened in early 1974 just a few months before he died at the age of 45, continues and develops this picture of a mythical Russia. The film has been described as 'not so much a movie as a melody', part of the actor–writer–director's 'synthetic thinking' where he can 'weave seamlessly various media – words, sounds, images, music – into one meaningful whole' (Givens, 1999, pp. 273–4). The film's music is a mixture of traditional folk song, modern folk stylisations, balalaika strings, popular song, band music and criminal song, all serving to highlight the contrast of town and country and the consequent reflection on the historical destiny of Russia, as the hero–martyr is carried to heaven accompanied by an angelic chorus.

Urban song is characterised by the bards, the phenomenally popular 'guitar poets' of the 1960s and 1970s. Vladimir Vysotskii (1938–80) is given several opportunities in films of the 1960s and 1970s to perform his own songs on screen, so giving Soviet cinema audiences a tantalising glimpse of a talent that was subjected to official restrictions (for instance, in Kira Muratova's *Brief Meetings* of 1967 and Iosif Kheifits's *My Only One* of 1975). Another guitar poet, Bulat Okudzhava (1924–2000), provided 'Your Honour, Madam Separation' ('Vashe blagorodie, gospozha razluka') for the extremely popular film *The White Sun of the Desert*, directed by Vladimir Motyl in 1969. Set in the blisteringly hot Central Asian desert during the Civil War, the film is about the Red Army officer Sukhov ('dry') liberating the harem of the local bey, Abdullah, and the soft guitar strings and sentimental lyrics offer a warm and comforting counterpoint to the aridness of the landscape. Okudzhava's song dislocates the narrative by removing it both in time and place: from the sun-baked deserts of Central Asia to the cultural metropolis of Russia, and from the Civil War to the Brezhnev period. Okudzhava also provided the music for another very popular film, *Belorussian Station* (1970), another exercise in nostalgia and loss.

A word should be reserved for the avant-garde, occasionally brilliantly evocative themes of Eduard Artemev that make use of Russian and Western sources (there is more than a hint of Pink Floyd in some of his scores). In Tarkovskii's films the electronic music adds an extra futuristic dimension to subject matter that is part allegory, part philosophical treatise and part existential despair.[5]

In short, music has been used by Russian film-makers not only as background, to heighten mood and sharpen emotional appreciation, but also within the diegesis and as an aid to characterisation and narrative commentary. Many films of the post-Soviet period have increasingly looked abroad for their creative inspiration, in an appeal to a youth audience that enjoys more exposure to Western culture than their parents ever did. The pulsating rock score of Balabanov's *The Brother* (1997) and its sequel *The Brother 2* (2000) is not only backdrop, but also maintains the excitement and tension of the narrative with its energetic drive and is even diegetic: the personal CD player saves Danila's life when it is hit by a bullet aimed at his chest. This use of rock music clearly emulates Western models (Tarantino's 1994 film *Pulp Fiction*, for instance), but it is above all *Russian* rock music, enhancing the nationalistic hubris of the *Brother* films.

Russian film, be it pre-Soviet, Soviet or post-Soviet, has its own cultural traditions and context. Directors have consistently seen themselves as part of an elevated national tradition, viewing film above all as an art form and seeing their professional task as one of education and the inculcation of moral values. They have done this through increased attention to both the sight and sound of their films.

Filmography

Agony ('Agoniia'), dir. Elem Klimov, 1975
Belorussian Station ('Belorusskii vokzal'), dir. Andrei Smirnov, 1970
Brief Meetings ('Korotkie vstrechi'), dir. Kira Muratova, 1967
The Brother ('Brat'), dir. Alexei Balabanov, 1997
The Brother 2 ('Brat 2'), dir. Alexei Balabanov, 2000
Earth ('Zemlia'), dir. Alexander Dovzhenko, 1930
The Fall of Berlin ('Padenie Berlina'), dir. Mikhail Chiaureli, 1949
Hamlet ('Gamlet'), dir. Grigorii Kozintsev, 1964
Happy Go Lucky ('Pechki-lavochki'), dir. Vasilii Shukshin, 1972
King Lear ('Korol Lir'), dir. Grigorii Kozintsev, 1971

Lieutenant Kizhe ('Poruchik Kizhe'), dir. Alexander Faintsimmer, 1934

Loyal Friends ('Vernye druzia'), dir. Mikhail Kalatozov, 1954

Maxim's Youth ('Iunost Maksima'), dir. Grigorii Kozintsev and Leonid Trauberg, 1934

The Meeting on the Elbe ('Vstrecha na Elbe'), dir. Grigorii Alexandrov, 1949

My Only One ('Edinstvennaia . . .'), dir. Iosif Kheifits, 1975

New Babylon ('Novyi Vavilon'), dir. Grigorii Kozintsev and Leonid Trauberg, 1929

Pulp Fiction, dir. Quentin Tarantino, 1994

Red Guelder Rose ('Kalina krasnaia'), dir. Vasilii Shukshin, 1974

The Return of Maxim ('Vozvrashchenie Maksima'), dir. Grigorii Kozintsev and Leonid Trauberg, 1937

Russian Field ('Russkoe pole'), dir. Nikolai Moskalenko, 1971

Volga-Volga, dir. Grigorii Alexandrov, 1938

The Vyborg Side ('Vyborgskaia storona'), dir. Grigorii Kozintsev and Leonid Trauberg, 1938

The White Sun of the Desert ('Beloe solntse pustyni'), dir. Vladimir Motyl, 1969

Your Son and Brother ('Vash syn i brat'), dir. Vasilii Shukshin, 1969

Notes

1. Denise J. Youngblood (1999) provides an excellent survey and analysis of pre-1917 cinema; on historical films and literary adaptations, see pp. 115–27.

2. Dovzhenko's contemporary Grigorii Kozintsev said that Dovzhenko's perception of the natural world was 'not that of the landowner, not even that of the artist, but that of the people', in that it was 'pantheistic, mythological nature'. Dovzhenko's natural world was 'without the fear of the elements, it was kind and wise'. (See Kozintsev (1983), II, 420.)

3. See, for instance, the brash and self-confident 1922 declaration of 'Eccentrism' by the Petrograd-based FEKS group (consisting of Grigorii Kozintsev, Leonid Trauberg, Sergei Iutkevich and Georgii Kryzhitskii). They may announce that 'the old painting is dead', but nevertheless admit their debt to pre-existing visual forms: 'From Cézanne to Picasso – the materialisation of the subject. Still lifes, landscapes, copying of signs, imitating raw materials, pasting objects on the surface of the brush. Pictures do not exist – it is angles, movements, subjects and colour that hit you from the frame.' (See Christie and Taylor (eds) (1994), p. 62.) Sergei Eisenstein would go on to express his admiration for the landscapes of Repin and Ivan Surikov, among others; see his speech 'The Problems of the Soviet Historical Film', in Taylor (ed.) (1998), p. 154.

4. As a final statement on the influence of art on film, it is interesting to note that the dress and physical appearance of Tsar Alexander III in Nikita Mikhalkov's *The Barber of Siberia* (1999), played by Mikhalkov himself, are almost identical to the Tsar as painted by Ilia Repin in his 'Reception of the Volost Foremen by Tsar Alexander III' (1884–5), as exhibited in the Moscow Tretiakov Gallery.

5. Vida T. Johnson and Graham Petrie note that in *Solaris*: 'The electronic sounds were used as reminders of the alien setting of the space station, while costumes, sets, dialogue and action reinforced the characters' inescapable links to earth.' For *Stalker* Tarkovskii rejected Artemev's first soundtrack, 'even though Artemev thought he had achieved the synthesis of Eastern and Western cultures that they had discussed as an intellectual framework for the film as a whole (he had taken a medieval tune and rescored it for Eastern intruments) . . . Finally, Artemev took one note of Indian music and then reworked it electronically.' (See Johnson and Petrie (1994), p. 57.)

CHAPTER TWO

The literary space

Theatre is 'seeming' whereas cinema is 'being'.

(Room, 1994, p. 128)

Screen 'translations' of works from literature have always been popular in cinema industries throughout the world and some of the world's greatest films have been based on literary works, novels in particular. The director looking to adapt a work of literature is faced with a similar dilemma to that of the maker of historical films: how faithful should he remain to the original material and how much should he 'update' it or make it relevant to a contemporary audience? Just how much does 'adaptation' actually depart from the text and is that, indeed, a good thing or not? Certainly, the enthusiasm with which early directors adapted works from the classical canon – Pushkin's *The Queen of Spades* (two versions: 1910 and 1916) and *The Stationmaster* (1918), Dostoevskii's *The Idiot* (1910), Tolstoi's *Father Sergius* (1917), to name but a few – testifies to the strong desire to make film more varied and challenging. Not only did these adaptations make the classics more accessible to the largely illiterate population, they also gave the new medium some measure of intellectual respectability.

When speaking of Soviet film, however, we are presented with a different set of problems and criteria. In adapting literary works for the screen, especially those from the pre-revolutionary past, directors were encouraged, indeed required, to add an ideological gloss to the finished cinematic product. Literature, even the classics, had to bear a clear political message.

Literature as film art

Before the Revolution, literary adaptations not only 'may have served an educational function of introducing less cultured audiences to the importance of these artistic monuments', but the best of them 'made a genuine contribution to the evolution of Russian film art' (Youngblood, 1999, p. 127).

Iakov Protazanov's *Father Sergius* (1917) is a case in point. Ivan Mozzhukhin (known as 'Mosjoukine' after his emigration in 1920) plays Prince Kasatskii, who enters a monastery on hearing on the eve of his wedding that his fiancée is mistress to the Tsar himself. He solemnly obeys his vows of chastity until tempted by a young woman who is lost and begs to stay the night. In order to mortify his own flesh, he chops off a finger. Years later, he finally succumbs to the advances of another woman, leaves the monastery in self-disgust and is arrested by the police for not having a passport and sentenced to Siberia. The film has very high production values, with a cast of hundreds at the Tsar's ball dancing the *mazurka* and extremely detailed and opulent costumes. There are also free-flowing moments of alcoholic and sensual abandon and much erotic (not to say Freudian) suggestiveness. Mozzhukhin also manages to portray a man tormented by both fate and his own inner demons ('the struggle between the spirit and the flesh', as the intertitles explain), a hapless figure unable to avoid destitution and despondency. *Father Sergius* was remade in 1978 with a wooden Sergei Bondarchuk in the title role and the emphasis very much on the sensual temptations testing the monk's faith. Thus, in ideology-speak, the hidden depravity of organised religion, and the hypocrisy of its practitioners, are amply demonstrated.

Given that film in Russia is high art, it is not surprising that the major writers of the nineteenth century have been accorded special attention: Tolstoi, Pushkin, Turgenev, Gogol, Alexander Ostrovskii, Lermontov and Chekhov have all been well served. A detailed list of adaptations is included in the filmography at the end of this chapter. Despite the reverence of directors towards the source material, most of these films remain simply filmic versions of the literary original, essentially theatrical and without much significant cinematic imagination and with few allowances made for a cinema audience.

A film with a definite contemporary resonance is Gleb Panfilov's *Vassa* (1983), based on the 1910 play *Vassa Zheleznova* by Maxim Gorkii. It is about a capitalist family faced with collapse and the efforts of the matriarch to keep it together. Despite a realistic portrayal of family life at the turn of the century and a powerful performance by Inna Churikova in the title role, the film, like the play, symbolizes the inner corruption and eventual demise of capitalism in Russia in the early twentieth century. It thus conforms to the prevailing ideological demands of the Soviet era, although it also plays to contemporary, that is, early 1980s', debates about the role and place of women as professional workers or domestic drudges.

Other adaptations similarly tried to update the literary material. In 1969 Andrei Mikhalkov-Konchalovskii filmed Turgenev's second novel, *A Nest of*

Valentina Iakunina, Olga Mashnaia and Iana Poplavskaia in Vassa *(Gleb Panfilov, 1983)*

Gentlefolk, which had been written in 1859. While sticking close to Turgenev's story of doomed love between Lavretskii, the Russian literary 'superfluous man' of wit and talent who can find no real fulfilment in society, and the moral and incorruptible young girl Liza, Mikhalkov-Konchalovskii allows his camera to sweep across great vistas and panoramas of an unspoilt Russian countryside and his depiction of male–female relationships has a palpable and quite daring eroticism. His *Uncle Vania* a year later featured some of the great actors of the day, including Innokentii Smoktunovskii, Sergei Bondarchuk, a young Irina Kupchenko and Vladimir Zeldin. It concentrates on the interaction of various characters and is predominantly shot indoors, with brooding passions and unresolved personal dilemmas. The film won considerable international acclaim.

The very existence of all these adaptations, which continue into the post-Soviet age, is clear evidence of the abiding love Russian film-makers have for their literary heritage. Moreover, literary adaptation can very often overlap as costume drama. Directors, as a general rule, have remained faithful to the plot, characterisation and even dialogue of the literary original, but there are some adaptations that are bold, innovative and distinguished.

Chapaev

The model of the Soviet art of adaptation was established in the 'golden age' by Vsevolod Pudovkin in his film of Gorkii's novel *Mother* (see Chapter 5) and Grigorii Kozintsev and Leonid Trauberg with their 1926 adaptation of Gogol's *The Overcoat*, with its self-conscious use of silhouette and shadow. Pudovkin's didacticism and obvious symbolism, and the startling cinematic images and powerful narrative development of both films, have left them as much emulated and widely admired classics of the genre. One of the most popular adaptations, however, is that by Sergei and Georgii Vasilev of Dmitrii Furmanov's novel *Chapaev*, made in 1934.

Furmanov's novel was first published in 1923. The author had served as political commissar in the 24th division of the Fourth Army, led by Vasilii Ivanovich Chapaev, a former peasant, in 1919, then fighting on the Eastern front. In the novel Furmanov, who died in 1926 aged 34, depicts Chapaev as a decisive man of action, a true hero loved and respected by his men and a dashing and fearless commander. Chapaev is, in Furmanov's account, a living legend:

> *His soldiers regarded him as the embodiment of heroism, although, as you see, there was nothing exclusively heroic as yet in his actions: what he did personally many others also did, but what these many others did no-one knew about, whereas what Chapaev did everyone knew about, minutely, with embellishments, with legendary details, with fabulous inventions.*

> *(Furmanov, 1966, p. 201)*

Furmanov's novel was one of the first to establish the Civil War hero as the 'positive hero', one of the key features of socialist realism that was to become enshrined in the early 1930s. Katerina Clark has clearly located the interaction of the two central characters within the 'spontaneity/consciousness' dialectic:

> *Klychkov, an educated, selfless working-class Party official, is the more solid, 'conscious' and efficient leader, less dashing than Chapaev but more reliable and, ultimately, more valuable. Chapaev, by contrast, is a semiliterate peasant leader and is quite explicitly identified as an example of the traditional 'spontaneity' of the peasant rebel, the* buntar'. *He is a Party member but is very confused about its ideology and its policies, is anarchic, self-seeking, and impetuous as a commander, and is a mob orator who can only speak illogically, 'from the heart'.*

> *(Clark, 2000, p. 85)*

Thus, in the course of the novel Chapaev, under the guidance of his political commissar Klychkov (who represents Furmanov himself), becomes increasingly aware of the greater struggle going on in society, beyond the next battle that he is involved in. It is for this struggle that he eventually becomes a martyr. Klychkov, too, learns from Chapaev that revolutions cannot be won through ideas alone and that emotions and quick thinking are just as important.

The Vasilevs' film stars the then relatively unknown Boris Babochkin in the central role, a role that was to make him famous. Babochkin did relatively little subsequently and would not achieve the same heights. His Chapaev is, like Furmanov's, a legendary hero, a man of the people, a man of energy and great drive. Babochkin's sheer physical presence adds to the sense of the man's raw power. But the role of political mentor is muted and he is absent in the second half of the film. Once Furmanov (the name reverts to the author of the novel) has impressed on Chapaev the need for discipline and reflection on the wider issues, he disappears from the action and the rest of the film concentrates on Chapaev's relationship with his acolyte Petka Isaev. The final scene when both are killed is melodramatic and powerful, given a tragic dimension by the sentimental musical score.

The film may have been made like a Hollywood Western, with suitably villainous bad guys and the cavalry coming over the hill at the end to defeat the Whites, but it was also a great critical success. The Party newspaper in November of that year proclaimed that 'the whole country will watch *Chapaev*'.[1] The film, probably more than the book, served to create the first real Soviet martyr–hero and in the visually exciting context of the Civil War showed 'the whole country' just what it was that people had fought and died for over a decade earlier.

Two films: *The Lady with the Lapdog* and *War and Peace*

It is to be expected that film versions of post-1917 literature, especially those conforming to the dictates of socialist realism, would remain faithful to the plot and ideological thrust of the original. What is of more interest is the way in which directors can add their own ideological glosses to pre-1917 literary works, thus giving these film versions a socio-political slant missing in the literary original. By way of example, Alexander Ivanovskii's 1935 film of Pushkin's (unfinished) novella *Dubrovskii* shows the peasant masses joining Dubrovskii's revolt against the tyrannical landowner Troekurov and even after the death of the hero they continue their revolt and right social wrongs. Pushkin is hijacked by Stalinist ideology, for in the original Dubrovskii does not die but flees abroad and after his disappearance the looting stops.

Similarly, *The Lady with the Lapdog* (1960) 'transfers' Chekhov's 1899 drama with great fidelity and is distinguished by the excellent playing of the two leads (Iia Savvina and Alexei Batalov). On the one hand, the peaceful, lyrical pacing, gentle musical score and the evocative Crimean setting help vividly recreate Chekhov's sardonic picture of the complexities of relationships for a modern audience. On the other, in certain background scenes the film serves up a depressing picture of the social ills (poverty, despair, moral corruption of the upper classes) of *fin-de-siècle* Russia. Kheifits's film, despite its closeness to Chekhov's text (right down to the dialogue), adds its own critical gloss to its depiction of Tsarist society, so that the old world is portrayed as morally redundant, beset by intractable social problems and, therefore, ultimately doomed.

The most celebrated adaptation of Russian literature is Sergei Bondarchuk's seven-hour, four-part *War and Peace*, made between 1965 and 1967. Sergei Gerasimov had adapted *Quiet Flows the Don* as an epic panorama in three parts a decade earlier (1957–8), with larger than life characters and heightened tension throughout. Bondarchuk's film is even grander, with a huge cast of characters (120,000 extras) and a broad sweep of both land and history. Tolstoi's novel covers the years 1805 to 1812, culminating in the Battle of Borodino and Napoleon's long wintry retreat from Russia. Within this historical canvas are interwoven the lives of fictional characters: Natasha Rostova, Pierre Bezukhov, Andrei Bolkonskii and dozens, if not hundreds, of minor or secondary characters, ranging from Napoleon himself to the resigned and wise peasant Platon Karataev.

Bondarchuk remains faithful to the essential grandness of Tolstoi's concept. The film opens and ends with aerial tracking shots of the Russian countryside, accompanied by suitably patriotic music. Certainly, production values are high, with costumes, interiors and external locations all appearing authentic. In peacetime, balls are attended by hundreds of guests. Battles, too, are fought out with thousands of extras and the director comes close to expressing Tolstoi's views on war by combining aerial shots of troop movements with a sure feel for combat as experienced at close hand. The sheer disorientation and devastation of a battlefield is convincingly evoked. But Bondarchuk also reproduces whole dialogues from the novel and often these are treated theatrically, with no sense of cinematic economy. The constant use of a voice-over that informs the viewer of the significance of events taking place on the screen reminds us that we are in the presence of 'great art'.

The film's theme, however, is not merely literary, but also patriotic. Russian troops are filmed against the backdrop of a church, with choral and orchestral music accompanying their efforts and it is the efforts of true, simple Russians that defeat Napoleon. Natasha Rostova is at one with her people, instinctively responding to balalaika music and her dancing watched approvingly by peasant women. Moscow is the 'holy capital', Russia is invaded not just by the French, but by 'the forces of Western Europe'.

The sheer scale aside, this is an uneven film, with most cinematic time given to Natasha Rostova, Pierre and Andrei Bolkonskii and lesser characters such as Anatole Kuragin and Nikolai Rostov underdeveloped. Furthermore, there are ideological touches, as in Kheifits's film. Russian and Austrian soldiers (but not their officers) show proletarian-like solidarity before the battle of Austerlitz and there is no mention in the film of Pierre's early dalliance with free-masonry, as if contact with a foreign creed might erode some of his Russianness – his Christian name notwithstanding. Bondarchuk's *War and Peace* contains some of the most thrilling and large-scale battle scenes ever filmed, but it remains a paeon to Russian military might and the strength of the Russian 'soul'.

Tolstoi or Dostoevskii?

The 1960s in particular saw the 'epics' of the nineteenth century given lavish screen treatment, film versions generally stretching to several hours: Dostoevskii's *Crime and Punishment* (1969), *The Idiot* (1958) and *The Brothers Karamazov* (1968). Tolstoi's *Resurrection* appeared in 1961. This novel was written in 1899, a stinging attack on the corruption of the upper classes and the inadequacies of the Russian legal system that sees a young prostitute sent to prison, then to Siberia. The film has even been seen allegorically, given that it was made during Khrushchev's de-Stalinisation policy. The director Alexander Mitta comments: 'And the staggering scenes in prison and the journey to hard labour in *Resurrection*? For the first time on the screen Russian lawlessness cried out so openly and furiously' (Mitta, 2000, p. 14). Soviet audiences would have had no difficulty in seeing the disconcerting parallels with the recent Stalinist past.

Still, even in such films the ideology is not far from the surface. Ivan Pyrev's *The Brothers Karamazov* makes no mention of the uplifting theme of children and the future with which Dostoevskii ends his novel, thereby adding to the feeling of gloom and hopelessness in pre-revolutionary Russia.

Nevertheless, these films appeared during what came to be called 'developed' or 'advanced' socialism, a term used to characterize the Brezhnev era that was supposedly a half-way house between socialism and communism, when the state was encouraging an upbeat, self-confident and occasionally aggressive foreign and domestic policy. These films were addressing a Russian audience, however, with the clear message, and a particularly Russian nineteenth-century one, that man was inwardly torn by doubt, failing to accomplish anything in life other than the destruction of that which he held dear. This reminder from Russia's literary past, or rather a continuing paradigm of beauty subverted and destroyed by evil, served to undermine the positivist ethos of the times.

Under the new freedoms of Gorbachev's glasnost directors were able to be bolder and show more scope for innovation in their films and their treatment of classical Russian literature gave them new, censorship-free possibilities. Mikhail Shveitser's 1987 film of Tolstoi's 1890 novella *The Kreutzer Sonata* offered a faithful rendering of the original plot, a harrowing and unflinching record of domestic violence in a loveless marriage and a powerful depiction of sexual jealousy, with careful attention to period detail. Shveitser's film also contains a relatively honest discussion of homosexuality, amounting to a call for its legalisation in the USSR (it was illegal until post-Soviet times). The film also challenged linguistic taboos by including a spoken obscenity (also contained in the original text) meant to be plainly heard by the audience. This scene provoked gasps of shock and outrage all round the cinema I watched it in on its release.

Adapting foreign classics

The best cinematic adaptations of foreign literature are arguably those of Grigorii Kozintsev. Kozintsev directed three films towards the end of his career that will probably account for the greatness of his reputation more than his socialist realist classics of the 1930s. These are *Don Quixote* (1957), with Nikolai Cherkasov in the title role, *Hamlet* (1964), starring Innokentii Smoktunovskii and *King Lear*, his last film in 1971, with Iuri Narvet as the king. All are memorable films in their own right and all feature powerful performances from the leading classical actors of the day. They all also tell us much about Soviet aesthetic values in the translation of foreign classics.

It is significant that for both *Hamlet* and *King Lear*, Kozintsev uses the Russian translations of Boris Pasternak. Pasternak spent much of the late 1940s and early 1950s working on translations of many of Shakespeare's plays (as well as Goethe's *Faust* and Schiller's *Maria Stuart*) and these renderings are still today considered to be masterpieces of poetic translation. This is all the more important in that in Pasternak's novel *Doctor Zhivago* (1957) the figure of Hamlet looms large. *Hamlet* is also the title of one of Pasternak's most famous poems. It was included in the novel as one of Zhivago's compositions. Pasternak's Hamlet is a man driven by destiny and forced by his times to play the role of Christ: thus is he immortalised in the hearts of others. It should also be pointed out that Pasternak translated Shakespeare's seventeenth-century English into twentieth-century colloquial Russian, thus making the language immediately accessible and comprehensible to a modern Russian audience.

Kozintsev's *Hamlet* impresses with its epic sweep, as much of the film is shot from a ground-level camera, giving both characters and architecture impressive stature. Elsinore is situated amid forbidding cliffs and battered by crashing waves, with massive portcullises and looming shadows. The ghost appears on the battlements as a physically huge presence, enveloped by a billowing cloak that seems to reach right out to the sea. This is a world that is doomed and the film is above all about corruption, betrayal and death. By ideological analogy this is the death of the old, aristocractic ways, the sweeping away of an outmoded order with Hamlet as the agent of social change. Innocence, in the form of Ophelia, is humbled, ridiculed and ultimately destroyed. Even her father Polonius connives in this as he uses her in order to find out more about Hamlet. Claudius is an unremittingly black villain, without the hint of remorse that Shakespeare suggests.

But the film, like the play, hinges on the character of Hamlet, who has much of the 'positive hero' about him. He is aware of the baseness of the world ('an unweeded garden') before he learns from the ghost of the circumstances of his father's death. Subsequently he becomes a resolute man of action, a solemn and focused righter of wrongs. Significantly, therefore, the 'to be or not to be' speech is not actually spoken by Hamlet; it is Hamlet's internal monologue used to justify his course of action. Not for him self-doubt and vacillation, but rather active resistance to tyranny and evil. Although Hamlet dies in the end, he is identified with social renewal, as he does away with a corrupt and decadent order that can be identified with feudalism.

Kozintsev brings to bear a few ideas of his own, none of which detracts from the film's impeccable ideological credentials. First, is Hamlet mad? Certainly, his hysterical laughter resounds through the corridors of Elsinore. It is his erstwhile friend Horatio, the only major character left alive at the end of the play, who instils in his grieving mind the idea of the ghost, and no one else sees the ghost apart from Horatio and his confederates (and all in the presence of Hamlet). Tellingly, the ghost does not make its second appearance in Gertrude's bedroom, neither does it speak again, as it does in the play. Is the ghost not simply an invention of Hamlet's troubled mind, put there by a scheming Horatio? Second, the anti-imperial theme is given an airing, with emphasis given to the Norwegian captain's words on the futility of invading a foreign land.

The class-based conflict of *Hamlet* is developed further in *King Lear*. If Kozintsev's Hamlet embodied the ultimately victorious forces of history and progress, here the director's emphasis is on the wronged hero's identification with his people. From the earliest shots in the film, the masses are portrayed in their silent suffering, victims of internecine strife and foreign invasion, their miserable lot made even worse by the court intrigues set in motion by Lear's division of his kingdom among his daughters and his rejection of Cordelia. The apocalyptic nature of the imagery in *Hamlet* gives way here to shots of wolves and rapacious dogs, symbolic of the greed and ruthlessness of the court. Significantly, Lear's redemption comes not through his madness, but rather through the reassertion of his link with the suffering people, first, in the hovel as he shelters from the storm and then in the final battle as he and Cordelia are captured. Only the Fool is left alive, alone and grieving in a devastated world. Kozintsev's *King Lear* treats the Shakespearean drama of madness, blindness, betrayal and death as a political conflict. Even Edgar, eventually victorious, is fired to bring about justice and peace not by the sight of his blinded father, but rather by the suffering refugees fleeing from war. Lear and Cordelia are captured as they are with their people and when they are both buried, the people come out in force to salute them.

It should be added that in purely aesthetic terms both films are magnificent, with the landscape and architecture given epic dimensions. However, these films are linked by their emphasis on madness and the destruction of peace and stability. The theme of madness is also in evidence in Kozintsev's adaptation of *Don Quixote*, although this time given an overt comic and satirical slant.

Cervantes' picaresque novel is presented as a mixture of burlesque and political satire, as the Knight of the Sad Countenance sees himself as the righter of social wrongs, the defender of the weak and oppressed. But he eventually achieves nothing and his help is spurned by all. His naivety and innocence are seen as a threat by the ruling aristocracy and church and the Duke himself says that Quixote's purity, loyalty and virtuous acts are comical, his notion of love is a mere figment of a fevered imagination. Sancho's brief reign as governor brings about a measure of justice based on sheer common sense and decency, but when he is evicted from his temporary grandeur he reveals social and political awareness of his environment. He attacks the aristocratic lackeys as 'parasites' and affirms his own identity as one of the simple, working people.

Cervantes' novel intends to ridicule and satirise the literary conventions of the day. Kozintsev has made a film that is a mixture of realism and comedy, about a deranged old man at the mercy of and abused by a venal and uncaring society that cares only for superficialities, with a cynical disregard for spiritual values or love. Furthermore, Sancho achieves a measure of political con-sciousness not out of place in the mindset of the socialist realist positive hero. Once again ideological imperatives are juxtaposed with aesthetic concerns.

The post-Soviet period

In post-Soviet times the literary heritage has remained one of the few bastions of certainty and national identity amid economic chaos and social and

political disruption. Reinterpretations of literature serve to remind a be-leaguered nation of their rich cultural heritage and can also make a statement about contemporary mores or the socio-political environment. Even amid the new commercial realities of post-Soviet Russia, writers and directors still strongly feel the pull of civic mindedness that has been a feature of Russian culture throughout its development.[2]

The cinematic treatment of pre-1917 Russian literature has seen some straightforward and literal adaptations, but some directors have taken the original text and 'transferred' it, in a variety of ways, to make it relevant for the modern age. Moreover, no longer are they governed by the political require-ment to 'doctor' the socio-political perspective. The original text can become a cipher for an exploration of Russia's historical destiny. Adaptations stripped of the need for a political context illustrate the various bold and challenging ways in which directors can adapt their source material and also show how cinema is adept at responding to the new challenges of post-Soviet Russia more immediately, and with more effect, than literature.

Among literary adaptations of the immediate post-Soviet period are Nikolai Dostal's *The Petty Demon* (1995), based on the 1908 novel of the same name by Fedor Sologub, Sergei Lomkin's *The Fatal Eggs* (1995), based on the 1925 satirical novella by Mikhail Bulgakov and a second version of *The Inspector General* (1996), directed by Sergei Gazarov.[3] This last film boasts a cast containing some of the leading stars of the 1990s, including Evgenii Mironov in the title role, with Nikita Mikhalkov, Oleg Iankovskii and Marina Neelova, and offers a faithful rendering of the motifs, characters and themes of the original. It falls down, however, in its sheer lack of discipline and its inability, given the comic possibilities of Gogol's text, to be funny. However, it has a topical dimension: Gogol's acerbic satire on corruption and bribe taking among government officials is not out of place in the chaotic and crime-ridden Russia of Boris Yeltsin.

Horses Carry Me, based on Chekhov's novella *The Duel* (1891), was directed in 1996 by Vladimir Motyl (he of *The White Sun of the Desert* fame). It transposes Chekhov's themes and characters to a modern, post-Soviet setting, with the emphasis on sex, sexual jealousy and betrayal, as if offering a statement on the moral corruption of the modern Russian intelligentsia that has sold its soul to commercialism. Another Chekhov adaptation, Sergei Snezhkin's *The Colours of Marigolds* (1998), offers more ambition in combin-ing two Chekhov plays, *The Cherry Orchard* and *Three Sisters*, in a post-Soviet setting, where the values of the past are threatened by the rampant commer-cialism of the present, and dreamers, in the end, have nowhere to escape to. The film is also visually striking, with much use of vivid colour (the title reminds us of Sergo Paradzhanov and his exuberant use of screen colour), dream and the absurd. Snezhkin has made an imaginative, unsettling film about greed, selfishness and betrayal, demonstrating a subtle awareness of the intricacies of Chekhov's texts and their relevance for the 'new' Russia.

An adaptation that speaks of considerable cinematic maturity is Valerii Todorovskii's *Katia Izmailova* (1994), also known as *Evenings Around Moscow*. It is based on the novella *Lady Macbeth of Mtsensk* by Nikolai Leskov. In Leskov's story of 1865, Katerina Izmailova is the bored wife of a well-to-do merchant who is much older than she and who often spends time away from home. She begins a passionate and uninhibited affair with Sergei, a steward on the estate. During one of her husband's absences her affair with Sergei is discovered by her father-in-law, Boris Timofeevich, whom she then poisons. The lovers then murder her husband on his return. A further victim of their spiral of violence is the child Fedor, Boris Timofeevich's nephew, who could benefit from the resulting inheritance. All the while Leskov emphasises the unbridled passion and desire Katerina and Sergei have for each other, at the same time subverting fashionable democratic ideas (a liaison between a noblewoman and a servant just won't work). Inevitably, they are caught by the police and sentenced to hard labour in Siberia. On the way to their place of exile, Sergei begins an affair with another female convict, Sonia, and taunts and humiliates Katerina in front of the other convicts. On a river crossing, Katerina seizes Sonia and jumps overboard with her. Both of them perish in the icy water. Leskov's novella is a bleak and uncompromising story of greed, lust and murder, set in the materialistic world of the merchant class. Roman Balaian's 1989 film *Lady Macbeth of Mtsensk* is a naturalistic and fairly literal rendering of the original, with the sex and eroticism, as well as the brutality and cynicism, of Leskov's original to the fore. It shows us a rotten, debased world, recognisably set in the Russian provinces of the nineteenth century, where the two murderous protagonists care only for money and sex and are ultimately doomed.

In Todorovskii's version the action is brought forward to the present and is set in the 'new Russian' world of affluence, stylish clothes, cars, fashionable furniture and opulent interiors. Katerina is working as secretary to her mother-in-law Irina Dmitrievna, a romantic novelist. She begins an affair with Sergei, a carpenter working in the house. Irina Dmitrievna had also been having an affair with him. When the affair is discovered by her mother-in-law, Katerina kills her. Her husband Mitia soon finds out about the affair and is killed by Sergei. His body is buried in the forest. Katerina and Sergei then begin to put their own ending to Irina Dmitrievna's last novel, but it is rejected by the local publisher. Their relationship does not last, as the restless Sergei rekindles his interest in a local nurse, Sonia. Katerina gets her revenge by driving her car off a bridge with both her and Sonia inside.

There are thus several significant departures from the original nineteenth-century text, in particular surrounding the personality of Katerina. The first

Vladimir Mashkov and Ingeborga Dapkunaite in Katia Izmailova *(Valerii Todorovskii, 1994)*

obvious departure is that instead of a hated father-in-law, Katerina kills her mother-in-law. In actual fact the killing is not the calculated murder by Leskov's cold-blooded heroine, but rather an impulsive, almost accidental act. Katerina seeks to assume Irina Dmitrievna's creative mantle and fame. Moreover, Katerina and Sergei try to replace Irina Dmitrievna's original text with a happy ending, the same happy ending Katerina would like to see in her relationship with Sergei. Life must thus imitate literature. However, the upbeat ending is rejected by the publisher; correspondingly, Katerina's life will not end happily.

The second important departure is in Katerina herself. In Todorovskii's film she is not the passionate, wilful *femme fatale* of Leskov's text. Rather, she is cold, aloof and calculating and even her suicide is not caused by the impulse of the moment, but a preconceived and well-planned act. She tries to make her life conform to literary paradigms, dominated by the 'happy end' of conventional romance. Life as literature is the film's major theme and it is significant that Sergei's initial seduction is conducted as Katerina is typing up Irina Dmitrievna's text. As Katerina says: 'I am not writing, I am retyping.'

The third and most telling departure is in the figure of the police chief Romanov, absent in Leskov's text, to whom Katerina confesses her crime. He dismisses her confession, saying he needs more evidence. Romanov is clearly based on Porfirii Petrovich, the investigator in Dostoevskii's *Crime and Punishment*, to whom the murderer Raskolnikov eventually confesses. Not only does Todorovskii introduce this character into his plot, he then subverts it: in Dostoevskii's novel Porfirii Petrovich waits for Raskolnikov to confess, knowing him already to be guilty, yet in Todorovskii's film Romanov rejects her confession as inadequate. Katerina's desire to become part of a literary tradition once more fails. Her aspiration to be a writer is also unsuccessful; the Dostoevskian baring of her soul is dismissed; finally, her own 'happy end' is destroyed by the discovery that her lover is fickle and shallow. Todorovskii's Katerina is no Lady Macbeth, doomed by the strength of her own passion and ambition, but rather a modern, self-aware woman with intellectual and cultural aspirations who is destroyed by the reality of the world around her.

Todorovskii, then, has made a film that gives more than a nod in the direction of the nineteenth-century literary tradition. Todorovskii refers to this tradition and effectively subverts then rewrites it. He has substantially revised and adapted the original text, in particular by adding some new elements, in order to give that text a relevance to the new Russia. The bones of Leskov's story are there, but the director has created a new, radically different narrative for the late twentieth century. The classical Russian literature of old, so often vaunted as a cultural and moral reference point, is seen as inadequate for the modern world, it can no longer guide or teach 'how to live'. Modern art forms,

Oleg Menshikov and Sergei Bodrov Jr. in Prisoner of the Mountains *(Sergei Bodrov Sr., 1996)*

such as cinema, can frame and illuminate individual lives, but no longer have to offer solutions.

It is thus no accident that the film makes direct reference to the cinema of America and France, arguably the leading cinematic nations in the world. The basic plot is a retread of James M. Cain's novel *The Postman Always Rings Twice*, itself made into two Hollywood films (1946, directed by Tay Garnett, and 1981, directed by Bob Rafelson), as well as providing the basis for Luchino Visconti's *Ossessione* of 1942, and the interment and disinterment of Mitia's body is reminiscent of Henri-Georges Clouzot's 1954 film *Les Diaboliques*. Valerii Todorovskii's film self-consciously refers not to nineteenth-century literature, but to twentieth-century mainstream cinema: away from the intellectual stagnation of the past and into the embrace of the popular culture of the present.

Prisoner of the Mountains is the title of a poem by both Alexander Pushkin and Mikhail Lermontov in the early nineteenth century, as well as a short story by Lev Tolstoi. In Pushkin's poem (1822), a Russian nobleman serving in the Caucasus is captured by Circassians and strikes up a relationship with a local girl. Pushkin's hero is full of admiration and respect for the dignity and strength of his captors. The girl falls in love with him and helps him to escape. Lermontov's poem (1828) revisits Pushkin's, but ends tragically when the Russian is killed within sight of his own camp and the girl is drowned in the Terek river. Lermontov is at pains to emphasise the grandeur and beauty of the mountains of the Caucasus. His most famous work, the 1840 novel *A Hero of Our Time*, is also set amid a military campaign in the Caucasus.

Tolstoi's story concerns a Russian officer, Zhilin, who is serving with his unit in the Caucasus during the nineteenth century. He is captured by the Tartars as he attempts to leave his fort to return to mainland Russia. They keep him in a remote mountain village in order to extort a ransom for his release from his family, and he is soon joined by a fellow officer, Kostylin, who is also being held hostage. They are both under the charge of Abdul-Murat, who has a young daughter, Dina. Zhilin and Kostylin try to escape and are captured, after which their Tartar captors become more brutal and uncompromising. One old man in the village has lost seven of his sons fighting the Russians and shot his eighth himself, after he had gone over to the Russian side. He wants Zhilin and Kostylin killed summarily. Zhilin, however, establishes a tenuous relationship with Dina, he makes her clay dolls and she eventually helps him to escape a second time, this time successfully.

Bodrov retains the plot and characters, but updates the setting to more recent times: the Chechen War.[4] There are, however, significant changes to Tolstoi's narrative. Zhilin and Sasha (i.e. not Kostylin) are ambushed and captured by rebels while out on a routine patrol. Abdul-Marat wishes not to ransom his prisoners, but to exchange them for his son, who is a prisoner of the Russians in the local garrison town. During their first, unsuccessful, escape attempt, Sasha kills two men. On their recapture Sasha is executed by the rebels. Abdul-Murat's son is killed by the Russians as he tries to escape, but Abdul-Murat finally allows Zhilin to walk away in an act of mercy.[5] The final shot of the film obviously borrows from Francis Ford Coppola's *Apocalypse Now* (1979), as Russian helicopter gunships fly over Zhilin's head on their way to destroy the village from which he has just been released.

The Russian troops throughout the film are portrayed as brutal, occupying forces, who think nothing of shooting at the locals and who trade their guns for vodka. Sasha, as played by Oleg Menshikov, regards the locals as little more than cannon fodder, vowing to return to the village in which he languishes at some future date to kill all the inhabitants. Only Zhilin, a raw conscript from a small town, treats his captors with respect and tries to understand them. Sasha, the professional and cynical soldier, represents the Russia of aggressive imperialism and oppression, Zhilin the values of meekness, humility and respect.

Abdul-Murat's gesture of mercy is an act of dignity and forgiveness. Here, too, Bodrov reworks Tolstoi's original, for, whereas Tolstoi makes no effort to understand the Tartars or their culture, Bodrov shows in detail the rebels' culture and their world and displays sympathy for their feeling of injustice.

Prisoner of the Mountains is a film that attacks Russia's aggression towards the smaller nations and cultures that are contained within its borders and is therefore not only about the Chechen War.[6] It is about war in general and the hatred it engenders, but it is even more than that. The nod to *Apocalypse Now* gives the film an intertextual reference point. Bodrov's film is fundamentally about intolerance and hate that bring about only suffering and the destruction of communities. It is also about Russia's search for identity in its post-imperial world, its attempt at self-definition through confrontation with an alien culture, 'the other'. Susan Layton has shown how the Russian literary treatment of the Caucasus in the nineteenth century helped construct Russia's own national identity:

> *The literary Caucasus was largely the project of Russian men, whose psychological needs it so evidently served. However, both sexes within the romantic era's élite readership could enhance their national esteem by contemplating their internally diversified orient. Effeminate Georgia fed the conceit of Russia's European stature and superiority over Asia. But knowledge of Russia's own Asian roots defied permanent repression, especially when a French consul in Tiflis or a visiting marquis in St. Petersburg was ever ready to castigate the tsars' 'rude and barbarous kingdom.' Under these conditions, Russians converted the Caucasian tribes into gratifying meanings about their own undeniable cultural and intellectual retardation* vis-à-vis *the West.*

> *(Layton, 1994, p. 288)*

Bodrov's film updates Tolstoi's text, but also addresses the same question posed by all the writers of the nineteenth century who explored the Caucasus, 'the other', in a search for the 'true' Russia. Russia's search for identity through its relations with non-Russians is made startlingly new and topical, especially with its reliance on other, non-Russian, cultural reference points.

Apart from its anti-war message, *Prisoner of the Mountains* is a film conscious of its own literary heritage. As if we didn't know, the title and author of the original work are scratched on a school blackboard in a scene featuring Zhilin's mother. After his execution, Sasha 'reappears' to Zhilin. The motif of the dead coming back to life to confront the living is common in Russian literature and has been treated by such writers as Pushkin, Gogol and Odoevskii in the nineteenth century and Bulgakov in the twentieth.

Both Todorovskii and Bodrov have taken 'hallowed' nineteenth-century literary texts, reshaped, rethought and reinvented them for the modern age. Such attempts are not always successful. Iurii Grymov's *Mu-mu* (1998), based on the 1852 story by Ivan Turgenev, stays close to the original plot within the milieu of nineteenth-century Russian serfdom, but adds modern motifs. Ostensibly the tale of Gerasim, a mute serf forced by his callous lady landowner to drown his beloved puppy – called Mu-mu, as it is the only oral sound Gerasim can produce – the film emphasises the sexual dissoluteness of the landed classes, with suggestions of masturbation, lesbianism and quirky cross-dressing. The director obviously wishes to marry the Russian literary heritage with the modern permissiveness of post-censorship Russia. Yet despite the crudity and naturalism of the images – phallic cucumbers, blood, sperm-like fluids slowly running down the wall, beheaded fish, lingering close-ups of raw meat – there is nothing new in the portrayal of the peasant masses as stupid and docile and our knowledge of the cruelties and iniquities of serfdom is not seriously enhanced.

Another largely unsuccessful adaptation that tries hard to capture period detail while attempting to meet modern tastes is Alexander Proshkin's *The Russian Rebellion* (1999), a faithful rendering of Pushkin's historical novel *The Captain's Daughter*. With an impressive budget that allows for some epic set piece battles and the inclusion of some of the major stars of the 1990s (Vladimir Mashkov and Sergei Makovetskii), the film concerns the peasant revolt led by Emelian Pugachev against Catherine the Great in 1773–4. Amid violence and sensuality and a portrayal of Catherine as dissolute and whimsical, a long way from the kind matriarch of Pushkin's story, the film's earnest efforts at authenticity tend to repel, its modernism seemingly a justification of excess.

The literary biopic is a curious sub-genre, rather more for what it has ignored than for what it has shown. Arkadii Naroditskii's *The Youth of the Poet* (1937) paid homage to Pushkin by concentrating on his childhood and school years. Despite the fact that one of the first Russian films, *The Departure of the Great Old Man* (1912), concentrated on the last days of Lev Tolstoi, Russian directors have been sparing in their studies of the lives of the great writers. Grigorii Kozintsev's *Belinskii* (1951) emphasises the radical critic's revolutionary credentials, with cameo appearances by Pushkin, Herzen, Gogol and Nekrasov. Sergei Gerasimov's *Lev Tolstoi* (1984) takes a long and pains-taking look at the writer's last days, but again is little more than cinematic hero worship. But there is no cinematic biography of other literary 'giants', such as Dostoevskii, Turgenev, Gogol, Bulgakov or Pasternak, to name but a few.

A very interesting foray into this area is provided by Alexei Uchitel's *The Diary of His Wife* (2000). This is a far from fawning examination of Ivan Bunin in French emigration, especially the years from 1933, when he was awarded the Nobel Prize, to his death in 1953. Andrei Smirnov portrays Bunin as an egocentric and boorish adulterer, surrounded by lesbians and drunkards, a mirror of the decadent emigration that would be in line with Soviet interpretations. By exploding the myth of the 'great' writer as repository of the nation's spiritual and moral values, Uchitel has made a film that is both challengingly iconoclastic and wittily irreverent.

The literary heritage, then, has played an important role in the development of Russian cinema, where among the many drab and theatrical adaptations, there have been occasional gems of individuality and true flights of cinematic imagination. In general, the hallowed integrity of the literary work and the writer have been observed and upheld, and only in post-Soviet times have directors chosen to update and rethink the canon. Literature remains in the past, but film moves it forward.

Filmography

(This filmography aims to provide a detailed list of film adaptations, including those not discussed in this chapter.)

Anna around the Neck ('Anna na shee'), dir. Isidor Annenskii, 1954

Anna Karenina, dir. Vladimir Gardin, 1914; Tatiana Lukashevich, 1953; Alexander Zarkhi, 1967

Apocalypse Now, dir. Francis Ford Coppola, 1979

Asia, dir. Iosif Kheifits, 1977

The Bad Good Man ('Plokhoi khoroshii chelovek'), dir. Iosif Kheifits, 1973 (based on Chekhov's *The Duel*)

Bela, dir. Stanislav Rostotskii, 1966

Belinskii, dir. Grigorii Kozintsev, 1951

Boris Godunov, dir. Sergei Bondarchuk, 1986

The Bride ('Nevesta'), dir. Grigorii Nikulin and Vladimir Stredel, 1956

The Brothers Karamazov ('Bratia Karamazovy'), dir. Ivan Pyrev, 1968

The Captain's Daughter ('Kapitanskaia doch'), dir. Iurii Tarich, 1928; Vladimir Kaplunovskii, 1959

Chapaev, dir. Sergei and Georgii Vasilev, 1934

The Colours of Marigolds ('Tsvety kalenduly'), dir. Sergei Snezhkin, 1998

The Cossacks ('Kazaki'), dir. Vasilii Pronin, 1961

Crazy Money ('Beshenye dengi'), dir. Evgenii Matveev, 1981

Crime and Punishment ('Prestuplenie i nakazanie'), dir. Lev Kulidzhanov, 1969

A Cruel Romance ('Zhestokii romans'), dir. Eldar Riazanov, 1984 (based on Alexander Ostrovskii's *Without a Dowry*)

The Darling ('Dushechka'), dir. Sergei Kolosov, 1966

Dead Souls ('Mertvye dushi'), dir. Leonid Trauberg, 1960; Mikhail Shveitser, 1984

The Departure of the Great Old Man ('Ukhod velikogo startsa'), dir. Iakov Protazanov and Elizaveta Thiemann, 1912

Les Diaboliques, dir. Henri-Georges Clouzot, 1954

The Diary of His Wife ('Dnevnik ego zheny'), dir. Alexei Uchitel, 2000

Don Quixote, dir. Grigorii Kozintsev, 1957

Dubrovskii, dir. Alexander Ivanovskii, 1935

Evenings on a Farm near Dikanka ('Vechera na khutore bliz Dikanki'), dir. Alexander Rou, 1961

The Fatal Eggs ('Rokovye iaitsa'), dir. Sergei Lomkin, 1995

Father Sergius ('Otets Sergii'), dir. Iakov Protazanov, 1917; Igor Talankin, 1978

Fathers and Sons ('Otsy i deti'), dir. Adolf Bergunker and Natalia Rashevskaia, 1958; Viacheslav Nikiforov, 1983

First Love ('Pervaia liubov'), dir. Vasilii Ordynskii, 1968; Roman Balaian, 1995

The Forest ('Les'), dir. Vladimir Vengerov, 1953; Vladimir Motyl, 1980

The Grasshopper ('Poprygunia'), dir. Samson Samsonov, 1955

Guilty without Blame ('Bez viny vinovatye'), dir. Vladimir Petrov, 1945

Hamlet ('Gamlet'), dir. Grigorii Kozintsev, 1964

Horses Carry Me ('Nesut menia koni . . .'), dir. Vladimir Motyl, 1996 (based on Chekhov's *The Duel*)

The Idiot ('Idiot'), dir. Petr Chardynin, 1910; Ivan Pyrev, 1958

The Inspector General ('Revizor'), dir. Vladimir Petrov, 1952; Sergei Gazarov, 1996

Katia Izmailova, dir. Valerii Todorovskii, 1994

King Lear ('Korol Lir'), dir. Grigorii Kozintsev, 1971

The Kreutzer Sonata ('Kreitserova sonata'), dir. Mikhail Shveitser, 1987

Lady Macbeth of Mtsensk ('Ledi Makbet Mtsenskogo uezda'), dir. Roman Balaian, 1989

The Lady with the Lapdog ('Dama s sobachkoi'), dir. Iosif Kheifits, 1960

Lev Tolstoi, dir. Sergei Gerasimov, 1984

Little Tragedies ('Malenkie tragedii'), dir. Mikhail Shveitser, 1979

The Living Corpse ('Zhivoi trup'), dir. Fedor Otsep, 1929; Vladimir Vengerov, 1952 and 1968

The Man in a Case ('Chelovek v futliare'), dir. Isidor Annenskii, 1939

A May Night or The Drowned Girl ('Maiskaia noch ili utoplennitsa'), dir. Alexander Rou, 1952

Mother ('Mat'), dir. Vsevolod Pudovkin, 1926

Mu-Mu, dir. Anatolii Bobrovskii, 1959; Iurii Grymov, 1998

My Affectionate and Tender Beast ('Moi laskovyi i nezhnyi zver'), dir. Emil Lotianu, 1978 (based on Chekhov's *The Shooting Party*)

A Nest of Gentlefolk ('Dvorianskoe gnezdo'), dir. Andrei Mikhalkov-Konchalovskii, 1969

The Nose ('Nos'), dir. Rolan Bykov, 1977

Ossessione, dir. Luchino Visconti, 1942

The Overcoat ('Shinel'), dir. Grigorii Kozintsev and Leonid Trauberg, 1926; Alexei Batalov, 1959

The Petty Demon ('Melkii bes'), dir. Nikolai Dostal, 1995

The Postman Always Rings Twice, dir. Tay Garnett, 1946; Bob Rafelson, 1981

Prisoner of the Mountains ('Kavkazskii plennik'), dir. Sergei Bodrov Sr., 1996

The Queen of Spades ('Pikovaia dama'), dir. Petr Chardynin, 1910; Iakov Protazanov, 1916

Quiet Flows the Don ('Tikhii Don'), dir. Sergei Gerasimov, 1957–58

Princess Mary ('Kniazhna Meri'), dir. Isidor Annenskii, 1955

Resurrection ('Voskresenie'), dir. Mikhail Shveitser, 1961

Rudin, dir. Konstantin Voinov, 1976

Ruslan and Liudmila ('Ruslan i Liudmila'), dir. Alexander Ptushko, 1972

The Russian Rebellion ('Russkii bunt'), dir. Alexander Proshkin, 1999

The Seagull ('Chaika'), dir. Iurii Karasik, 1970

The Shot ('Vystrel'), dir. Nikolai Trakhtenberg, 1966

The Stationmaster ('Stantsionnyi smotritel'), dir. Alexander Ivanovskii, 1918; Sergei Solovev, 1972

The Steppe ('Step'), dir. Sergei Bondarchuk, 1977

The Storm ('Groza'), dir. Vladimir Petrov, 1934

The Storm ('Metel'), dir. Vladimir Basov, 1965

Taman, dir. Stanislav Rostotskii, 1959

The Three Sisters ('Tri sestry'), dir. Samson Samsonov, 1964; Sergei Solovev, 1994

Uncle Vania ('Diadia Vania'), dir. Andrei Mikhalkov-Konchalovskii, 1970

The Vacancy ('Vakansiia'), dir. Margarita Mikaelian, 1981 (based on Alexander Ostrovskii's play *A Profitable Position*)

Vassa, dir. Gleb Panfilov, 1983

Vii, dir. Konstantin Ershov, 1967

War and Peace ('Voina i mir'), dir. Sergei Bondarchuk, 1965–7

The Wedding ('Svadba'), dir. Isidor Annenskii, 1944

Without a Dowry ('Bespridannitsa'), dir. Iakov Protazanov, 1936

The Youth of the Poet ('Iunost poeta'), dir. Arkadii Naroditskii, 1937

Notes

1. '*Chapayev* is a great event in the history of Soviet art. *Chapayev* invisibly and powerfully multiplies the links between the Party and the mass. *Chapayev*, a work of art of great quality, demonstrates convincingly and eloquently the organising role of the Party and shows how the Party subdues the elements and moves them along the road of Revolution and victory.' (See 'The Whole Country is Watching *Chapayev*', in Christie and Taylor (1994), pp. 334–5.)
2. Nevertheless, it should be noted that some of the greatest Soviet films are adaptations of Soviet literature, including *Quiet Flows the Don*. Mark Donskoi's *Maxim Gorkii Trilogy* (1938–40) is a superb example of realism, with an explicit ideological content, but is only partly devoted to post-1917 literature.

3. In a survey of the cinema, V. Pritulenko characterized the recent trend of screening the literary classics as the 'new escapism', which sees directors in 'flight from actuality and into another reality, the saving bosom of literature'. (See Pritulenko (1996), p. 71.)

4. Bodrov affirms that work on the screenplay actually began before the outbreak of the Chechen War. See his interview, Bodrov (1996a). For further discussion of this film, see Gillespie and Zhuravkina (1996) and Graffy (1998).

5. The theme of the 'noble savage' of the mountains, notably absent in Tolstoi's story but not in Pushkin's poem, is also present in the 1978 Soviet TV production of *A Prisoner of the Caucasus*, directed by Georgii Kalatozishvili and starring Iurii Nazarov and Vladimir Solodnikov as the captured Russian officers. The ending, when Zhilin's life is spared, is similar to that of Bodrov's film. It was shown in Great Britain on BBC TV in 1980 and repeated in 1982.

6. Bodrov himself said that he initially wanted to make the film in Bosnia; see Bodrov (1996a). In another interview, he does not hide the fact that the film criticises Russian imperial attitudes. (See Bodrov (1996b).)

CHAPTER THREE

The Russian film comedy

As everyone knows, laughter does not lend itself to falsification. It is easier to squeeze out a tear than a smile. You can lead a horse to the water but you can't make it drink.

(Genis, 1999, p. 22)

A theoretical preamble

Laughter and comedy have been staple ingredients of cinema since its birth. If a film is funny, it will bring in the crowds. If it can combine comedy and education, it will serve a useful social function as well as entertaining. Genuine laughter is the joyous expression of the emotions of an individual and/or collective and it is democratic in that it unites and binds people of varying backgrounds and social strata. Furthermore, laughter can simply amuse as an innocent artistic form of entertainment or it can be more subversive by ridiculing prevailing mores or ideology. Laughter can therefore also be a dangerous expression of freedom, an awareness that the object of laughter is funny because it is transient and that there exists a greater truth. It is therefore not fortuitous that the country that gave the world the concept of 'democracy' – ancient Greece – also gave the world the first artistic smile in its visual art. The ancient Egyptians, Indians and Mesopotamians allowed only their deities to smile, but it was in Greek art and in particular sculpture of the fourth and fifth centuries BC that the smile was first bestowed not on gods, but on ordinary mortals, a demonstration of the preoccupation of Greek art 'with the human and with the gods' proper place in the world of men (rather than vice versa)' (Boardman, 1986, p. 309).

The pioneering study on the function of laughter in culture was carried out by Henri Bergson in his essay entitled *Laughter: An Essay on the Meaning of the*

Comic, first published in 1900. Bergson argues that the collective need for laughter is a social force that counters evil. Bergson was writing, however, in a relatively untroubled time. Mikhail Bakhtin in his essay 'Forms of Time and of the Chronotope in the Novel' (1937–8), and in particular *Rabelais and his World* (written 1940, published 1968, edition used 1984) demonstrates that laughter is the people's response to a closed, authoritarian discourse, a life-affirming statement of the people's truth. Bakhtin establishes that the people's laughter is a great liberating force, the victory of the future over the past and the defeat of ossified hierarchies by the vibrant dynamics of folk humour. Furthermore, Bakhtin wrote his study in the dark days of the 1930s and the obvious and intended similarities between the dogmatic oppression of Stalin's Russia and Catholic France have not been missed by commentators. Bakhtin says of Rabelaisian laughter:

> *The extraordinary force of laughter in Rabelais, its radicalism, is explained predominantly by its deep-rooted folkloric base, by its link with the elements of the ancient complex – with death, the birth of new life, fertility and growth. This is real world-embracing laughter, one that can play with all the things of this world – from the most insignificant to the greatest, from distant things to those close at hand. This connection on the one hand with fundamental realities of life, and on the other with the most radical destruction of all false verbal and ideological shells that had distorted and kept separate these realities, is what so sharply distinguishes Rabelaisian laughter from the laughter of other practitioners of the grotesque, humor, satire and irony.*
>
> (Bakhtin, 1981, p. 237)

Dmitrii Likhachev has taken Bakhtin's study of Rabelais and applied it to medieval Russian culture. To Likhachev laughter is both destructive and creative: it subverts the senseless and absurd social laws that oppress and humiliate and reasserts the truth of a world where man is inwardly free and all men are equal. Here, too, he emphasises the essential democratic nature of laughter, where the world of order, stability, piety and established hierarchies is opposed by an 'anti-world' of poverty, drunkenness, hunger and anarchy. The anti-world is the real world turned upside down, where fools speak the truth and nakedness represents unadorned reality:

> *The function of laughter is to lay bare and display the truth, to divest reality of its outer clothing of etiquette, ceremony, artificial inequality and the whole complex system of signs of its given society. This laying bare makes people equal . . . Stupidity is the mind freeing itself of all conventionality, all forms and habits.*
>
> (Likhachev, 1987, pp. 356–7)

I will return to these precepts later in this chapter. Andrei Tarkovskii's film *Andrei Rublev* (1965) offers a striking confirmation of laughter as protest, where, in one of the opening episodes, some monks (including Rublev) and peasants, while sheltering from the rain outside, are treated to some bawdy and irreverent songs by a jester in a tavern. In Likhachev's anti-world, the tavern stands in opposition to the church, drunkenness to asceticism, the jester to the monk. The Grand Duke and his secular authority are the butt of much of the jester's jokes, who is then denounced by one of the monks. The jester is taken away, beaten and tortured by the Grand Duke's men: half his tongue is cut out, a clear signifier of the authorities' fear of the power of the word.[1]

The studies by Bakhtin and Likhachev on the role of laughter in culture across the centuries are relevant for our study in that the great comic works of Russian literature – from Nikolai Gogol to Anton Chekhov and, in the twentieth century, Mikhail Bulgakov, Venedikt Erofeev, Vladimir Voinovich and Sergei Dovlatov – have a riotous, satirical edge that is directed towards officialdom and the values advocated by society's ruling elite. Here, too, laughter is subversive, affirming the people's truth as well as rejection of and liberation from authoritarian discourse. It remains to be said, of course, that Bulgakov, Erofeev, Voinovich and Dovlatov were writers in confrontation with the Soviet regime and their works were not recognised or published until the years of glasnost.

Given the particular ideological demands on film-makers after the Revolution, the genre of comedy was particularly difficult. Soviet critics, especially in the 1920s, tended to dismiss or deride comedy films that had, as they saw it, insufficient ideological content. It is not only in the Soviet Union, however, that comedy has been treated with disdain and suspicion. In Western countries, too, critics have often treated film comedy as cheap and 'lowbrow' entertainment, offering little spiritual sustenance or moral insights.

Soviet comedy film-makers needed to tread a fine line between making people laugh, on the one hand and being ideologically acceptable to the vigilant critics, on the other. The ideological foundation for film comedy, based entirely on class antagonism, was provided by Anatolii Lunacharskii, the Commissar for Enlightenment, in 1924:

> *While man is weak before his enemy he does not laugh at him, he hates him, and if occasionally a sarcastic, hate-filled smile appears on his lips, then this is laughter poisoned with bile, laughter that sounds unsure. But then the oppressed grow, and laughter resounds louder, firmer. This is outraged laughter, this is irony, biting satire. In this laughter is heard the swish of the lash and occasionally the peals of the impending thunder of battle. This is how Gogol' began to laugh, the tears still wet in his eyes, and this is how Saltykov began, trembling with indignation.*

And then?

And then laughter becomes more and more contemptuous as the new order feels its power. This contemptuous laughter directed downwards from above is jolly, aware already of its victory, already heralding relaxation, is as essential as the most genuine weapon. It is the wasp's sting that is driven into the body of the dark sorcerer, recently killed but who is preparing to return from his tomb, it is the hammering in of hard nails into the black coffin of the past.

(Lunacharskii, 1924, p. 62)

'Contemptuous laughter' is hardly the stuff of knockabout comedy or slapstick farce, although it may serve the needs of a totalitarian state. Still, during the so-called 'stagnation years' of 1964–85 the ideological importance of the film comedy was still emphasised: 'Soviet film comedy has been formed as an art form of high social resonance, participating in the process of the moral education of Soviet people, the builders of Communism' (Vlasov, 1970, p. 3). In other words, the Soviet film comedy was, first and foremost, to reassure Soviet citizens that they lived in a secure and stable society and that the problems faced by capitalist societies were largely irrelevant for them. The very idea of film 'comedy', therefore, was generically distinctive: a film need not be funny, as long as it was light-hearted, uplifting and, above all, optimistic.

Comedies of the 'golden age'

One of the earliest Soviet comedies, *The Extraordinary Adventures of Mr West in the Land of the Bolsheviks*, directed by Lev Kuleshov in 1924, was blessed with these requirements. It certainly made people laugh and it also contained a clear political message as it showed an American businessman, Mr West, arrive in Soviet Russia attended by his cowboy bodyguard, Geddy. Audiences were encouraged to laugh at the outrageous slapstick escapades of Geddy, replete with six guns and ten-gallon hat, thousands of miles from the sunny prairie and let loose in wintry Moscow. The political message is conveyed with Mr West's enlightenment, as he initially suspects the Soviet Union as a dark and dangerous place inhabited by Bolshevik 'barbarians'. These suspicions are realised when he is kidnapped and held to ransom by a criminal gang. He sees the 'real' Soviet Union and its people when he is rescued by the police. The heroic policeman is dressed in full-length leather coat, the uniform of the Cheka, the dreaded secret police. Kuleshov's film may offer some satirical asides on Soviet life, but this is nevertheless a fairly safe film in ideological terms; the laughter is largely at the expense of the uncomprehending Americans, West and Geddy, and the happy end reinforces the idea that

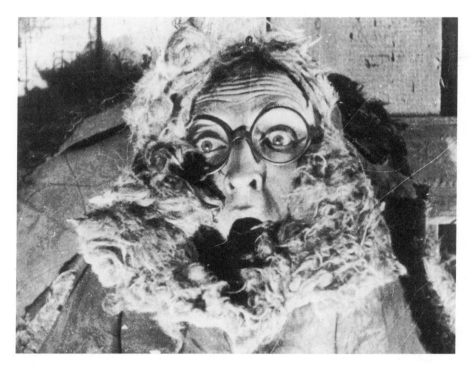

Porfirii Podobed in The Extraordinary Adventures of Mr West in the Land of the Bolsheviks *(Lev Kuleshov, 1924)*

the country is safe in the hands of the Bolsheviks, who want only to be understood correctly by Western powers.

Both Vsevolod Pudovkin and Alexander Dovzhenko tried their hand at comedies in their early work. Pudovkin's *Chess Fever* (1925) treats the hero's chess mania in true comic fashion, as he loses his girlfriend and even plays chess with himself, but it also features the world chess champion José Capablanca as himself, persuading the heroine of the joys of chess! Dovzhenko's *Love's Little Berry* (1926) is a light-hearted farce about the wayward hairdresser Jean who, after a series of mishaps with twin babies, learns the error of his ways and accepts responsibility by settling down with his girlfriend Liza. However, the film ends with a joke at Jean's expense: the baby ('love's little berry') he had imagined to be his in fact belongs to Liza's aunt. Both these films are short and display a light touch that would be missing in the subsequent work of both directors.

Boris Barnet, who played the cowboy Geddy in *Mr West*, went on to direct some important early comedies himself, especially *The House on Trubnaia* (1927). However, the central figure in the development of Soviet film comedy in the 1920s is Iakov Protazanov, who had cut his directorial teeth back in the pre-revolutionary years. Between 1925 and 1930 he made films which had great commercial success, but which were not so enthusiastically received by the critics as they tended towards 'entertainment' to the detriment of 'content' (i.e. ideology).

Don Diego and Pelageia (1929) is on the surface a comedy of misunderstanding, as the Pelageia of the title is arrested and imprisoned simply for crossing the railway track at the wrong place. She is the victim of an uncaring and impersonal bureaucracy and is released only due to the tireless efforts of her husband and the local komsomol activists. The film ends on a comic note when both the elderly Pelageia and her husband ask to be accepted into the komsomol – the communist youth league – but the subtext of individuals at the mercy of the state and arbitrarily subject to repression is one that was far from funny in the reality of the late 1920s.

Most of Protazanov's comedies starred Igor Ilinskii, the greatest Russian comic actor of all, whose success would continue until the 1960s. In *The Festival of St Jorgen* (1930), Ilinskii (together with Anatolii Ktorov) plays a criminal on the run who takes refuge in a nun's habit and creates all sorts of comic mayhem in the religious community which he adopts. Protazanov is a master at creating situations that, through misunderstandings and confusion, can be used by different characters for their own ends, but with comic and farcical results. Another example is *The Trial of the Three Million* (1926), which also starred Ilinskii and Ktorov and which centres on the search for the 'three million' in the house of a rich Western banker, with thieves, clergy and businessmen all cleverly parodied as they pursue their own venal ends.

The comedies of socialist realism

The coming of sound brought a new type of comedy to Soviet screens. Critics and Party ideologues called for a mass cinema, one that could both instruct and entertain and one that rejected the directorial autonomy of the 1920s that created too many films ordinary workers often failed to appreciate or comprehend. In particular, sound could be used to comic effect, sometimes at the expense of visual slapstick. The first Soviet comedy blockbuster was Grigorii Alexandrov's musical comedy *Cheerful Fellows* of 1934. *Cheerful Fellows*, itself a jolly hybrid with aspects such as animated title sequences borrowed from Hollywood and its rip-roaring gusto of slapstick humour, is the first in a long line of musical comedies that was to stretch through the 1950s and whose effects could still be felt in films of the 1970s. *Cheerful Fellows* is also a 'safe' film in that it offers no challenges to the prevailing ideology or socialist realist metatext: everyone is happy in the workers' paradise. Indeed, it was singled out for praise by the Party leadership. Boris

Shumiatskii, the head of Soviet cinema from 1930 up to his arrest and execution in 1938, praised the film's 'cheerfulness, its joie de vivre and its laughter' and called on other film-makers to follow suit:

> In a country building socialism, where there is no private property or exploitation, where the classes hostile to the proletariat have been liquidated, where the workers are united by their conscious participation in the construction of socialist society and where the enormous task of liquidating the remnants of the capitalist past is being accomplished by the Party even in people's consciousness – in this country comedy, apart from its task of exposure, has another, more important and responsible task: the creation of a cheerful and joyful spectacle. [. . .] The victorious class wants to laugh with joy. That is its right, and Soviet cinema must provide the audience with this joyful Soviet laughter.
>
> (Shumiatskii, 1994, pp. 368–9)[2]

Nevertheless, the knockabout comedy in *Cheerful Fellows* is striking for its sheer anarchic, madcap vitality and is one of the last purely apolitical comedies of the decade.

Alexandrov's *The Circus* (1936), *Volga-Volga* (1938) and *The Shining Path* (1940) were similar attempts to transplant the Hollywood comedy on to Soviet soil. *The Circus* contains vivid musical numbers combined with slapstick comic routines and was particularly praised by Soviet critics, with its clear portrayal of the evils of capitalism, the positive internationalism of Soviet people and its clear ideological focus: 'Through irony and laughter the film clearly foregrounds the idea of the new life, the awareness of youth and happiness. The entire film is infused with the image of the Motherland, appearing in the songs, the sets and in the whole style of *The Circus*' (Shumiatskii, 1994, pp. 368–9). *Volga-Volga* (reputedly Stalin's favourite film: he even presented a copy as a gift to a rather bemused President Roosevelt) features a superb comic performance by Ilinskii as the obstructive and petty-minded Stalinist bureaucrat Byvalov. In both *Volga-Volga* and *The Shining Path* Soviet peasants sing happily, content with their lot (despite the miserable state of agriculture historians tell us actually existed in the 1930s).

Furthermore, in *The Circus* and *Volga-Volga* there is very little characterisation or plot ingenuity; in the former, the American Marion Dickson (Liubov Orlova) finds the Soviet Union a place of tolerance and political enlightenment, whereas the latter film shows how village musicians can achieve success and recognition in the capital. In *The Shining Path* the village girl Tania Morozova (again Orlova) discovers true satisfaction and happiness in her work and traverses 'the shining path' that leads her inexorably onwards and upwards until she is awarded a medal by the supreme leader himself in

Rural talent on its way to fame in Moscow in Volga-Volga *(Grigorii Alexandrov, 1938)*

Moscow. It is a Soviet Cinderella tale of rags to riches and dreams come true. Alexandrov revels in animated sequences, especially at the beginning and the end of each film, visual tricks and illusions all giving the impression of heroes and heroines at play and at ease with themselves and Stalin's Russia. However, these comedies contain little actual laughter; rather, the Soviet viewer is encouraged to smile in contentment at the essential justness of life under Stalin.

Ivan Pyrev's collective farm comedies are significantly different from those of Alexandrov. *The Rich Bride* (1937) and *The Swineherdess and the Shepherd* (1941) also feature optimistic songs, affirmation of the new and a blond, blue-eyed alternative to Liubov Orlova in Marina Ladynina (Pyrev's wife). Here, too, peasants break into song at the drop of a hat and the lingering shots of the peaceful Russian countryside all reinforce patriotic sentiment and encourage the myth of political legitimacy: Stalin = the state = Mother Russia. These films are hymns to the glory of socialist labour in the fields, as women gather in the wheat and men manifest their masculinity by mastering the machinery.

In *The Rich Bride* we see that the cultural level of the village is astoundingly high, as it has its own orchestra, the hairdresser prefers to practise on his trumpet rather than cut hair and everyone joins in the communal waltz in the triumphant culmination. In *The Swineherdess and the Shepherd* the sun also shines, Ladynina smiles and sings her way through the film (much as in *The Rich Bride*) and the viewer is persuaded that a Russian country girl and a shepherd from Dagestan can fall in love and find each other, despite the tremendous distances and psychological and cultural barriers between them. Pyrev's films are generally more plot driven than those of Alexandrov and rely on the boy-meets-girl scenario that most viewers would readily identify with and accept. The sweet narrative overlay helps the audience more easily to digest the film's ideological underpinning.

The role of the musical comedy in raising the cultural level of the viewer can be seen in films by Alexander Ivanovskii. *A Musical Story* (1940) and *Anton Ivanovich Gets Angry* (1941) are notable in their attempt to bring some levity to the solemn world of classical music and to make that world accessible to the average movie-going Soviet worker – even a taxi driver can become an acclaimed opera singer. Furthermore, these films reflect the inclusive cultural policy of the leadership. If the films of Alexandrov and Pyrev combined classical, popular and folk music without preferring one over the other, Ivanovskii erodes boundaries within classical music. *A Musical Story* features the person and the voice of the leading tenor of the day, Sergei Lemeshev, while *Anton Ivanovich Gets Angry* does away with generic hierarchies, putting such different genres as opera and operetta on an equally valid footing (even Johann Sebastian Bach himself approves).

Other gentle comedies of this time, such as *A Girl with Character* by Konstantin Iudin (1939) and Tatiana Lukashevich's *The Foundling* (1939), were similar feel-good movies where real conflicts do not arise. In these films of 'high Stalinist culture' (Clark, 2000, p. 91) true love is just around the corner and a five-year-old girl who is lost and wandering about Moscow is inevitably returned to her parents by kind-hearted, honest Soviet people. The sun shines, people express their joy in songs and the Communist Party, under the benevolent gaze of Comrade Stalin, leads society steadily onwards. This is humour at the service of the state, reinforcing the myth of legitimacy and stability and ensuring that, if Soviet citizens can smile and feel happy, they must be secure in their society.[3] There is a darker side, however: the Stalinist musical comedy of the 1930s and early 1940s also coincided with the years of the greatest terror and it is likely that the urban, cinema-going population looked in these films for not only a legitimisation of Stalin's rule, but also a release from the pressures and insecurities of life outside the movie theatre.[4]

During the war, comedies that were made inevitably sang the patriotic tune, such as the series of a dozen 'combat cinema collections' that appeared in 1941, where leading actors and actresses of the day played out humorous shorts ridiculing the enemy and asserting the right and the might of their homeland. In the years from 1945 to the death of Stalin in 1953, the film comedy suffered from the crisis in film production (*malokartine*) that was a feature of the immediate post-war years, although some comedies were made, including Semen Timoshenko's *The Silent Ace of the Skies* (1945) and Grigorii Alexandrov's 1947 film *Spring*, starring his wife Liubov Orlova and the renowned Nikolai Cherkasov. Alexandrov's film is of interest in that it shows the Soviet drive for scientific discovery (solar energy) merging with the artistic impulse (the cinema), against a background of male–female relationships where in the end the woman is reconciled with domesticity.

By far the most significant of the 'comedies' of the post-war period up to the death of Stalin, however, is Pyrev's *The Kuban Cossacks*, made with Ladynina in 1949. Subsequently sharply criticized by Nikita Khrushchev in 1957 for its 'falsification' of reality, this is nevertheless a 'poetic hymn to collective farm labour, characterising this labour as joyous, festive and happy' (Iurenev, 1964, p. 432). Like similar pre-war offerings, it is not actually funny, but it does not need to be. Rather, it is intended as a whole-hearted affirmation of the quality of life under Stalin.

Unlike Pyrev's films of the 1930s, *The Kuban Cossacks* does not contain much plot, simply a series of romantic interludes in an otherwise unbroken stream of images of pastoral bliss, lovingly filmed in colour. The camera lingers on rolling fields with ranks of smiling, singing peasants all working to bring in the harvest. Most of the peasant men have medals and decorations and where else but in a socialist country would you meet a lowly peasant able to quote Shakespeare? In the village market there are all sorts of goods on sale, including fruits and vegetables, household items, bicycles, guitars, radios, vases, books, even a grand piano. The men are dressed in traditional Cossack attire, the women in suitably demure flowery dresses and old and young alike rejoice in the abundance and prosperity of a collectivised rural economy.

Pyrev's idyllic picture of post-war rural life is light years away from the reality. Richard Taylor notes:

The opening and closing sequences of The Kuban Cossacks *use conventions familiar from the Hollywood musical to distance the audience from any expectation of reality: they depict a stylized countryside and suggest what life in the Soviet Union could be like, 'if only'. We should not forget that the film is set in the postwar period, indeed less than five years after a war that brought unparalleled devastation to the Soviet countryside and that compounded the dislocation and starvation deliberately self-inflicted during the period of actual collectivization in the early and middle 1930s, only just over a decade earlier. So the film is intended to offer the vision, anticipated by Lunacharskii, not of reality as it is, but 'of reality as it will be'. The film is therefore well within the guidelines of socialist realist practice. This fantasy element is confirmed by the vision of plenty offered in the autumn fair sequences that are framed within the opening and closing sequences. But here the fantasy is not a faraway magic capital like Moscow, it is literally down on the (collective) farm, in the Potemkin village: it constitutes that 'preview of the coming attractions of socialism'.*

(*Taylor, 1999, pp. 157–8*)[5]

The Kuban Cossacks is pure fantasy, an escape from what was by all accounts a very drab and desperate rural existence in the early post-war years and a projection of future, or at least imagined, prosperity. It reflects the state's explicit ambition to turn the fairytale into reality. It can, nevertheless, be compared with post-depression Hollywood products. An obvious example here is *The Wizard of Oz* (1939), where Judy Garland's Dorothy abandons the real world of black-and-white drudgery down on the farm in Kansas for the technicolor splendour of the Yellow Brick Road leading to the Emerald City. There is, however, a crucial difference between the film and the book written by L. Frank Baum in 1900. In Victor Fleming's film Dorothy lives on quite an affluent farm and Uncle Henry and Auntie Em have a posse of farmhands. Dorothy flees the real world in her dream simply because of the threat to her dog, Toto, from a nasty neighbour. In the book Dorothy and her relatives live a hand-to-mouth existence and her utopian dream-fantasy is her only means of escape from a grinding poverty and greyness that have made her aunt and uncle old before their time. Is there really that much difference between the Judy Garland vehicle, with its memorable tunes and the dream of a better life somewhere over the rainbow and Pyrev's film, designed to show Stalin that all was well in the countryside and that the country was flourishing under his rule (i.e. there's no place like home in Stalin's Russia)? Certainly, in both cases the cinematic fairytale aided social cohesion.

The problem of Soviet film comedy can be seen in clearer focus in the late 1940s, in comments by a leading film critic of the time. Dmitrii Eremin, one of the editorial board of the influential monthly journal *Iskusstvo kino*, made it clear in 1948 that the true task of the Soviet comedy writer was not to be funny, but to educate (I have tried to maintain the turgid style of the original):

The greatest danger for the comedy writer is the strictly professional desire to make the comedy simply funny, and not to achieve a great artistic effect. The main desire for the Soviet comedy writer should be the desire to portray – in a witty comedic form – lively and authentic characters, that is, to achieve an artistic and vivid depiction of life. Through a system of totally positive characters, developed in the depiction of the instructive and funny, the ideological and creative task of the

Soviet comedy writer can be expressed with as much content and subject matter as any other dramatic genre.

(Eremin, 1948, p. 12)

In other words, there was not really much difference between the genre of comedy or, say, the literary adaptation. From the early years of sound to the death of Stalin, the state regarded film comedy as a propaganda tool, with the emphasis on solid ideological content and a secondary consideration of whether it was actually entertaining. Comedy was above all meant to raise a contented smile, to persuade Soviet citizens that they lived in a prospering state and that life under Stalin had indeed become better and more cheerful.

After Stalin: the emergence of satire

Stalin died in March 1953. As ever in Soviet Russian culture, the beginning of one age meant the rejection of the conventions of the previous. For the first time since the 1920s social satire made itself felt in film comedy of the mid-1950s. Soviet film-makers began exploring the legacy of Stalinism and its effects on the psyche and behaviour of people in what became known as the 'thaw'. Mikhail Kalatozov's 1954 comedy *Loyal Friends* is an important and largely successful attempt to address this legacy. A genuinely funny, occasionally hilarious account of three childhood friends who, in middle age, take a raft trip down the Iauza river, it contains mild criticism of demagogic officials and the inhumanity of the old system. Moreover, the film can be seen as an allegory of individual rebirth and social regeneration, as the trio shake off the superficial officiousness acquired in the course of their adult years – Stalinism – and recapture the innocence and goodness of their younger years. In the year following Stalin's death, the film offers clear pointers for spiritual and moral revitalisation, realised in a comic and gently satirical context.

The film's key scene is the arrest and interrogation of one of the friends, the civil engineer Professor Nestratov, on suspicion of being a member of a criminal gang. This classic case of mistaken identity may be milked for its full comic effect, but it has a dark subtext. The detailed interrogation, the policeman's assumption that mere suspicion is proof of guilt and Nestratov's release only secured by the *deus ex machina* of a telephone call from Moscow have a serious correlation with the recent past. Not many innocent Soviet citizens would have been saved by a highly placed friend's telephone call in the course of their interrogation during the Stalin terror.

Loyal Friends also marks the point where satire and narrative comedy begin to take over from the false optimism of the musical comedy. Eldar Riazanov's first major film was *Carnival Night*, released in 1956, and another that relied on narrative twists rather than simply songs. Igor Ilinskii plays Ogurtsov, the Stalinist director of a 'house of culture' that is preparing a spectacular New Year's Eve show. The young students defy the mind-numbing strictures of Ogurtsov, who demagogically insists on mediocre uniformity in all artistic endeavour, and manage to put on a show full of freshness and originality, at the same time debunking Ogurtsov's status. Clearly a film of its time – the thaw and the beginning of de-Stalinisation – *Carnival Night* is a successful comedy with some hilarious moments, as well as a carnivalesque rejection of the old world and a youthful celebration of the new. The setting of New Year's Eve allows much fun to be poked at Ogurtsov, so that he becomes a stage buffoon by the end of the proceedings. The film has much visual flair and exuberance, offering a happy, smiling post-Stalin collective where old and young alike can find romance and where the pleasures of the flesh – champagne, dancing, singing, laughing – promise a new order.

The carnival, however, may be short lived. Ogurtsov is essentially the same Stalinist bureaucrat as Byvalov, played by Ilinskii in *Volga-Volga*. If, at the end of Alexandrov's film, Byvalov simply fades from view as his bureaucratic mindset becomes redundant, in *Carnival Night* Ogurtsov has the last say. After the closing credits he reappears on screen to address the viewer directly, denying responsibility for what has gone before – but also offering a veiled warning that he and his kind may yet return.

In the 1970s and 1980s Riazanov made comedies with a more dangerous, political edge, becoming bolder and more pronounced towards the end of the so-called 'stagnation' period. In 1967 he made *Keep an Eye on Your Car*, for instance, a sympathetic portrait of a car thief with some gentle and ideologically harmless humour aimed squarely at the new consumerism of Soviet society. His *An Irony of Fate or Enjoy Your Bath* (1975), however, went a step further in not just presenting a romantic comedy, but one that had significant social comment. It was voted the best film of 1976 and the star, Andrei Miagkov, was voted in a magazine poll the best actor that same year. It is still a phenomenally popular film in Russia and continues to be shown every year on Russian television on New Year's Eve.

The plot is as follows. Miagkov plays Zhenia, a Muscovite who is about to get married. Traditionally, he and three friends go to the bathhouse on New Year's Eve, before the real celebrations begin. Inevitably, of course, he gets drunk and ends up boarding a plane for Leningrad. There he takes a taxi to what he believes to be his own street in Moscow, finds the right house and apartment and his key fits the lock. However, he has actually found his way into the Leningrad flat of Nadia, who turns up to find a strange man asleep, without his trousers on, in her bed! Much farcical confusion ensues, but eventually, after the inevitable misunderstandings and painstaking explanations, Zhenia and Nadia fall in love. This denouement is, of course, highly contrived, but what Riazanov has done is to show how a little bit of magic can illuminate the depersonalised, soulless Soviet city and rehumanise communities that have no identity or individuality, where the street names, house numbers and even their construction are the same, where keys fit the locks of houses in streets of the same name but in different cities.

The attributes of carnival and barely suppressed anarchy are evident in *An Irony of Fate*. In defiance of social convention, the four men drink vodka in the bathhouse on New Year's Eve. This results in spatial confusion, whereby the two metropolitan centres, Moscow and Leningrad, become indistinguishable and the intoxicated Zhenia undermines and eventually deflates the pomposity and claim to moral authority of Ippolit, Nadia's officious boyfriend.[6] The culture of vodka drinking and male bonding continues to be an important narrative component in post-Soviet cinema (of which more later).

Riazanov has given many topical subjects the comic treatment in his films since the 1970s. In *An Office Romance* (1977) he shows the blossoming romance between an office junior Novoseltsev (again played by Miagkov) and his female boss (Alisa Freindlikh), thus locking into current male concerns of female emancipation and the perceived threat to male dominance of the workplace. It also throws out some satirical asides at the pampered classes whose connections get them foreign travel and Marlboro cigarettes and who callously and cynically attempt to use these connections to manipulate people.

The film is structured around two romances, one an honest and sincere affair, the other used by the interestingly named Samokhvalov ('Self-aggrandiser') for his own selfish ends. Samokhvalov as played by Oleg Basilashvili is an easily recognisable type from 1970s' Russian culture: a cynical, self-serving bureaucrat who uses everyone, including his friends, for personal advancement and gain. When Samokhvalov is slapped, it is the comeuppance his type gets in film, if not in real life. As Novoseltsev tells him at the end: 'You'll go far' ('Далеко пойдете', with the formal second person plural now replacing the previously more intimate 'ty' form of address).

A Station for Two (1982) is set in a railway halt in the back of beyond and here Riazanov explores the limits of the permissible. He also makes some telling points about the increasing social tensions that were becoming obvious in late Soviet society. He may overtly criticise those who deal in the black market, but he allows those characters to make the point that the black market supplies goods the official retailers cannot, although they are in great demand. Liberal sexual mores are also held up to scorn, but with a tantalising glimpse of the possibilities on offer to the average Soviet male who may be tempted by predatory females to stray from the straight and narrow. The country here is filmed as an admittedly benevolent police state, but even here true love will find a way – even through the barbed wire of a labour camp.

Riazanov's most perceptive and acutely observed film, however, is *The Garage*, made in 1979, about a group of car owners whose garage access is suddenly threatened. The car owners are mainly workers, academics and administrators from the aptly named 'Scientific Research Institute for the Protection of Animals from the Environment' and the meeting takes place in the museum which features exhibits of rare animals, birds and fish. Riazanov makes use of comic juxtaposition several times to frame a particular character next to a stuffed exhibit: the corrupt and ultimately callous market manager is juxtaposed with a lion, the bellicose Karpukhin stands next to a model of a carp and the hapless chairman of the meeting (played by Valentin Gaft in a brilliant comic performance of increasing exasperation) seeks refuge beneath the swinging figure of a fish whose gaping mouth perfectly captures his helplessness at the mounting anarchy of the situation.

In the film, four of the staff are arbitrarily deprived of their garage space, as a major road project will reduce the number of garage spaces available for the Institute's cooperative. Those who initially lose out are the most vulnerable and defenceless members of the meeting, including Khvostov (Andrei Miagkov), who has lost his voice and is unable to protest, at least vocally; the humble research worker Guskov, recently denied a trip to Paris and here represented by his loquacious wife; and a war veteran who has recently retired. The four rebel against this decision, made by management with no consultation, steal the key and lock everyone in the building overnight. Eventually, after much discussion and soul searching, the collective decides to exclude those who have no moral right to a garage space. These are the two members of the cooperative who are not Institute staff, such as the venal market manager and the well-connected professor's son, as well as the officious and, as it becomes clear, corrupt deputy director of the Institute Anikeeva (Iia Savvina). Indeed, her car is stolen in the course of the meeting and she therefore has no further need of a garage space! Democracy apparently rules as the others then draw lots to decide who loses the last place. The short straw is left for the character, played by Riazanov himself, who has slept throughout the whole meeting and who is thus deprived of his car space through sheer inaction.

Riazanov has made another carnivalesque, cleverly allegorical film about a collective that cuts itself off for one night from the outside world, rids itself of the corrupt members and self-seeking authorities and reinvents itself from the bottom up. The weak rebel against a rigid authority and in the course of the film attract most of the others to their side. Those who represent the tyranny of authority (such as Karpukhin) repeat Stalinist phrases such as: 'I am of the majority, I am for order and discipline, everything is founded on the likes of me.' Laughter comes at the expense of authority and established order and is especially raucous when one of the staff punctuates the proceedings with loud bursts on his trombone, deflating all attempts at solemnity and platitudes.

The Garage is an extremely bold film for its time and one that goes beyond carnival. Here established hierarchies are overturned and narrative closure heralds a new order. It is also very funny, with good ensemble acting from Riazanov's favourite crop of actors (apart from Miagkov, leading roles are played by Georgii Burkov, Liia Akhedzhakova, Svetlana Nemoliaeva and Semen Farada), with some telling one-liners and a general encouragement to anarchy and rebellion.

The late 1950s saw the emergence of another talent who, together with Riazanov, is undoubtedly the dominant figure in Soviet and Russian comedy of the post-Stalin period. This is Leonid Gaidai. Both directors also embody differing approaches to the film comedy. If Riazanov's films rely on verbal sparring and wit, Leonid Gaidai's films are primarily visual, based on the hearty slapstick and knockabout comedy beloved by millions of moviegoers the world over.

Leonid Gaidai began directing films in the late 1950s. His first film, *The Fiancé from the Other World* (1958), was savaged by the censors and reduced in length by almost a half. Subsequently Gaidai kept away from overt political comedy, although he got away with several political asides in his films, usually in the form of throwaway one-liners containing double meanings that would be understood by a Soviet audience. He could thus include jokes about the average citizen's urge to inform on his neighbour, the power of the police and the regimentation of society. But on the whole Gaidai's humour is similar to the purely visual comedy of the silent age. Riazanov's satire loses its edge with time, as what was funny in 1979 may be lost on a new generation, but Gaidai's apolitical knockabout style still raises a chuckle decades later.

Leonid Gaidai made his name in the 1960s with a series of comedies about Shurik, a hapless and comically pitiful character who may bumble and bluster, but who always wins through in the end. In the 1970s Gaidai consolidated his reputation with his adaptation of the classic Soviet comic novel *The Twelve Chairs* (1971), written by the duo Ilia Ilf and Evgenii Petrov in the 1930s, and the hit comedy *Ivan Vasilevich Changes Profession* (1973), where the hero Timofeev travels back in time to meet Ivan the Terrible and brings him back to modern Moscow, with much fun had at the expense of Soviet bureaucratic pomposity.

His films of the 1960s, such as *Barbos the Dog, Moonshiners* (both 1961), *Operation 'Oo-oh'* (1965) and *The Girl Imprisoned in the Caucasus* (1966), were phenomenally popular, with the last two reaching over 70 million viewers each. In all these films three stooge-like comic villains (played by Iurii Nikulin, Evgenii Morgunov and Georgii Vitsin), see their attempts at petty crime – poaching, illegal vodka distilling, burglary, kidnapping – come to nought through a combination of their own bungling and incompetence and sometimes by the redoubtable Shurik (Alexander Demianenko). These are simple comedies with amiable would-be conmen trying their luck and coming to grief. The villains look to make illegal earnings and so raise their material status in true capitalistic fashion, but they offer no threat to the social fabric, neither do they encroach on the prevailing ideological norms. The peoples of the Soviet Union, in true internationalist fashion, are shown to be united, they work together to defeat villainy, the proclaimed modern emancipated status of women triumphs over backward notions of Caucasian patriarchal conservatism and the letter of the law is upheld.

Gaidai's most famous film is *Diamond Arm*, made in 1968 with an array of well-known comic players: Iurii Nikulin, Andrei Mironov, Anatolii Papanov and Nonna Mordiukova. Nikulin plays Gorbunkov, who goes on a tourist trip to the West (Istanbul, Marseille), falls foul of some villains and returns home with his arm in plaster, inside of which, unbeknown to him, is a stash of illegally smuggled diamonds. Despite the fact that the vast majority of Soviet citizens at that time would never be offered a trip to the West, Gaidai has made a subtle film that provides the staple criticism of Western mores, but also, and more significantly, gently mocks the Soviet paranoia of the West. Mordiukova, in particular, as the house manager and staunch defender of official values and morality, is the butt of much of the humour. *Diamond Arm* is a witty satire of the officially encouraged fear and suspicion of all things Western, at the same time providing some tantalising snippets of Western exotica, such as striptease. (Mironov's character alludes to the pleasures of the flesh early in the film when he sings a song 'The Island of Bad Luck', where the natives walk about 'in their birthday suits'.)

Another director specialising in comedies in the 'stagnation period' is Georgii Daneliia. His *Mimino* (1978) is qualitatively different from similar offerings of the day as there is a clear ideological thrust here which is missing, or at best muted, in the films of Gaidai. Mimino is the central character (played by the Georgian actor Vakhtang Kikabidze), a pilot serving the mountainous villages of Georgia. He yearns to be an international pilot and sets off for Moscow to realise his dream. When he is in Moscow, a chance encounter enables him to do this and we get some insights into the general low-level corruption that people need in order to get things done in the big city. This is in contrast to the worthy, wholesome values of rural Georgia. Eventually Mimino realises that he really does belong back home and returns to his rustic but honest homeland.

This is a film that gives an ideologically impeccable picture of a society where all conflicts and problems can be resolved through friends or the goodness of people, sometimes complete strangers. *Mimino* was made at a time when Jewish emigration from the USSR was at its height and official propaganda, if it made any mention of the exodus at all, would remind hard-working Soviet citizens that life in Israel was bad and dangerous and it would be much better for honest Soviet citizens to remain at home. Mimino talks on the telephone to a Georgian living in Tel-Aviv who yearns to return to his native Georgia and who bursts into tears when they sing Georgian songs together. Nostalgia is akin to patriotism.

The foreign influence

A few words should be said about the foreign imports into Russia during the 1970s and 1980s. Certainly, more and more Western films were shown in Soviet cinemas, as were films from Africa and especially India. Western comedies would be shown that depicted the class divisions of capitalist society or which simply appealed to Russian tastes, such as the custard-pie throwing slapstick of Blake Edwards's *The Great Race* (1965), the sexual confusions of Billy Wilder's *Some Like It Hot* (1959), the film farces of the French actor-director Pierre Richard and the anarchic, occasionally very tasteless comedies of Coluche (Michel Colucci). The Soviet Union showed the Dustin Hoffman smash hit *Tootsie* to its audiences in 1983, presumably to convince Soviet citizens that in the USA the only way for an unemployed actor to get a job is to dress up as a woman. The idea that a man must degrade himself to such an extent and deny his own sex in order to survive in the West was obviously one that had great appeal to the Soviet cultural ideologues. Nevertheless, it seems certain that the film's main appeal to Soviet moviegoers lay not in the ideological slant imposed on it by officialdom, but in its blurring of sexual identities. This was a theme that had great relevance for a Russia itself experiencing, in the words of a writer of the time, the anxieties and uncertainties of 'the universal process of the feminization of men and the masculinization of women' (Lipatov, 1978, 5: 139).[7]

The same issue had been raised in Soviet cinema in Viktor Titov's 1975 film *Hello, I'm Your Aunty!*, based on Brandon Thomas's farce *Charley's Aunt*. It is an adaptation that would be more at home in the theatre, being based in one set and deriving its humour from the cross-dressing of the central character and the confusions that arise all around. The film is played with an eye for the risqué possibilities of a man dressed up in a woman's clothing who evades the amorous attentions of a (male) judge and at the same time sorts out the emotional lives of those around him. But it also has a clear ideological function: set in the USA in the early twentieth century, the film makes clear pronouncements on the capitalist system, where people use and abuse each other for financial gain. It is an example of a Soviet film that not only adapts its Western material, but also significantly distorts and appropriates it for its own ideological ends. Still, it is interesting, alongside the phenomenal success of *Tootsie* in Soviet cinemas, to note the continuing Russian fascination with cross-dressing and gender confusion, which goes as far back as Protazanov's *The Festival of St Jorgen* of 1930.

The post-Soviet comedy

Perhaps surprisingly in the years since the collapse of the Soviet Union and despite economic meltdown, misery and hardship for the majority of the population and general uncertainty about the future, the comic tradition in Russian cinema has remained robust. Still, this is a new type of comedy that eschews smugness and pseudo-optimism and one that rather tends towards anarchy, black humour and bad taste and the pleasures of life, especially vodka. This 'carnivalisation' also serves to reassess the Soviet experience and a significant film in this respect is Vladimir Levin's *The Pioneer Girl Mary Pickford* (1995).

The film had been in gestation for a long time before it was actually completed and released. Its production at the Odessa film studio in the late 1970s was halted by Goskino and it was made only in post-Soviet times. An ironic take on the 'heroic comedy', it is a very clever and witty film set in the late 1920s, with the 11-year-old Olia Evtushenko playing Shurka, a young girl who wants to be a film star like Mary Pickford, with wealth and fame in the Hollywood manner. Except that this is provincial Russia and the communist youth leaders do not approve of those who express individualistic leanings to the detriment of the collective. The ominous, threatening undertone of official rhetoric, with its persecution and psychological torment of the young girl, is nevertheless simply a backdrop for a satirical debunking of official Bolshevik values, as demonstrated by young Shurka. The inclusion of documentary footage reminds us of the grinding, prosaic reality behind the bombast and the deportation of a priest and a well-off family show that behind the surface laughter and cheers there is a ruthlessly efficient ideology at work. Shurka's indomitable will and good humour pervade the film and Levin the director has produced a damning indictment of the Soviet regime not through piling on the horrors and butchery, but through the gentle humour of a young girl determined to make her own way in the world. Shurka says at the end that she has twelve smiles, but the camera freezes on her smiling face as the final credits roll: this may be her first and last smile in a society becoming dangerously intolerant of the individual.

Certainly film-makers in 1990s no longer felt the need to glorify the achievements of the state. The artist's need to serve the state had been superseded by the desire to show life warts and all (generally with emphasis on the warts) and a desire to use the new-found artistic freedoms to the full. Directors such as Dmitrii Astrakhan, Iurii Mamin and Alexander Rogozhkin have also demonstrated that, although budgetary constraints offer significant obstacles, it is possible to produce funny films that have something to say about the national condition in a time of crisis.[8]

One of the major films of the 1990s, and one of the great comedy hits of the past two decades, is Rogozhkin's *The Peculiarities of the National Hunt*, an enormously popular film of 1995. Rogozhkin has followed this success with sequels made to the same formula, with the same actors reprising their roles (see filmography). A Finn joins a group of Russians on what he thinks will be a traditional Russian hunt. What he gets, however, is a vodka-fuelled comic adventure with very little hunting. They only manage to capture a cow. In fact, the picture we get of Russian men is very dispiriting: unable to do anything but drink and talk, they achieve nothing, have little or no drive and seem content to exist in an alcoholic stupor. In one scene the hunters become the hunted, as a bear interrupts their communal washing in the bathhouse and, more annoyingly for them, drinks their vodka. In *The Peculiarities of the National Hunt in Winter Time* (2000) there are some very funny visual and sound jokes, such as when the hapless hunters think they hear the mating call of a stag, when the sound is in fact the toot of a passing train, and when a man and woman are literally joined together when their lips are frozen to the cup they both try to drink from.

Iurii Mamin made films in the early 1990s that could be seen as wrily satirical asides on the turbulent contemporary social and political situation in Russia. *Kiss the Bride!* (1998), however, is gentler and less ironic towards the hapless characters caught up in various stories of marital and erotic bliss. As people wait for the bride to arrive at a registry office, they tell Chaucer-like tales of how individuals got together, or failed to get together, in a series of comic, occasionally hilarious vignettes. There is no denying the violent reality all around, but even a fairly vicious street mugging is given a comic slant as a man beaten and stripped naked by thugs is transformed into an Adonis for a love-starved neighbour.

There is a gentle humour to this film, but there is also a number of paradoxes. Mamin removes the artificiality and hypocrisy of marriage as a state of so-called bliss. Marriage as an institution may be mocked, but people of all creeds and cultures need it to find happiness. Relationships fail only because of the inconstancy of women, while Russian men are basically decent and unassuming, needing something to believe in and look to the future. People flock to get married and so to affirm their faith in the future, but the film's foregrounding of excess suggests that people live only for the moment, with all thoughts of an uncertain tomorrow blocked out. Mamin's humour can be truly surreal: where else but in Russia would someone attend a wedding dressed in deep-sea diving gear?

In some ways *Kiss the Bride!* resembles Pavel Lungin's 2000 film *The Wedding*, in that it shows a group of Russians determined to have a carnival and enjoy themselves to the full despite their straitened material circumstances. Both films also lock into a post-Soviet concern with masculinity, as exemplified by Rogozhkin's 'hunters'. With the collapse of super-power status since 1991, Russian men have become disempowered, unable to achieve their goals and content to wallow in alcohol. Lungin's film foregrounds competing masculinities as two men vie for the love of the honest Russian girl Tania, who has come back to her rural roots from a modelling career in Moscow. These two men represent the Russia of the 1990s, Misha the decent working-class lad, Vasilii a 'new Russian' wheeler-dealer with all the trappings, power and arrogance of affluence. That she chooses Misha is an expression of faith in the power of endurance and that honest Russian values will win through. Rogozhkin's hunters achieve nothing but a monumental hangover, Mamin's men are at the mercy of their womenfolk and Lungin's are basically honest and good natured.

Real laughter in Russian culture, as noted by Dmitrii Likhachev and Mikhail Bakhtin, is a life-affirming counter to the dead hand of authoritarian, closed discourse of the rulers. Combining the bawdy, abrasive and irreverent, it is a liberating force that affirms the truth of the people as opposed to those who tyrannise them. Bakhtin's study of Rabelais shows how humour can be subversive, established hierarchies can be overturned by the carnival and the fool can become king for a day. In post-Soviet comedy the concept of masculinity and its accompanying discourse of power and empowerment are both deconstructed and definitively debunked.

This applies not only to the equation of male potency and political power, but to culture, too. On first viewing Alexei Balabanov's *Of Freaks and Men* (1998) one can be forgiven for thinking that it is an extended sick joke at the expense of the audience. It is certainly grotesque, a comedy of the blackest sort, but it also overturns existing hierarchies and challenges fundamental cultural assumptions. It is set in St Petersburg in the early years of the twentieth century and, in apparent homage to the early years of cinema, is shot in black and white, with intertitles. However, it soon becomes apparent that the new medium is not for the enlightenment of the people or for the development of a new art form, but simply as a means of making money, and fairly dirty money at that.

Viktor Ivanovich and his boss Iogan sell pornographic photographs, then graduate to pornographic films once the moving image can be captured on camera. They use as their subjects the weakest and most vulnerable: a pair of Siamese twin boys, a blind widow and Liza, a young girl suddenly left destitute. Innocence is corrupted and defiled in images that are alternately repulsive and grotesquely funny. St Petersburg society of the so-called 'silver age' of Russian culture does not seek artistic sophistication or aesthetic delight, but rather depravity and debauchery.

Of Freaks and Men is a film that is very aware of its own cultural credentials. In particular, it offers a deconstruction of St Petersburg as a centre of artistic achievement. There is little evidence of any culture or erudition of any sort, but there is a gathering of dirty old men watching a naked woman being thrashed with birch twigs. Outdoors the camera lingers on the topography of St Petersburg, the canals, the Neva river and the embankment. Characters' names also invoke the city as past capital of the country: the cameraman Putilov bears the same name as the Petrograd munitions factory that was one of the Bolsheviks's centres of working-class support in 1917; Dr Stasov, the adopted father of the Siamese twins, shares his surname with Vladimir Stasov, St Petersburg's most eminent nineteenth-century art critic. Scenes of depravity are accompanied by music from the ballet of *Romeo and Juliet* written in 1936 by Sergei Prokofev, an inhabitant of Leningrad. The epilepsy that Iogan suffers from links him with both the person and the work of Fedor Dostoevskii, another inhabitant of that city.

Balabanov's film is therefore more than an exercise in very twisted humour. It debunks the notion of cinema as an art form and the elevated notions of culture associated with St Petersburg and the 'silver age' (approximately 1890–1917). Since 1991 comedy and humour, then, have been used in order to confront the past and as vehicles to convey apprehension at the consequences of social collapse and dislocation.

Filmography

Andrei Rublev, dir. Andrei Tarkovskii, 1965

Anton Ivanovich Gets Angry ('Anton Ivanovich serditsia'), dir. Alexander Ivanovskii, 1941

Autumn Marathon ('Osennii marafon'), dir. Georgii Daneliia, 1979

Barbos the Dog ('Pes Barbos'), dir. Leonid Gaidai, 1961

Carnival Night ('Karnavalnaia noch'), dir. Eldar Riazanov, 1956

Cheerful Fellows ('Veselye rebiata'), dir. Grigorii Alexandrov, 1934

Chess Fever ('Shakhmatnaia goriachka'), dir. Vsevolod Pudovkin, 1925

The Circus ('Tsirk'), dir. Grigorii Alexandrov, 1936

Dear Elena Sergeevna ('Dorogaia Elena Sergeevna'), dir. Eldar Riazanov, 1989

Diamond Arm ('Brilliantovaia ruka'), dir. Leonid Gaidai, 1968

Don Diego and Pelageia ('Don Diego i Pelageia'), dir. Iakov Protazanov, 1929

The Extraordinary Adventures of Mr West in the Land of the Bolsheviks ('Neobychainye prikliucheniia mistera Vesta v strane bolshevikov'), dir. Lev Kuleshov, 1924

The Festival of St Jorgen ('Prazdnik sviatogo Iorgena'), dir. Iakov Protazanov, 1930

The Fiancé from Another World ('Zhenikh s togo sveta'), dir. Leonid Gaidai, 1958

A Forgotten Tune for Flute ('Zabytaia melodiia dlia fleity'), dir. Eldar Riazanov, 1987

The Foundling ('Podkidysh'), dir. Tatiana Lukashevich, 1939

The Garage ('Garazh'), dir. Eldar Riazanov, 1979

The Girl Imprisoned in the Caucasus ('Kavkazskaia plennitsa'), dir. Leonid Gaidai, 1966

A Girl with Character ('Devushka s kharakterom'), dir. Konstantin Iudin, 1939

The Great Race, dir. Blake Edwards, 1965

The 'Happy New Year' Operation ('Operatsiia "S Novym godom!"'), dir. Alexander Rogozhkin, 1996

Hello, I'm Your Aunty! ('Zdravstvuite, ia vasha tetka!'), dir. Viktor Titov, 1975

The House on Trubnaia ('Dom na Trubnoi'), dir. Boris Barnet, 1927

An Irony of Fate or Enjoy Your Bath! ('Ironiia sudby ili s legkim parom!'), dir. Eldar Riazanov, 1975

Ivan Vasilevich Changes Profession ('Ivan Vasilevich meniaet professiiu'), dir. Leonid Gaidai, 1973

Keep an Eye on Your Car! ('Beregis avtomobilia!'), dir. Eldar Riazanov, 1967

Kiss the Bride ('Gorko!'), dir. Iurii Mamin, 1998

The Kuban Cossacks ('Kubanskie kazaki'), dir. Ivan Pyrev, 1949

Love's Little Berry ('Iagodka liubvi'), dir. Alexander Dovzhenko, 1926

Loyal Friends ('Vernye druzia'), dir. Mikhail Kalatozov, 1954

Mimino, dir. Georgii Daneliia, 1978

Moonshiners ('Samogonshchiki'), dir. Leonid Gaidai, 1961

Moscow Doesn't Believe in Tears ('Moskva slezam ne verit'), dir. Vladimir Menshov, 1979

A Musical Story ('Muzykalnaia istoriia'), dir. Alexander Ivanovskii, 1940

Of Freaks and Men ('Pro urodov i liudei'), dir. Alexei Balabanov, 1998

An Office Romance ('Sluzhebnyi roman'), dir. Eldar Riazanov, 1977

Operation 'Oo-oh' ('Operatsiia "Y"'), dir. Leonid Gaidai, 1965

The Peculiarities of National Fishing ('Osobennosti natsionalnoi rybalki'), dir. Alexander Rogozhkin, 1998

The Peculiarities of the National Hunt ('Osobennosti natsionalnoi okhoty'), dir. Alexander Rogozhkin, 1995

The Peculiarities of the National Hunt in Winter Time ('Osobennosti natsionalnoi okhoty v zimnii period'), dir. Alexander Rogozhkin, 2000

The Pioneer Girl Mary Pickford ('Pionerka Meri Pikford'), dir. Vladimir Levin, 1995

Prediction ('Predskazanie'), dir. Eldar Riazanov, 1993

The Rich Bride ('Bogataia nevesta'), dir. Ivan Pyrev, 1937

The Shining Path ('Svetlyi put'), dir. Grigorii Alexandrov, 1940

The Silent Ace of the Skies ('Nebesnyi tikhokhod'), dir. Semen Timoshenko, 1945

Some Like It Hot, dir. Billy Wilder, 1959

Spring ('Vesna'), dir. Grigorii Alexandrov, 1947

A Station for Two ('Vokzal dlia dvoikh'), dir. Eldar Riazanov, 1982

The Swineherdess and the Shepherd ('Svinarka i pastukh'), dir. Ivan Pyrev, 1941

Tootsie, dir. Sydney Pollack, 1982

The Trial of the Three Millions ('Protsess o trekh millionakh'), dir. Iakov Protazanov, 1926

The Twelve Chairs ('Dvenadsat stulev'), dir. Leonid Gaidai, 1971

Volga-Volga, dir. Grigorii Alexandrov, 1938

The Wedding ('Svadba'), dir. Pavel Lungin, 2000

The Wizard of Oz, dir. Victor Fleming, 1939

Notes

1. 'The buffoon embodies the anarchic creative spirit of the people, their earthiness, and their instinctive resistance to hypocrisy and the arrogance of power: church and state combine to suppress him' (Johnson and Petrie, 1994, p. 87).

2. In that same year (1935), however, the film had been criticized in the pages of *Literaturnaia gazeta* (28 February, 6 March and 16 March) for the 'formalism' of the central, and very funny, fight scene, which purportedly had nothing to do with the film's content and was therefore redundant.

3. Rostislav Iurenev, author of the standard history of Soviet film comedy, is gushing in his praise of *The Foundling*: 'The director T. Lukashevich and camerman S. Sheinin have succeeded in creating a bright, attractive image of the socialist city Moscow with its large houses, trams, stations, cars, gardens and the incessant stream of passers-by who affectionately, attentively and affably encounter the little seeker of adventure. The kind-hearted city is the film's protagonist. The broad streets are full of noise and people. The windows of large houses are cordially thrown open. The greenery of the avenues, the new tall bridges, the slender contours of the ancient Kremlin towers . . . And everywhere there are people, cheerful, kind people, ready to treat the child with affection and comfort, even adopt her.' (See Iurenev (1964), p. 328.) It is interesting to note that another comedy by Konstantin Iudin, *Four Loving Hearts*, a harmless comedy about two couples who eventually find true love and made in 1939, was labelled as 'lacking in ideas' (*besideinyi*), banned and was not shown until 1944.

4. For discussion and statistical information on Soviet cinema in these years, see Maya Turovskaya (1993), 'The Tastes of Soviet Moviegoers during the 1930s', in Lahusen with Kuperman, pp. 95–107.

5. Taylor (1999), pp. 157–8. Moreover, the film's original title was *A Cheerful Market* (*Veselaia iarmarka*), and was intended by Pyrev and Nikolai Pogodin, the author of the screenplay, as a comedy, but Stalin changed the title because he wanted 'a real picture of the life of the Kuban' village'. (See Mariamov (1992), p. 113.)

6. Stephen Hutchings states that *An Irony of Fate* 'is, in fact, a carnivalesque film in which official order is, for one sane night, overturned (Ippolit is ejected and ridiculed), the jester (Zhenia) becomes king, and the outside world of vodka and laughter replaces the polite, inside, bureaucratic "court"'. (See Hutchings (2000), p. 245.)

7. For more discussion of the battle of the sexes in film, see Lynne Attwood, 'Gender Angst in Russian Society and Cinema in the Post-Stalin Era', in Kelly and Shepherd (1998), pp. 352–67.

8. For discussion of the films of Astrakhan, see Julian Graffy, 'Dmitri Astrakhan: Popular Cinema for a Time of Uncertainty', in Beumers (1999), pp. 161–78.

CHAPTER FOUR

The course and curse of history

Time present and time past
Are both perhaps present in time future
And time future contained in time past.

(*T. S. Eliot,* Burnt Norton)

Background: the problem of 'history'

Pierre Sorlin comments: 'The historical film is a dissertation about history that does not question its subject – here it differs from the work of the historian – but which establishes relationships between facts and offers a more or less superficial view of them' (Sorlin, 1980, p. 21). Every national film culture likes representing its own past on the screen. Major events from the past have often been the staple diet of world cinema – witness the myriad films about the Second World War, the Russian Revolution, the American West, the lives of the English kings and queens. Yet in order to speak to a new generation, these films must have a contemporary relevance, and the historical film is rarely, if ever, a true representation of the past, for the film-maker must select and organise his material in order to be in tune with the modern consciousness. In Western cinema, a historical film must, above all, sell. Whether it is actually a true representation of the events it depicts is not actually that important to the producer and director. Contrariwise, the Russian historical film is of interest to the viewer above all in what it tells him not about the past, but the present.

There are countless examples of historical films across the globe that are fast and loose with the facts. In the conditions of the Soviet Union, the film had to have primarily an ideological purpose, and 'history' was determined from above. History, indeed, was deemed to have reached its logical, class-based culmination with the October Revolution and it was only a matter of time before other states followed and adopted the Soviet form of government. For the Marxist-Leninist leadership, the war had been won, even if some important battles still needed to be fought and history, as we know, is always written by the victors.

Film-makers, therefore, had to use history to legitimise the current leadership and the Marxist-Leninist reading of world and in particular Russian history. The past, then, was rewritten to fit in with the present. Even in post-Soviet cinema, this paradigm remains valid. Historical films of the 1990s have addressed a modern audience all too familiar with the facts of the recent past and are part of a debate about post-totalitarian identity and what Russians themselves prefer to call their 'destiny'.

In Soviet Russia, history was a particular problem. Coming to terms with the past – learning the truth – is the key to understanding the present, but that 'truth' was always subject to the Party's control and manipulation. Russia's preoccupation with its own history, especially during the Soviet period, offers an eerie echo of the Party's slogan in *Nineteen Eighty-Four*: 'Who controls the past controls the future: who controls the present controls the past' (Orwell, 1954, p. 31). Therefore, the Russian historical film, be it pre-1991 or subsequent, is not only about representing the past or visualising it as a means of entertainment or instruction. Rather, it is there to legitimise the present, to explain past events in the light of present-day realities and so point to the future. Thus, there is in Russian cinema a constant effort to reinvent history.

The Soviet regime engaged in Orwellian 'reality control' and the appropriation of Russian history. History was constantly revised and updated to serve the current leadership's interests (thus, the subsequent airbrushing from photographs of Party leaders who fell out of favour with Stalin). As Russians are fond of saying, 'There is nothing as unpredictable in Russia as her past' and those involved in Russian culture have for decades been at pains to explore Russia's troublesome historical legacy in order to comprehend better the contemporary reality around them. For decades observers have repeated Gogol's question from the end of *Dead Souls*: 'Russia, where are you heading?' ('Русь, куда же несешься ты?'). In post-Soviet times this question remains just as relevant, perhaps even more so.

Stalin's nationalisation of history

It is therefore no surprise to learn that among the first Russian films were historical studies, such as V. Romashkov's *Stenka Razin* in 1908 and Vasilii Goncharov's *The Defence of Sevastopol* in 1912. Directors of the 'golden age' of Soviet cinema chose the February and October Revolutions of 1917 to create a vast historical tableau which combined epic cinematic vision with a treatise on historical progress. Thus, Sergei Eisenstein's hymns to revolution (*Battleship Potemkin*, 1926 and *October*, 1927) recreate on film the Marxist-Leninist interpretation of historical development, where the exploited masses rise against their masters and thereby raise the political consciousness of the nation. In the face of tremendous violence and suppression by the authorities, they eventually win through – if not in the past, then certainly in a projected future. *Battleship Potemkin*, therefore, is not only about events of 1905, but also looks forward to the coming victory in October 1917, from which point mankind progresses in a qualitatively different manner and direction.

Eisenstein's films of the 1920s have been rightly praised for their innovative camera and editing ('montage') techniques and the boldness of their cinematic language. Eisenstein deliberately foregrounds the mass as the mover of history, crowds seethe and surge towards the Winter Palace, victory is above all a collective march towards the workers' promised land. Vsevolod Pudovkin trod much the same ideological ground in *The End of St Petersburg* (1927), but with more concern expressed in his films for the fate of the individual caught in the huge tide of impersonal historical forces. Esfir Shub, too, depicted the Revolution in all its vigour and dynamism with her brilliantly organised collage of documentary clips, *The Fall of the Romanov Dynasty* (1927).

It is interesting to compare the style of both Eisenstein and Pudovkin in their historical films of a decade later. In Eisenstein's 1920s historical films individuals serve only as martyrs to the greater cause, such as Vakulinchuk in *Battleship Potemkin* or the unnamed fallen soldier in the assault on the Winter Palace in *October*, lying wounded on the wet ground but urging his comrades forward despite his wounds. By 1938, however, leaders of men were back in fashion. His Alexander Nevskii unites the Russians of Novgorod to defeat the Germans on the battle on the ice of Lake Peipus. The film also has a contemporary resonance as an assertion of Soviet Russian nationalism and its readiness to fight the Fascist threat of the late 1930s. It is an ironic fact that the film was briefly banned during the Soviet-German non-aggression pact of 1939–41. Still, the fighting scenes are sanitised, Russians merrily hack their way through massed ranks of armour-clad Teutonic knights, whose mettle and conviction waver before the cheery but dogged determination of their foe. Eisenstein's refusal to show the thick of battle in all its brutality is in contrast to the scenes in Pudovkin's 1939 film *Minin and Pozharskii*, about the defence of Moscow from the Poles by Russians led by Prince Pozharskii and the peasant Minin in the seventeenth century. Pudovkin's battles are full-blooded, wounds are painful and there is a clear sense of the confusion and fear of the battlefield.

The leader figure is even more to the fore in *Ivan the Terrible* (Part One, 1944; Part Two, 1945, but released only in 1958). Ivan is obviously meant to be an allegorical representation of Stalin, an interpretation encouraged by the tyrant himself. In his opening speech at the magnificently filmed coronation sequence, Ivan makes it clear to various representatives from foreign lands and his own nobles ('boyars'), all resplendent in comically exaggerated attire and often filmed in grotesque close-up, that he intends to be a strong Tsar who will unite the country against its enemies, both external and internal. Substitute 'Stalin' for 'Ivan' and we have an apologia for the terror of the preceding decade. In Part One Ivan carries out his self-appointed task by defeating the Tartars at Kazan, but then sees his wife murdered by his internal enemies.

Still, strong leaders are loved by the people, for when Ivan leaves Moscow to seek solace in isolation following the death of his wife, the people of Moscow come out en masse to beg him to return. In a superbly realised scene, Ivan's head fills the screen, looking down on his massed subjects bowed in supplication below and thus dominating them. There could be no clearer indication of Stalin's total control of the state and its people.

In Part Two Ivan's paranoia is leading to insanity, a cinematic statement, on Eisenstein's part, tantamount to a suicide note. Indeed, it is well documented that Stalin summoned both the director and the star, Nikolai Cherkasov, to a late-night meeting in the Kremlin in February 1947, where he proceeded to lecture the two on the significance of Ivan in Russian history.[1]

The key scene in the second part of *Ivan the Terrible* is the dance of the *oprichniki*, Ivan's secret police who ravaged the country as the Tsar's agent in destroying the power of the boyars (and as such an obvious representation of Stalin's NKVD). This scene is the only one in both surviving parts of the film shot in colour, and is about ten minutes long. The dominant colours are gold, black and red, as the *oprichniki* ('the men apart') are dressed in black, singing boastful songs about hacking their enemies to pieces and urged on by a crazed Ivan with cries of 'Burn! Burn! Burn!'.

Eisenstein here has created an 'anti-world' that corresponds to that defined by Dmitrii Likhachev in the previous chapter. Likhachev examines how medieval laughter is directed at everything that is considered sacred, honourable or pious. As the sign system of the established order is subverted and destroyed, there comes into being an 'anti-culture', an 'anti-world' that is the very opposite of prevailing 'normality'. The anti-world is one of poverty, drunkenness and hunger, as opposed to the prosperity and orderliness of the world of the rulers. In the anti-world, the tavern replaces the church, the prison takes the place of the monastery, drunkenness replaces asceticism. The anti-world emphasises illogicality, unreality and the 'real' world is thus turned upside down. The impossible becomes possible, the absurd and the foolish become the norm. Words, too, lose their meaning and folk sayings, rhymes, aphorisms and oxymoron take the place of 'rational' discourse.

Ivan's *oprichniki* are part of this 'anti-world', murderers dressed in monks' clothing. Their carousing is the anti-ritual of monastery life. Ivan himself dresses as a fool and pretends to be one in front of the halfwitted Prince Vladimir. Ivan acts as if he is humble and lonely, the drunkenness of his followers represents the anti-fast and their celebration of murder and destruction the anti-liturgy. The monastery becomes the tavern, with buffoonery and evil mirth and the fool becomes king for a day, as Ivan clothes Vladimir in regal robes.

Ivan's anti-world not only parodies and subverts established hierarchies of the time. This closed world of oppression and terror is also Stalin's and Prokofev's score with its slightly off-note, rising strings suggests the tyrant's increasing mental instability. The false pretender Vladimir is killed by an assassin who mistakes him, dressed in Ivan's clothes, for the Tsar and Ivan himself presides over the murder. In the final analysis it is Stalin's world that is condemned and demonised. It is not surprising that Stalin did not like it (even if he understood it), but it is surprising that Eisenstein was not made to pay dearly.

The leader as embodiment of the will of the people is the main theme of Vladimir Petrov's *Peter the First* (1937–8). Peter as portrayed by Nikolai Simonov is above all a man of the people, a larger than life character (as history tells us physically he was) at one with the ordinary folk and apt to burst into a large grin that identifies him as in spirit a simple man. So much, in fact, does he see himself as protector of the Russian people that he even orders the execution of his own son Alexei (Nikolai Cherkasov), who had been plotting with some of the nobility against him. Peter's sentencing of his own son to death is historically accurate.

Both *Ivan the Terrible* and *Peter the First* clearly place Stalin within a continuum of popular but ruthless Russian rulers, men who embodied the will and spirit of the Russian nation and who had to be cruel to be kind. It was above all the task of the Soviet film-maker of historical dramas in the 1930s and 1940s to harness the perceived glories of the past in order to legitimise the present, and their most popular forum was through the lives of great men.

Stalin through the looking glass: the heroic biography

The individuals who helped make Russia a strong and respected nation were all, of course, mirror images of the Great Leader himself. Thus, between 1943 and 1953 the theme of history became reduced to recounting the lives of individuals from Russian history as if they were positive heroes from a socialist realist 'master plot'. Peter Kenez explains that the preoccupation with individual heroes from Russian history was not only a reflection of the Stalin cult: 'They also expressed in the clearest form the xenophobic message of

Stalinist ideology. Russian scientists, musicians and admirals have always been the greatest; and Russian talent and virtue have always shone. The films, therefore, bolstered patriotism' (Kenez, 1992, p. 240).

These films are more than mere biopics in that they are designed clearly as heroic biographies. General Kutuzov, for instance, in the 1943 film by Kozintsev and Trauberg (*Kutuzov*), is the embodiment of the will, determination and bravery of the Russian people during their momentous struggle with Napoleon in 1812 (read Hitler in 1943). It is a wartime patriotic flag waver, but is also has a distinct anti-Western stance. The foppish general Barclay de Tolly, complete with a comical foreign accent, bemoans the climactic battle of Borodino as a defeat, whereas wise old Kutuzov sees it and the subsequent abandonment of Moscow to the French as part of a wider scheme to wear down and exhaust the enemy. This plan, of course, works. A contrast to the Westernised de Tolly is General Bagration, a real Russian who drinks and jokes with his men. These men, significantly, go into battle not with cries of 'For the Tsar!', but 'For the Motherland!'. In the Second World War Soviet soldiers would storm the enemy shouting 'For Stalin!'.

There is nothing personal or private about Kutuzov, his whole being is taken up with saving Russia. The same is true of the surgeon and scientist Nikolai Ivanovich Pirogov in another of Kozintsev's films (*Pirogov*, 1947). Pirogov is revered by young medics who do not hesitate to call him 'genius' and 'brilliant' and he is feared and resisted by older (and corrupt) doctors in thrall to suspect Western methods. Pirogov works not for personal gain or status, but for the good of Russia. So, having discovered ether as an anaesthetic to be used in surgery, he travels to the Crimea to save Russian lives in the war there with the English. Pirogov also has no personal life, we know of no family or home, he exists only for his work and for the cause of Russia. Often his gaze is directed, in 'positive hero' fashion, into the distance, where he can presumably glimpse the 'radiant future'.

The hero of Pudovkin's *Admiral Nakhimov* (1946) is another wise and far-seeing man of the people, liked by his men but not his fellow officers, he is instinctively at one with his men and intuitively understands them. He has an almost miraculous ability to claw victory from the jaws of defeat and the adulation of his men borders on the mystical (so much so that they gladly throw themselves in the way of bullets meant for him).

Nakhimov not only sees the need to modernise the Russian navy and to move from wind power to steam, but he can also divine future historical and political developments: the coalition of England, France and Turkey against Russia and the beginning of the Crimean War. It is no surprise to learn that he has no personal life or family, other than Russia itself. His is 'a warrior's achievement' for which he dies on the battlefield: 'eternal glory for a great patriot', the end of the film tells us.

Admiral Nakhimov does not ignore its immediate socio-political context of the beginning of the Cold War, with hysterically anti-Russian English, aloof and arrogant, duplicitous and cowardly but able to recognise Russia as a 'great nation'. This context is also evident in another film by Pudovkin, *Zhukovskii* (1950), tracing the life and work of 'the father of Russian aviation' Nikolai Egorovich Zhukovskii from 1886 to 1917. Zhukovskii is devoted to his work and the greatness of Russia, refuses to compromise for commercial reasons and is opposed by those working for foreign interests, such as Russian capitalists and the Imperial Court in the First World War. Zhukovskii differs from other heroic Russian patriots, however, in that he has a settled family life, with a dutiful wife who looks on her husband with a mixture of reverence and awe, humbly appreciative of the great work he is doing for Russia and so providing him with a stable and well-organised household.

Zhukovskii opens with Levitan-like canvases of the Russian countryside, the patriotic motif asserted from the start as the camera lingers over tranquil fields, the sky and the trees. Similar scenes feature in Leo Arnshtam's film of the life of the composer Mikhail Glinka (*Glinka*, 1946). The film follows him from 1812, when he is a young boy inspired by the sounds of Russian church bells and the strength and determination of the Russian peasant in defeating Napoleon, through to 1842 and his opera of Pushkin's *Ruslan and Liudmila*, which Glinka composed surrounded by the idyllic Russian countryside. Arnshtam's film is a straightforward Stalinist parable, with a linear narrative and the hero's drive towards consciousness in socialist realist fashion. Glinka serves the Russian nation, he has no self-doubt, no aberrations and no moments of sudden insight. Although of landowning stock, he is in awe of folk music and choral singing, his creative fire further stirred by his acquaintance with Pushkin, whose enraptured face is caught bathed in ethereal light as he listens to Glinka's opera. Glinka also has a wife, but she is flighty and more interested in dashing young cavalry officers. Her superficiality is shown in her totally indifferent response to news of Pushkin's death.

Glinka does have certain interesting features, however. First, it condones the composer's adultery as he goes off with a girl who really understands 'culture'. Second, there is a moment of allegorical absurdity when Glinka's opera *Ivan Susanin* is played for the first time. The assembled dignitaries in the theatre begin to laugh and mock the nationalist elements, as if a serious opera could ever be written on a Russian theme, but then the Tsar begins applauding. Everyone joins in and no one wants to be the first to be seen to stop – a curious contemporary reference to the fawning reception the Party's Central Committee accorded Stalin's speeches, when the member who was the first to stop applauding would fear for his life at the hands of the ever-vigilant security services.

Modest Musorgskii, in Grigorii Roshal's film of 1950, is also shown drawing his inspiration from Russian life and the pain and suffering of the masses. He is seen working together with Stasov, Rimskii-Korsakov, Balakirev, Dargomyzhskii and Borodin for a future of freedom and justice. Others regard him with adoration, and the greatest acclaim is from the people, the *narod*. Music should be the 'property of the people,' he asserts, and his mentor Vladimir Stasov (played by Nikolai Cherkasov) is similarly forthright: 'What do we want? We want original Russian realistic art.' And that is what they get. Musorgskii has no life outside his music, he lives only for it. He spends days and nights without food or drink, agonizing over his operas *Boris Godunov* and *The Khovanshchins* and all foreign (i.e. Western) influences and claims to cultural superiority are denigrated.

Such treatment of the historical personage is in vivid contrast to what was practised just a decade earlier. *The Deputy from the Baltic*, directed by Alexander Zarkhi and Iosif Kheifits in 1936, is dedicated to the work of the Russian botanist Kliment Timiriazev. Timiriazev in the film goes under the name of Professor Polezhaev (played by Nikolai Cherkasov) who in 1918 accepts the Revolution, despite the condemnation of most of his bourgeois colleagues. He is feted as a national hero by the Bolsheviks. Polezhaev is suitably cantankerous and doddery for his age, but also unassuming and modest. More importantly, he is recognisable as a human being, with a settled home life and spacious apartment and given to occasional outbursts of indignant anger. As played by Cherkasov, the viewer can believe in Polezhaev as a character and his conversion to the Bolshevik cause is all the more convincing.

Civil War heroes also came under the cinematic spotlight. Dovzhenko's Nikolai Shchors (*Shchors*, 1939) is an embodiment of sheer will, devoted to Lenin and the Bolshevik cause and subordinating his personal life to the goals of the Revolution. He has a wife, but only communicates with her via telegrams. Alexander Faintsimmer's Grigorii Kotovskii (*Kotovskii*, 1950) is also at one with the people, a Robin Hood figure before the Revolution and avenging angel during the Civil War. Kotovskii is fearless and dashing and can even find time to propose marriage during a battle. Like Chapaev before him, he is loved by his men, an embodiment of their wishes and ambitions. Unlike Chapaev, he is more politically aware than his commissar.

But *Kotovskii* also contains subversive hints that at least ripple the veneer of ideological orthodoxy. In pre-revolutionary Russia both political prisoners and hardened criminals are herded together and prisoners are transported to Siberia in the same 'Stolypin' railway carriages that would be used decades later to take the condemned off to Stalin's Gulag. Furthermore, the language used in these scenes is heavily reliant on prison slang. Could Faintsimmer, in these dangerous times, have been not just excoriating the Tsarist past, but even alluding to the oppressive nature of the contemporary regime?

Yet the most obvious source for the heroic biography was Vladimir Lenin himself. In the 1930s there were several famous attempts to foster the cult of Lenin and make him into a larger-than-life hero. The first of these was Dziga Vertov's quasi-documentary *Three Songs About Lenin*, made in 1934, composed of a series of interconnected images proclaiming Lenin as the leader of the world revolution, the creator of the Soviet state and just about the most important man in world history. Shots of a statue of Lenin dominating the landscape are intercut with pictures of Soviet industrial achievements in the early 1930s: the huge metallurgical factories in Magnitogorsk, the dam across the Dnieper river.[2]

This was followed by semi-fictional films in the late 1930s. In 1937 Mikhail Romm made *Lenin in October*, following the great man's struggle for the victory of Bolshevism and two years later continued with *Lenin in 1918*, following the Civil War years. In both films Lenin was played by Boris Shchukin. Here Lenin is not only resolute in political matters, but, much as Vertov had shown him, kind and unassuming in his dealings with ordinary citizens. Mere mortals look on Lenin with love and devotion in their eyes and Stalin, played respectively by Mikhail Gelovani and Semen Goldshtab, is appropriately placed alongside or just behind him in key scenes, the dutiful servant and inheritor of the baton. These films tell us little about the historical background of Revolution and Civil War that we did not already know, neither are they meant to provide insights into the man's character, but they do cement the mythological status of Lenin as the father of the nation, the leader as almighty and untouchable.

We in the West have little cause to patronise Stalinist cinema's preoccupation with great heroes. In Hollywood of the late 1930s and early 1940s there was a spate of biopics of famous people from the USA and Western Europe, although without the nationalist trappings. These include *The Story of Louis Pasteur* (1936), *The Story of Alexander Graham Bell* (1939), *Edison the Man* (1940), *Dr Ehrlich's Magic Bullet* (1940) and *Madame Curie* (1940), all films of generally good quality about individuals who have changed our lives for the better. Hollywood thus gets the credit for the invention of electricity and the telephone, as well as the cure for venereal disease.

Mark Donskoi's *The Village Schoolmistress* (1947) is a heroic biography of a different caste, as it is fictional and about a woman. Vera Maretskaia plays Varvara Vasilevna, who decides to work as a schoolteacher in a village in order to bring light to the darkness of a rural community blighted by drunkenness and ignorance. This is pre-revolutionary Russia, characterised by patriotic images of rolling fields, rivers and sky. Her conviction and sheer will change the backwardness and inherent violence of village life, but her idealism borders on political commitment: she does not teach the children the lyrical or love poetry of the nineteenth-century poets Afanasii

Fet or Fedor Tiutchev, but rather the socially committed verses of Nikolai Nekrasov.

The injustices of the Tsarist past are paraded before us: political repression and the unwillingness of school officials to allow poor and rich children in the same class. Justice and freedom for all come with the new world of the Bolsheviks. The film spans three decades, through to the years of collectivisation, as class enemies want to kill our heroine and burn down the school, and into the war years. Varvara Vasilevna has no personal life after the death of her husband, she simply serves the Motherland and finds true emotional fulfilment when she is recognised by the Supreme Soviet and awarded the Order of Lenin, which coincides with victory in the War. In other words, Varvara Vasilevna's cinematic biography is very similar to that of other Stalinist heroes, with the proviso that hers is fictional. The brazen artificiality of the master plot is there for all to see.

The thaw and after

Not surprisingly, the films of the thaw years tended to ignore history and concentrate on the present. The most significant films of the years 1954–64 were concerned with the spiritual and moral regeneration of post-Stalin society and so were set very palpably in the present or in a past that could still be remembered and relived, the War. Some minor historical films were produced, but it was in the 1960s that the historical theme was to re-emerge and with a qualitatively different approach to its subject matter.

Perhaps the oddest Soviet historical film is Fridrikh Ermler's *Before the Judgement of History* (1964). Made as a documentary, it features the continuing dialogue between the real-life 86-year-old Vasilii Vitalevich Shulgin and an actor playing the part of a Soviet professor of history. Shulgin was one of the most ferocious anti-Bolshevik leaders of the White armies during the Civil War and had been present at the Tsar's abdication. Here he revisits the Soviet Union for the first time in 40 years and his views on the course of Russian history are consistently challenged and countered by the orthodox professor. The intent of the film is to show the recantation, or at least admission of error, by a former class enemy of the regime and thus to prove the legitimacy of the regime. It is therefore not surprising that the filming was particularly closely followed by the KGB. Several scenes had to be rewritten and reshot.[3] Still, after the film ends we know that Shulgin remains unrepentant and he recounts certain facts that would have been unpalatable had they not been told by an ideological foe, such as the fact of the Red Terror during the Civil War. The film's blatant attempt to manipulate history does not work, as the attempt to legitimise the Soviet version of recent history collides with the brick wall of

Nonna Mordiukova about to exercise revolutionary justice in The Commissar *(Alexander Askoldov, 1967)*

eyewitness testimony. In the confrontation of state propaganda and historical fact, there can be only one winner.

The 1960s saw the completion of two other major historical films, Tarkovskii's *Andrei Rublev* (1965) and Alexander Askoldov's *The Commissar* (1967), and both were to suffer censorship problems. Tarkovskii's film will be discussed in Chapter Nine; Askoldov's film, although set in the past, is very much about the present. It challenges the official myths of revolutionary sacrifice for the good of the cause and explores other topical issues. In particular, the fate of the Jews and the role of women in the Soviet state are subject to particular scrutiny.

The film is based on a 1934 story by Vasilii Grossman entitled 'In the Town of Berdichev'. It is set in the Russian Civil War, where a detachment of Reds led by the political commissar Vavilova (Nonna Mordiukova) enters the town of Berdichev in Ukraine. Vavilova takes great pains to be accepted and respected by the young men under her command, hiding her sex under a huge, billowing greatcoat and showing maximum ruthlessness in her summary execution of the so-called deserter Emelin, who is sentenced to death because he had merely visited his wife for a few hours in a neighbouring village.

Vavilova cannot hide her femininity for long, however, as she is pregnant. Her commander (played by Vasilii Shukshin) even half-jokingly threatens to have her shot for deserting the revolutionary cause. She is billeted with a Jewish family headed by Efim Magazannik (Rolan Bykov) and his wife, significantly named Mariia. Their happiness and the obvious love they have for each other is in stark contrast to the coldness of Vavilova and the harmony of their family life is a counter to the savagery of the conflict going on around them.

This savagery is given harrowing symbolic representation in the games played by the Magazanniks' children. They act out scenes that are all too familiar in the adult world of the Civil War, such as a mock pogrom that includes the simulated gang rape of their elder sister. War as a child's game negates the promise of a better future. These children are victims of the chaos around them, but Vavilova's child, when he is born, becomes a victim of his own mother's ideological commitment to the cause. She abandons him to the care of the Magazanniks and goes off to rejoin her unit and continue the struggle.

Is it worth it? One of the film's themes is that of the futility of fighting for a political cause. The film's imagery and symbolism combine to confirm this in a series of increasingly powerful vignettes. As Vavilova gives birth, she remembers the father of her child, another political commissar. She recalls his death and the death of many others, as well as surreal scenes of blind men struggling to find their way in a Central Asian desert and soldiers armed with scythes mowing the desert sand. Riderless horses race past rows of graves and the cries of Vavilova giving birth mingle with those of men as they die. When her (unnamed) lover is killed, he bares his chest to the oncoming bullets in a parodic reprise of the famous culmination of Alexander Dovzhenko's 1928 film *Arsenal*, when the revolutionary Timosh rips open his shirt to confront his firing squad. Timosh remains untouched by their bullets, but here there is no such mythological invincibility and the man falls dead.

Askoldov's film calls into question those ideals that formed the basis of the Revolution and Civil War and debunks any notion of heroism or the noble cause itself. Vavilova may blindly affirm her commitment to this cause, but she betrays herself as a mother and her own young child. The last we see of her is when she strides across a field that is being torn apart by bombs and we know that she will never see this child again. The child becomes a symbol, not of the emerging new world as the official mythology would have us believe, but of the destruction of ideals and human suffering. Askoldov also foregrounds an astonishing 'flash forward', as Vavilova sees a long line of Jews dressed up as Second World War concentration camp inmates entering a charnel house. This, then, is the fate awaiting the Magazanniks in the future, where the family and notions of domestic love are also destroyed. For

Askoldov, as for Grossman, there is no difference between the destructive tyranny of the Bolsheviks and that of the Nazis.

The Commissar, made in 1967, was Askoldov's first film. It was, of course, immediately banned and he was not allowed to make another film. It was released only under Gorbachev and even then not without some hiccups, first shown at the Moscow Film Festival in 1987 and released in the USSR only at the end of 1988.[4] There can be little doubt that no other Soviet director has made a single feature of so much import and lasting significance.

Given the resurgence of the Soviet film industry in the 1960s and 1970s, it is surprising that relatively few historical films were made. A quick look at the production figures for these years shows that between 1964 and 1985 each year between 130 and 158 films were made.[5] Hardly any of these were historical films of any lasting merit, as the past was again becoming a tricky area in these years. Nikita Mikhalkov's *A Slave of Love* (1976) reflects the hidden dangers of dealing with history. The film is set in the Crimea in 1917, as a film crew tries to shoot a film. Revolutionary events begin to impinge: history in the making has two meanings. Mikhalkov's film is caught between the need for ideological orthodoxy and its desire to celebrate a rapidly disappearing world.

The most celebrated historical fim, however, was Elem Klimov's *Agony*, made in 1974 but released only in 1981. It depicts the last years of the reign of Tsar Nicholas II and in particular focuses on the personality and role of Grigorii Rasputin in the downfall of the old order. Surprisingly, the Tsar is not shown as a bloodthirsty autocrat, out of touch with his people and society, but rather as a weak man unable to impose his will on Rasputin or his wife and, as such, historically doomed. Klimov is careful to film the massacre of 1905 in black and white, so giving it a documentary authenticity. The inference here is clear: there certainly was political oppression, but if it were not for the wilful and scandalous behaviour of the Siberian priest, the monarchy may not have collapsed. The film suggests a subtle rejection of the Leninist dictum that the old order was doomed by overwhelming historical forces and the figure of Rasputin was simply one manifestation of the corruption of the Tsarist regime.

An entirely different approach to history can be found in Andrei Mikhalkov-Konchalovskii's four-part *Siberiade* (1979–80), an attempt to present a mythical history of Siberia throughout the twentieth century. The passage of real time is shown in the use of newsreel and documentary footage, but Konchalovskii's real interest is in the elemental life of the people of the *taiga*, the vast area of virgin forest, shot in naturalistic detail. Progress is measured by the constant sounds of trees being felled to make way for roads or the building of oil wells to exploit Siberia's natural resources, all depicted as physical damage inflicted on the body of nature. There are uncomfortable views of historical events: villagers rejoice in the dekulakisation campaign at the end of the 1920s as it gives them a chance to rob the rich of their furs and valuables. The film contains a great sense of the sensuous physicality of life, the erotic enjoyment of life's pleasures and the mystical, shamanistic traditions of Siberia. It is, moreover, a film that refers not so much to the facts of history for its 'truth', but rather engages in the mythical construction of Siberia as a space that exists simultaneously in the past and the present.

Ancestral memory and the denial of history: Sergo Paradzhanov

Sergo Paradzhanov is, alongside Andrei Tarkovskii, the great *auteur* of post-Stalin Soviet cinema. Of Georgian–Armenian descent, he does not strictly belong to Russian national cinema, but his preoccupation with ancestral and cultural memory places him firmly within the 'film and history' debate.

Born in Tbilisi in 1924, where he studied music during the war years, he graduated from the State Film School (VGIK) in Moscow and worked initially in Kiev and then in Armenia and Georgia. He suffered considerable official persecution in the course of his life, including imprisonment, and died in 1990. Paradzhanov's film art is a rejection of the entire historical experience of the twentieth century, a turning away from history as the correct arrangement of events and personalities and an exploration of history as cultural identity, using visual images, music and folklore.

Shadows of Our Forgotten Ancestors was made in 1964 and takes us not only into the past, but also to a distant and almost inaccessible geographical location. The film is set among the Gutsul people of the Carpathian mountains in northern Ukraine (it is filmed in Ukrainian). The Gutsuly are a people who observe the rituals of Orthodox Christianity, but whose lives are governed by a paganistic relationship with the natural world. Barbarism, adultery and murder coexist with an elemental enjoyment of the natural world, as children dance naked and invoke the earth spirits. The exuberant colours of folk costumes are complemented by the sounds of folk music and church bells.

Nature gives life and also takes it away. A woman dies as she tries to save a lamb from drowning and a man is killed by a falling tree. Life is celebrated as the birth of a lamb or a rustic wedding. Man and nature coexist uneasily and the threat of a storm brings disharmony to the human world. The storm is averted by a sorcerer, who claims a bride as his prize, leading to unhappiness and death. Paradzhanov's first major film is a kaleidoscope of imagery, colour and sound in which a remote people, cut off in time and distance, provide a counterpoint to and a commentary on modern civilisation. The film is arranged as a series of Pasolini-like tableaux, all highlighting the Gutsul people's elemental perception of the world, a people literally a century away from industry and what is accepted as progress.

The Colour of Pomegranates (1969) has a similar structure. It is another celebration of pre-modernity that takes as its initial premise the life of the eighteenth-century Armenian poet Sayat-Nova, with a folk music soundtrack and an array of folk costumes and vivid colour splashed across the screen. The poet is the repository of the nation's soul and culture and although Christianity provides the rituals of spiritual life, its symbolism is constantly undermined. The poet physically resembles Christ, but the Biblical narrative is grotesquely literalised as sheep flock into a church and artificial angels have no wings. We learn little about Sayat-Nova's life, apart from his beginnings as a weaver, and Paradhzanov seems much more interested in providing an extravaganza of colour and sound, filmic expression of a nation's time-less culture and its sensuous link with the natural world – the colour of pomegranates is red, the same as blood.

The Legend of the Suram Fortress (1984) is also about myth and folklore and is presented again as a series of tableaux with intertitles. Legend stipulates that the Suram fortress will crumble before its enemies unless a sacrifice is made. Sacrifice demands the ultimate unselfish deed and the folkloric belief that 'good deeds are not forgotten' can apply only in a world and time untouched by materialism and rational belief (i.e. the twentieth century). Paradzhanov again floods the screen with vivid colours, with a soundtrack dominated by Caucasian folk music and the rugged mountain landscape, as well as being the major force in these people's lives, provides a magnificent scenic backdrop.

Paradzhanov celebrates pre-industrial civilisation where man's bond with his native land and his spiritual and cultural links with his ancestors are not lost. Russian directors have concentrated on recognisable events and people from the past, but Paradzhanov rejects rationalism and the consequent materialism of the modern world itself, looking back to a time when past and present were part of an organic and elemental unity of life. For Paradzhanov, history is above all a narrative of the human soul developing in harmony with its natural landscape, fed and nurtured by memory of the past.

The rediscovery of history: the glasnost years and beyond

With the freedoms afforded by Gorbachev's new 'openness', the exploration of history often overlapped with a desire to settle political scores. Both the historical and political merged, as new films were made exploring the Stalinist past and those that had been banned under Brezhnev came to the screen, often for the first time. Within a few years many important films dealing with the recent past were released.

Alexei German's *My Friend Ivan Lapshin* had been completed in 1982 but was released before Gorbachev's accession to power, in 1984. It is set in the mid-1930s, but structured retrospectively, through the memories of an old man living in the present and recalling his childhood past, in particular his 'friend', the policeman Ivan Lapshin.

Although the plot of the film concerns Lapshin's hunt for the criminal gang led by a certain Solovev, German's camera concentrates not so much on the cops-and-robbers story as on the minutiae of life in a communal apartment in a provincial town. Set in winter, the film captures the sheer drabness of life, accentuated by Tarkovskian switches from colour to black and white images. The finale, where Lapshin cold bloodedly shoots a disarmed and surrendering Solovev, is all the more disturbing when set against the dull grey hues of the surrounding houses and fields. Yet, although the film is set in the Stalin years, there is no mention of the Great Leader himself, although there is ample evidence of the spirit of the times through the use of posters and placards adorning windows and walls. History is made up of the small things, of failed romances and the pressures of communal living, not the 'bigger picture' of politics and historical landmarks.

With the end of the Cold War the 'end of history' was announced as the merging of previously antagonistic political and social systems and the victory of consumer-led capitalism. In the last years of the Soviet Union's existence, however, the end of history was taken by some in a much more literal sense. Karen Shakhnazarov's *Zero City* (1990) paints an absurdist, at times surreal picture of a provincial town ('Zero') where the secretary to a local factory boss sits naked at her desk and the exhibits in the local museum, covering major events in world history as well as the lives of noted individuals from the town, are frighteningly lifelike. Historical progress comes in the form of imported Western trends, such as rock and roll and those who oppose it can only contemplate (but not actually commit) suicide. As the hero Varakin tries to flee, he is caught at the end of the film adrift in a boat on a river enveloped in fog, going, like Zero City itself, nowhere. Russia in the last throes of Soviet socialism is caught between the Scylla of market-led Western liberal democracy and the Charybdis of strong statehood and the identification of the individual with the state.

The cinematic debunking of Stalinism continued apace after 1991, but in films that pursued an agenda very different from Gorbachev's avowed aim of restoring Leninist 'norms'. Perhaps the most famous of these films was Nikita Mikhalkov's *Burnt by the Sun*, if only because it won the 1994 American Academy Award for Best Foreign Picture. However, in many ways a more significant picture was Pavel Chukhrai's *The Thief*, similarly, but unsuccessfully this time, nominated for an Oscar (in 1997). Mikhalkov continued the historical debate with his epic *The Barber of Siberia*, released in 1999.

Chukhrai's film starts with the birth of Sania at the side of a road during the war years. We then board a train in 1952, where Tolian, a soldier, makes the acquaintance of Katia, Sania's widowed mother. Tolian and Katia consummate their relationship within a few hours there and then on the train. They begin to live together. In the course of the next few months Tolian shows himself to be quite a brutal father figure, but he and Sania inevitably grow closer and Tolian tells the young boy that he is in fact Stalin's son, showing him a tattoo of the dictator inscribed on his chest. It soon becomes clear that Tolian is a professional thief and he begins to use the boy in order to get access to private apartments. Later Katia dies as a result of a miscarriage and Tolian falls foul of the police. About ten years later Sania, now in a children's home, accidentally comes across Tolian at a railway halt and, confronted by old memories, wets himself. That night, Sania shoots Tolian with the gun he had secretly kept since Tolian's arrest all those years ago. Fast forward 30 or so years to the present, or at least an imagined near future where post-Communist Russia is consumed by civil strife and Sania is the commanding officer of a unit evacuating a bombed-out town. He comes across a drunken old man whom he takes to be Tolian, but he is mistaken. Sania leaves on a train, offering vodka as medicine to a young mother and her child, just as he had been befriended 50 years before. Chukhrai's film is not only about fatherhood but also the legacy of Stalin, the failure of the body politic to exorcise the ghost and his continuing destructive influence.

The Thief is also a film about another father, that of the director himself. Grigorii Chukhrai made *The Ballad of a Soldier* in 1959. *The Thief* can be seen very much as the son rewriting his father's film, as it contains none of the heartstring pulling of *The Ballad of a Soldier*. Russia in the later film is a desolate and bomb-blasted wasteland, its people demoralised and destitute. The train here brings about dislocation and strife, it is a means of escape for Tolian. In *The Ballad of a Soldier* it offered a means of reconciliation and reunion with home and family. *The Thief* sees the sins of the 'father' visited on his 'son' and offers a grimly realistic picture of life in communal apartments in the early post-war years, in stark contrast to the sun-drenched village homes of *Ballad*. Grigorii Chukhrai made a film that touched the heart. His son has raised questions about Russia's historical destiny in the latter half of the twentieth century, presuming the country and its people to be on a collision course with catastrophe.

The Barber of Siberia is a cunningly made film with a double agenda: to show to the West a positive and hearty image of Russia and its people and to show Russians how fickle and dangerous Westerners are. On the one hand, late nineteenth-century Russia is shown here as a land where people eat caviar by the spoonful at the Shrovetide fair, Tsar Alexander III toasts his officers with vodka and the young Russian officer cadets are boisterous and spirited

Julia Ormond, Richard Harris, Alexei Petrenko and Oleg Menshikov in The Barber of Siberia *(Nikita Mikhalkov, 1999)*

but pure of spirit and honour bound. The epitome of these virtues is 18-year-old Alexei Tolstoi, rather incongruously played by Oleg Menshikov (who was pushing 40 at the time!). Westerners, by way of contrast, represented by Mrs Callahan (Julia Ormond), are scheming, opportunistic and dangerous or, like Mr McCracken (Richard Harris), hell bent on destroying Russia's landscapes in order to make money.

Mikhalkov's vision of late imperial Russia, then, is largely mythical, with little sense of social deprivation and political tensions. Rather, Russia is seen as spiritually pure as the white snow that so frequently fills the screen and at the mercy of perfidious Westerners all too ready to abuse its hospitality and kindness.[6] Russian markets overflow with foodstuffs, caviar is plentiful and vodka is drunk not to escape from life, but in order to celebrate it. In other words, this is an image with which post-Soviet Russians deprived of a sense of history can identify, as well as a warning for Russians towards the end of the twentieth century, a message not too far removed from that in *Burnt By the Sun*.

Burnt by the Sun is about the arrest and subsequent execution of a respected army officer during Stalin's purges of the 1930s. Brigade Commander Kotov is an honest-to-goodness Russian man of the soil, loved by his men, a man who loves his country and comrade Stalin in equal measure. He is betrayed and finally destroyed by the recently returned émigré Mitia, a man of Western airs and values (i.e. duplicitous and cold blooded). Mikhalkov's film is shot in a sun-soaked rural retreat with characters dressed in white. An innocent way of life is about to be disrupted and destroyed forever: it is the beginning of the end of another Russian idyll.

The curse of history – especially recent history – continues to fascinate film-makers, and not only in Russia. A Russia–France co-production, *East West* (1999), confronts the fate of those exiled Russians who, in 1946, chose to return to the Soviet Union in the wake of Stalin's exhortations. They travel with their foreign relatives, idealistic lambs being led to the slaughter. Once on Soviet soil rape, torture, execution or the Gulag await them or else they are forced into a humiliating hand-to-mouth existence under constant surveil-lance by the secret police. Another similarly forthright analysis of recent history is in Alexander Sokurov's *Moloch* (1999), a portrayal of the last days of Hitler and his close entourage (Bormann, Goebbels). This is, above all, a restrained psychological study of major twentieth-century historical players, showing men usually depicted as monsters as fairly ordinary people. Sokurov picks one of the key historical moments of the last century and succeeds in removing from it the customary hysteria and obloquy to present us with a series of flawed but recognisable human beings.

Sokurov's film is concerned with the end of things. Similarly, Gleb Panfilov's *The Romanovs* (2000) looks at the Russian royal family's last years, culminating in their blood-spattered massacre in 1918, and provides an affirmation of faith in the monarchy as a symbol of lost Russian greatness and the tragic fate of the family as a symbolic martyrdom. Indeed, the film ends with actual footage of the official Orthodox canonisation of the royal family in August 2000. What is of significance here is that whereas Elem Klimov's 1975 film paid much attention to the lascivious figure of Rasputin, Panfilov does not mention him. He has other targets. Tsar Nicholas II is a victim not so much of the Bolsheviks (foul-mouthed boors and thugs), as of his own generals, dismayed that he is reluctant to carry on the war with Germany. Kerenskii is here portrayed as a vainglorious, opportunistic upstart – not unlike the image of him presented by Eisenstein in *October*. The Tsar, in contrast, instinctively feels at one with his people, denying that he gave the order to shoot on protesting workers on Bloody Sunday in 1905, but accepting responsibility all the same as the 'little father' of the nation.

Panfilov's film is undeniably powerful, showing the royal family as a deeply loving and close-knit unit. The end of imperial Russia is nothing short of a disaster for Russia. But it is also a selective picture, for it tells us little of the poverty and social conflicts of the time. In this respect it follows in the footsteps of Stanislav Govorukhin's controversial documentary *The Russia We Have Lost* (1992), a lament for the lost pageantry and glory of imperial Russia that also remains significantly silent, for instance, on the role of Grigorii Rasputin in tarnishing the image of the court.

The Stalinist night is literally realised in Alexei German's *Khrustalev, My Car!* (1998), with most of the film shot in darkness outdoors or in dimly lit interiors. The use of black and white photography emphasises the gloom and despair evident everywhere. It is set in the last days of Stalin's rule, late February 1953, as the tyrant lies dying. Like *My Friend Ivan Lapshin*, it is related retrospectively, this time by the son of the main character, Doctor Klenskii. Klenskii is also a secret police official and is arrested, deported to Siberia and then brought back to tend the dying leader, but to no avail. German's film is a nightmarish vision of a society ruled by force, where human relationships are defined only by power and violence and where there is little difference between the inmates of an asylum and those who treat them. Violence both verbal and actual is an everyday fact of life and the human body (especially male) is subjected to every kind of indignity. As an exercise in the 'aesthetic of the ugly', a common feature of 1990s culture, the film remains unsurpassed, as characters spit, swear and vomit in an absurd, grotesque picture of collective madness.

Sokurov's *Taurus* (2000) is, like *Moloch*, concerned with the everyday lives of important historical figures. Lenin lies dying after suffering a stroke, now a figure of fun and derision by those attending him, even his wife Nadezhda Krupskaia. This is as far as is possible from the heroic image of Lenin presented in the films of Mikhail Romm. What we are confronted with here is a frail and pathetic creature, forced to witness his own physical and mental

Mariia Kuznetsova and Leonid Mozgovoi in Taurus *(Alexander Sokurov, 2000)*

degradation. Stalin visits in a show of comradely support, but can barely conceal his contempt for the near-dead man before him. Lenin's only joy comes as he nears death, sitting in his garden, listening to the birds singing. Sokurov's achievement in both films is to show two of the most important historical players of the twentieth century – Lenin and Hitler – as mere mortals, at the end ordinary people, and it is therefore no accident that the same actor, Leonid Mozgovoi, plays both roles.

These films can be located within a post-Soviet cultural discourse that confronts the past and seeks to reassess and reinvent history, as with Chukhrai and especially Mikhalkov. German and Sokurov are not merely debunking mythology, as set out in a deliberately unsettling aesthetic style, but are also dismantling the architectonics of tyranny. The state is no longer able to control and direct 'history' and the meaning of history is no longer as clear cut as it once appeared.

Filmography

Admiral Nakhimov, dir. Vsevolod Pudovkin, 1946

The Agony ('Agoniia'), dir. Elem Klimov, 1975

Alexander Nevskii, dir. Sergei Eisenstein, 1938

Arsenal ('Arsenal'), dir. Alexander Dovzhenko, 1928

The Ballad of a Soldier ('Ballada o soldate'), dir. Grigorii Chukhrai, 1959

The Barber of Siberia ('Sibirskii tsiriulnik'), dir. Nikita Mikhalkov, 1999

Battleship Potemkin ('Bronenosets Potemkin'), dir. Sergei Eisenstein, 1926

Before the Judgement of History ('Pered sudom istorii'), dir. Fridrikh Ermler, 1964

Burnt by the Sun ('Utomlennye solntsem'), dir. Nikita Mikhalkov, 1994

The Colour of Pomegranates ('Tsvet granata'), dir. Sergo Paradzhanov, 1969

The Commissar ('Komissar'), dir. Alexander Askoldov, 1967

The Defence of Sevastopol ('Oborona Sevastopolia'), dir. Vasilii Goncharov, 1912

The Deputy from the Baltic ('Deputat iz Baltiki'), dir. Alexander Zarkhi and Iosif Kheifits, 1936

East West ('Vostok Zapad'), dir. Régis Wargnier, 1999

Dr Ehrlich's Magic Bullet, dir. William Dieterle, 1940

Edison the Man, dir. Clarence Brown, 1940

The End of St Petersburg ('Konets Sankt-Peterburga'), dir. Vsevolod Pudovkin, 1927

The Fall of the Romanov Dynasty ('Padenie dinastii Romanovykh'), dir. Esfir Shub, 1927

Glinka, dir. Leo Arnshtam, 1946

Ivan the Terrible ('Ivan Groznyi'), Parts One and Two, dir. Sergei Eisenstein, 1944–5

Khrustalev, My Car! ('Khrustalev, mashinu!'), dir. Alexei German, 1998

Kotovskii, dir. Alexander Faintsimmer, 1950

Kutuzov, dir. Grigorii Kozintsev and Leonid Trauberg, 1943

The Legend of the Suram Fortress ('Legenda Suramskoi kreposti'), dir. Sergo Paradzhanov, 1984

Lenin in 1918 ('Lenin v 1918 g.'), dir. Mikhail Romm, 1939

Lenin in October ('Lenin v Oktiabre'), dir. Mikhail Romm, 1937

Madame Curie, dir. Mervyn LeRoy, 1943

Minin and Pozharskii ('Minin i Pozharskii'), dir. Vsevolod Pudovkin, 1939

Moloch ('Molokh'), dir. Alexander Sokurov, 1999

Musorgskii, dir. Grigorii Roshal, 1950

My Friend Ivan Lapshin ('Moi drug Ivan Lapshin'), dir. Alexei German, 1984

October ('Oktiabr'), dir. Sergei Eisenstein, 1927

Peter the First ('Petr pervyi'), Parts One and Two, dir. Vladimir Petrov, 1937–8

Pirogov, dir. Grigorii Kozintsev, 1947

The Romanovs ('Romanovy, ventsenosnaia semia'), dir. Gleb Panfilov, 2000

The Russia We Have Lost ('Rossiia, kotoruiu my poteriali'), dir. Stanislav Govorukhin, 1992

Shadows of Our Forgotten Ancestors ('Teni zabytykh predkov'), dir. Sergo Paradzhanov, 1964

Shchors, dir. Alexander Dovzhenko, 1939

Siberiade ('Sibiriada'), dir. Andrei Mikhalkov-Konchalovskii, 1979–80

A Slave of Love ('Raba liubvi'), dir. Nikita Mikhalkov, 1976

Stenka Razin, dir. V. Romashkov, 1908

The Story of Alexander Graham Bell, dir. Irving Cummings, 1939

The Story of Louis Pasteur, dir. William Dieterle, 1936

Taurus ('Telets'), dir. Alexander Sokurov, 2000

The Thief ('Vor'), dir. Pavel Chukhrai, 1997

Three Songs About Lenin ('Tri pesni o Lenine'), dir. Dziga Vertov, 1934

The Village Schoolmistress ('Selskaia uchitelnitsa'), dir. Mark Donskoi, 1947

Zero City ('Gorod Zero'), dir. Karen Shakhnazarov, 1990

Zhukovskii, dir. Vsevolod Pudovkin and D. Vasilev, 1950

Notes

1. A verbatim account of this discussion, also attended by Molotov and Beria, can be found in Bergan (1997), pp. 340–4.
2. That this is a film by the former avant-garde documentarist Dziga Vertov is, at times, hard to believe. Vertov here lays his art squarely at the service of the Stalinist

state and little of his previous experimental techniques remain. Still, there remain some nuggets: there is a remarkable shot of a parachutist landing inside a building, seen from the parachutist's own point of view, and an aircraft's exhaust seems to sweep away the untidiness of the natural world below it.

3. For details of how the film was 'corrected', see the report by A. V. Romashov, head of the State Cinematography Committee, in Fomin (1998), pp. 154–6. Interestingly, Romashov recommended that the film be shown abroad, but for domestic consumption only in 'closed auditoria'.

4. See Lawton (1992), pp. 115–18.

5. Zemlianukhin and Segida (1996), p. 6.

6. Mikhalkov's appeal to Russian nationalistic emotions is very ironic, given that the film itself was shot in English and, in the version released to Russian audiences, Mikhalkov himself does the voice-over. In other words, the director above all has his eye on Western sales, with the Russian consumer clearly in second place – not an approach likely to endear him to the Russian cinema-going public.

CHAPTER FIVE

Women and Russian film

Oh, how sweet it was to be alive! How good to be alive and love life! And how he longed to thank life, thank existence itself, directly, face to face, to thank life in person.

This was exactly what Lara was. You could not communicate with life, but she was its representative, its expression, the gift of speech and hearing granted to inarticulate being.

(Pasternak, 1992, pp. 351–2)

Pasternak is one in a long line of Russian authors who have worshipped the feminine ideal and who saw in women a symbol of purity that sharply contrasts with the grimness of the world and the perceived lack of courage and honour among men. We can look back to the nineteenth century – Turgenev, in particular – to see how male characters put their women on pedestals and we can note that these pedestals proved to be remarkably resilient in the twentieth century. Pushkin makes his captain's daughter (Masha Mironova) a model of domesticity and virtue, while Dostoevskii's Sonia Marmeladova in *Crime and Punishment* offers the penitent hero Raskolnikov the only true way to spiritual rebirth. The sparkling and dynamic Natasha Rostova in Tolstoi's *War and Peace* symbolises the vitality of Mother Russia, for whose survival her brother Nikolai and eventual husband Pierre fight Napoleon. Barbara Heldt has commented on male preoccupations with female virtue in Russian literature, in this deliberately extended quotation:

There is no lack of general pronouncements about how women act or feel or think in Russian literature: these, however, have been overwhelmingly made by men. The unflattering have been more than amply 'balanced' by the flattering. In fact, in Russian fiction the elevation of the Russian woman is matched only by the

*self-abasement of the Russian man. His is a long and tortuous road to enlighten-
ment, while she grasps the essentials of life, if not immediately then certainly
firmly and intuitively when the time comes (to fall in love). For the male writers
who dominate the tradition of fiction (including the novel, the novella or povest'
as it is called in Russian, and the short story), woman is a kind of paradigm
or shorthand. There is no novel of gradual female development, of rebirth or
transformation as we find in Austen or Eliot; while some male characters learn
and grow through intellect or experience, the changes in women are mysterious
givens of nature, of Womanhood. The heroines of male fiction serve a purpose
that ultimately has little to do with women: these heroines are used lavishly in a
discourse of male self-definition.*

(Heldt, 1987, p. 2)

Early years: active women in films by men

One of the more interesting aspects of Soviet cinema is that, whereas films
about history or ideology, and even comedies, had to reflect and encourage
official policy, films about women, sometimes written and directed by
women, could be highly individualised.

One of the earliest stars of the pre-revolutionary Russian cinema was Vera
Kholodnaia, who died in the Crimea in 1919 of influenza at the age of 26. She
was phenomenally popular in her short career and documentary footage of
her funeral shows thousands of people paying their last respects. Richard
Stites notes: 'The former dancer with the sad grey eyes animated the cellu-
loid world she dwelled in, a world of tainted money, opulent restaurants,
champagne picnics, luxury autos careening through the night, and illicit love
leading to tragedy' (Stites, 1991, p. 245). She was the first real Russian female
superstar who showed audiences, especially the women in them, the joys and
rewards a modern woman could have.

In the 1920s female roles were not all continuations of the passive, suffering domestic stereotypes that were still very common in pre-revolutionary
film and literature (and with which we in the West are also familiar).
Certainly, in films such as Iakov Protazanov's *The Man from the Restaurant*
(1927) the gifted daughter of Skorokhodov is subjected to sexual harassment
by the owner of the restaurant in which she plays the violin, and as such
represents the exploited classes (including the waiters) who are at the mercy
of the pre-revolutionary bourgeoisie. *The Devil's Wheel*, directed in 1926 by
Kozintsev and Trauberg, features Valia as the recognisable love interest with
little psychological depth. Zina, the 'cigarette girl from Mosselprom' in the
1924 film of that name directed by Iurii Zheliabuzhskii, may be the main

character, but she is hardly active in deciding her own fate, neither does she show much self-awareness as a woman trying to get ahead in the male-centred world of film-making.

But the dominant trend in these years was to show strong, active women, decisive characters who often sort out the problems of the men around them. One such is the Anna Sten character Natasha in Boris Barnet's *The Girl with the Hatbox* (1927), who has both initiative and drive to look after her grandfather, defeat the wiles of her landlady Irène and finally find true love with Ilia. Edith in Lev Kuleshov's *By the Law* (1926) is the strongest and most sober minded of the trio that find themselves isolated in a hut during the Yukon gold rush, with her husband Hans and their murderous captive Michael. Michael had killed another two prospectors at the beginning of the film and Hans wants to execute him in revenge. Edith, however, insists that justice should be carried out 'by the law'. Kuleshov's film is, above all, a study in character and how people behave in an extreme situation. Edith's initial strength evaporates with time and she agrees with her husband that Michael should be executed. They botch the hanging and Michael escapes.

In the films of the 'golden age' it is the image of the politically active woman that is best remembered. In *New Babylon* (1927), directed by Kozintsev and Trauberg, set during the Franco-Prussian War of 1870–1, it is the women of Paris who rescue the cannon in the name of the beleaguered communards, an anachronistic projection of the much-vaunted emancipated status of women after the October Revolution. The heroine Louise dies defiantly, calling out 'Long live the Commune' as she is executed by the bourgeois authorities along with the other representatives of the working class. Marfa Lapkina, the heroine of Eisenstein's *The General Line* (also known as *The Old and the New*, 1929), progresses from downtrodden peasant to spiritual leader of the village community and then to politically committed tractor driver, triumphing over both class enemies and the sullen suspiciousness of the other villagers. It is on her initiative that the peasants form themselves into a cooperative, thereby freeing themselves from the whims of the 'kulaks' who have exploited them.

Perhaps the most significant portrayal of a woman shaking off her shackles and gaining political commitment in these years is Pelageia Vlasova in Pudovkin's *Mother* (1926). Pelageia witnesses – unwittingly contributes to – the arrest and imprisonment of her son Pavel for hiding guns and deals with the subsequent loss and loneliness by giving herself to the cause of the proletarian revolution of 1905. She carries aloft the revolutionary banner, fire in her eyes as she gazes confidently at the ranks of enemy cavalry about to cut her down, aware that she is about to enter legend. What is important in this film is not only the coming to consciousness of a previously downtrodden woman, but also the convincing portrayal of Pelageia by Vera Baranovskaia,

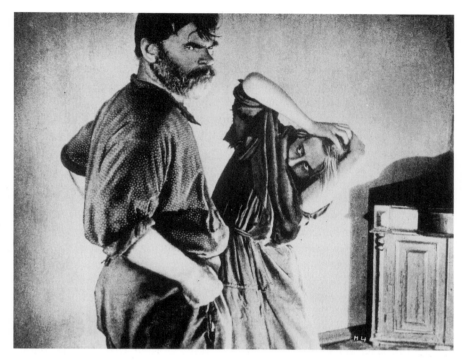

Alexander Chistiakov and Vera Baranovskaia in Mother *(Vsevolod Pudovkin, 1926)*

who succeeds in conveying a range of emotions, from fear and despair to confidence and faith in the cause, and it is largely on the back of this performance that the film continues to impress and move.

Early Soviet films were careful not to cast women as merely sexually alluring objects for the gratification of the male gaze, but neither were they feminist beacons proclaiming their own independence from male value systems. Woman's newly established emancipated status was consciously identified with the causes of social progress and/or political struggle. Women were long seen as the victims of a patriarchal, deeply conservative order and in the new world promised by the 'dictatorship of the proletariat' they were (literally, in Pelageia's case) to be the standard bearers of equality and freedom.

From Stalin to stagnation: the rediscovery of domesticity

The Revolution was meant to free women from domestic slavery, but in the 1930s the cause of female emancipation was one the successors of Lenin treated with typical bombast but also equivocation. The woman was entitled to work and be financially independent, but she should not forget bringing up the children and providing the centre of the nuclear family: the 'double' burden that many Russian women bear to this day. The emerging female stars of the 1930s may have had a feistiness that would represent a certain amount of personal independence, but narrative closure would place their achievements within a patriarchal political structure.

It was no accident that Liubov Orlova and Marina Ladynina became the dominant female stars of the 1930s and 1940s: both were married to the major directors of these years, Grigorii Alexandrov and Ivan Pyrev respectively. Richard Taylor adds:

> *One reason for the privileging of women in the countryside was the need to encourage them to play a greater part in collective, as opposed to domestic, labour in the light of male migration to the cities and the consequent labour shortage in rural areas. Another resulted from the context in which these musicals were made: by male directors to showcase the acting, singing and dancing talents of their wives. Yet another was to emphasise that women were equal and thus to underline the superiority of the Soviet way of life.*

> (Taylor, 2000, p. 22)

Both Orlova and Ladynina portrayed working women, thereby demonstrating to the Soviet viewer that men and women were equal in the professional sphere and therefore the 'woman question' was solved. As blonde and blue-eyed stars, they also gave the Soviet viewing public a taste of what Hollywood must have looked like, especially as Western cinema was out of bounds by the late 1930s. They thus conveyed twin but mutually compatible signals: the prospects for working women in Stalin's Russia were good and the Russian working woman could be as glamorous as a Hollywood starlet.

There were, of course, other female stars. Valentina Serova offered a more youthful alternative to both Orlova and Ladynina – she was ten years younger than Ladynina and 15 years younger than Orlova – with her blonde hair and fresh-faced features the embodiment of Russian female virtue and innocent vitality. In films such as *A Girl with Character* and *Four Loving Hearts* (directed by Konstantin Iudin, in 1939 and 1941 respectively), Serova, still in her early twenties, makes her characters wilful and self-motivated. In both these films she has a 'character' of her own that can both solve the problems in animal husbandry, despite the inefficiency of the farm management and find true love.

Vera Maretskaia had appeared in the silent films of Iakov Protazanov and Boris Barnet, but achieved particular fame in *A Member of the Government*, made in 1939. She plays Alexandra Sokolova, a downtrodden peasant woman who becomes politically conscious and is appointed chair of the collective farm, in the teeth of resistance from the men and especially her husband Efim. She becomes the embodiment of progressive forces in the countryside, carrying out Party policy and bringing into line the recalcitrant rural workforce, especially the men. Efim leaves her and goes to earn a living in the town, unable to countenance his wife as a socially and politically active individual. The scene when he leaves is filmed with great emotional power and is shot entirely from the viewpoint of Alexandra.

Significantly, it is the other women in the village who understand better than their men that the collective way offers a better life. Efim returns several years later, expecting to find the farm rundown and in chaos, but is surprised to see it flourishing to such an extent that his wife offers him pies that would only normally be eaten on a Sunday, and this on a Friday. The director Kheifits himself has commented on the importance of the scene of Efim's return:

> But this business-like and ordinary 'No, Friday' contains all of Alexandra's inner triumph, her victory over her husband, his self-assurance and his pride. To be sure, he did not believe in her strength and ability to build a new life, about which she 'perhaps had been dreaming of for a hundred years'. And now he has come midweek, on a Friday, and is eating pies that would normally be eaten on a festive occasion.

(Kheifits, 1966, p. 35)

Sokolova not only survives an assassination attempt by class enemies in the village, but she is upwardly mobile and never loses her political beliefs. She is eventually elected to the Supreme Soviet, where she brings everyone to their feet with her speech where she, 'a simple Russian peasant woman (baba), beaten by my husband, cursed by the priests, shot at by enemies, but still alive', expresses her faith in the Party, the future and Soviet power. Closure thus brings into focus the film's twin thematic strands: the self-fulfilment of a politically conscious peasant woman from the masses and the benign, paternalistic authority of the Party standing in contrast to the patriarchal tyranny of the old ways.

There were some very different actresses in these years. One of the great comic geniuses of Soviet film was and indeed remains Faina Ranevskaia, specialising as the irrepressibly bossy harridan, with Rostislav Pliatt or Erast Garin usually her hen-pecked foil. In films such as Tatiana Lukashevich's *The Foundling* (1939) she steals every scene, dominating and haranguing to great comic effect the poor Pliatt, and we are actually sorry to see her plans defeated as the wicked stepmother in Nadezhda Kosheverova's 1947 film *Cinderella*. Indeed, as she leaves the stage we hope that she will yet get her revenge.[1]

After Stalin: the rediscovery of womanhood

It is generally acknowledged that with the death of Stalin and the onset of the 'thaw' from 1953 Soviet cinema reclaimed its humanity and concern for the 'little man'. This concern can be extended to the 'little woman', too. The figure of Veronika (played by Tatiana Samoilova, who would play Anna Karenina ten years later) in *The Cranes are Flying* (1957), is a superbly directed and acted picture of human frailty, weakness and beauty. Veronika loses her parents in a bombing raid during the war, then her fiancé Boris and then establishes a relationship with Boris's best friend Mark, even though he has raped her. Audiences were invited not to condemn Veronika for her human weakness, but to sympathise and understand.

These were important years for reintroducing women as human beings with emotions and fears with which the female audience could identify. It took a female director, however, to articulate what it was like to be a woman in post-Stalin Russia. Larisa Shepitko's *Wings* still looks like a remarkable film and its central theme of the role and place of women in society has not aged. Nadezhda Petrukhina is a war hero, now a headteacher, who finds it difficult to fit into the modern world. She is happy only when she recalls her past glory. Shepitko consistently films her as an outsider, whether this be in a male-dominated beerhall or at her adopted daughter Tania's house, where she looks into the room occupied by men from the doorway, or as she is prevented from entering a restaurant on her own after 6 pm. She herself has a masculine haircut and dresses in dark, official-looking suits. The only time she enjoys any real communication is with the waitress Shura, when they talk, eat, drink, sing and dance together, men symbolically excluded as they stand outside behind closed doors, peering in. Nadezhda is seen as little more than a museum exhibit and she can, in the end, only escape by getting in a plane and flying away. As Lynne Attwood comments, 'she is free at last of the constraints placed on women' (Attwood, 1998, p. 361).

Shepitko's film offers a convincing and sympathetic picture of female loneliness and social alienation. Kira Muratova in *Brief Meetings* (see p. 92) also concentrated on the plight of women at the emotional mercy of men. In male-directed films of these years the status and role of women generally was secondary to more symbolic or 'bigger' issues. Askoldov's *The Commissar* (1967) is in this respect exemplary: apparently an exploration of femininity in a man's world, the film soon becomes an indictment of revolutionary values and the denial of humanity (rather than just womanhood). Andrei Mikhalkov-Konchalovskii did much the same in *The Story of Asia Kliachina, Who Loved but Did Not Marry* (*Asia's Happiness* for short, made in 1967), where the heroine consciously chooses not to take up the offers of marriage that come from two men and decides to have her baby and bring it up alone. She has her baby in a field at night, thus becoming an integral part of Mother Nature – another example of a male director putting his heroine on a (symbolic) pedestal.

A blockbuster such as Vladimir Menshov's *Moscow Doesn't Believe in Tears* (1979) focuses on various interpretations of a woman's place, but decides that it is with her man, even if he does earn less than she does. Menshov's film takes a male-centred reductive view of what a woman wants in a relationship and is rather at odds with the conclusions of other male directors. Iosif Kheifits made *My Only One* in 1975, based on Pavel Nilin's story *Stupidity*. It is about a young loving couple Kolia and Tania Kasatkin, who experience estrangement when she takes a lover and they eventually divorce. The director refuses to condemn his heroine for her flightiness, for although she deeply loves her husband she is rather weak and in thrall to her rascally music teacher Boris Ilich (played by heart-throb troubadour Vladimir Vysotskii). Kolia remarries, but begins drinking heavily and Tania falls ill. The film ends on a sad note, as both realise that they have lost each other forever through sheer 'stupidity'.

Vadim Abdrashitov's *A Word for the Defence* (1976) sees a female defence lawyer Mezhnikova trying to clear her client Valentina Kostina of the attempted murder of her boyfriend Vitalii. Mezhnikova and Valentina grow closer as they talk about the nature of male–female relationships and Mezhnikova increasingly examines her feelings for her own fiancé. Valentina obviously still deeply loves Vitalii and is given a suspended sentence. Mezhnikova realises that she does not possess such a depth of feeling and that she is not in love at all.

The fraught nature of male–female relationships is treated with more than a hint of irony by Ilia Frez in his 1985 film *The Personal Case of Judge Ivanova*. Judge Ivanova of the title (played by the well-known Natalia Gundareva) specialises in divorce hearings, spending her working day telling couples how to live together or granting them a divorce. Life imitates art when her husband Sergei goes off with a younger woman, the piano teacher of their teenage daughter Lena. As she herself comments: 'How many people have I split up and I didn't know what it was like.' The film does not flinch from showing the emotional fallout of a disunited family, especially the negative effect on Lena (she is 16 at the end of the film). There is no happy ending, as Sergei leaves and Lena runs away from home. We see her at the end in the airport, staring out at the runway, wondering whether to go or to return home. It is not explicitly stated, but there is a clear hint that Sergei's dalliance was provoked by his wife spending long hours away from the home (especially the kitchen) and Ivanova's attempts to get him back are doomed from the start. Her own mother is not surprised, saying that men are weak and it is understood by both women that a man is always liable to run off with a younger and more attractive woman.[2]

The bitter-sweet comedy *Autumn Marathon* (1979) turns the tables on the male roué. It concerns the trials and tribulations of a university teacher, Buzykin (Oleg Basilashvili). He is in his mid-forties and his inability to take crucial decisions leads to his abandonment by both his wife and younger mistress. The same happens to Sergei Makarov (Oleg Iankovskii) in Roman Balaian's *Dream Flights* (1982), a man just turned 40 who cannot rid himself of an infantile inability to forge relationships. His wife throws him out, his younger lover finds another (younger) man, even the lonely spinster who has loved him for years abandons him. Alone and forgotten by everyone, in the last scene he finds himself a womb-like haystack in which to seek refuge. In Brezhnev's Russia, it was not only the economy that was stagnating, but male–female relationships, too.

Female stars of the 'stagnation' period

Vera Alentova, the star of *Moscow Doesn't Believe in Tears*, went on to make other important films in subsequent years and won several prizes (including, in 1992, the accolade of People's Artist of the Russian Federation). But the most admired female star of the 1970s and early 1980s was Liudmila Gurchenko, a regular with Eldar Riazanov ever since *Carnival Night* in 1956. In her films from the 1960s to the 1990s she not only gave Russian women a lesson in how to get beyond the age of 40 and remain attractive and sexy, but she also played vulnerable women of a certain age in dead-end relationships, with whom most of the female audience could sympathise and identify. Even in her fifties she maintained her grace and sexual allure, being the envy of every other Russian woman (and admired by men, too). She retained enough glamour to get away with going topless in Riazanov's 1999 film *Old Nags*.

Klavdiia Vavilova in *The Commissar* is played by Nonna Mordiukova, a very popular actress whose most memorable roles have been as strong mother figures. Even in relatively minor roles, such as in *Diamond Arm* (1968) and *A Station for Two* (1982), she displays a sure feel for comedy and satire. However, her most powerful roles are in Nikita Mikhalkov's 1983 film *Kinfolk* and Denis Evstigneev's 1999 film *Mama*, in many ways its sequel.

Kinfolk was controversial at the time of its release for its frank portrayal of dysfunctional families. Mariia Vasilevna travels from the provinces to the town to find her daughter now separated from her husband. She tries to reconcile them but ultimately fails. Mordiukova portrays Mariia Vasilevna as a headstrong and impulsive character out of place in the city, a woman with a ready smile and instinctive feel for what is right. She realises in the end that basic goodness alone cannot achieve goals and that human relationships are more complex than she first imagined. As Mordiukova writes in her autobiography: 'The idea of the film was clear: to show that it does not do to hurry destroying a family, and how much people lose when they break with their kinfolk and the place where they were born. But it only seems that it is so clear and simple' (Mordiukova, 1998, p. 342).

Mama stars not only Mordiukova but some of the most bankable male stars of the late 1990s: Oleg Menshikov, Vladimir Mashkov and Evgenii Mironov. They are among the five surviving sons of Polina Iureva (Mordiukova), one-time stage performers who, under their mother's leadership, had once tried to hijack a plane to the USA and a better life. Now many years on, their mother finds them scattered across the length and breadth of Russia and the 'near abroad' of post-Soviet times and succeeds in uniting them once more in Moscow. They rescue the crippled Menshikov from an asylum and eventually return to their roots in provincial Shuia. The film starts with Iureva's memories of a sun-soaked Shuia railway station in wartime and ends in sunshine with the family together again on the same station. The film's link with Mordiukova's earlier films is made clear when she sings to herself the same lullaby she had sung to her new-born baby as Klavdiia Vavilova in *The Commissar*.

Perhaps the most important female star of the 1960s through to the late 1980s is Inna Churikova, whose most significant films have been made with her husband, the director Gleb Panfilov. She began making films in the early 1960s, but her trademark became strong-willed and determined characters. In *The Debut* (1970) she plays a provincial actress, Praskovia, chosen to play Joan of Arc in a film. As her relationship with Arkadii, a married man, deteriorates, the confusions and weaknesses of real life are contrasted with the solemn, focused and resilient nature of Joan of Arc, tortured and finally burnt at the stake for her beliefs and refusal to compromise.

In another Panfilov film, *I Wish to Speak* (1976), Churikova plays Uvarova, a strong-willed provincial bureaucrat with unwavering faith in the Party. A more substantial role, however, is as Sasha, a French-speaking tour guide in *The Theme* (1979), a natural and plain-speaking innocent who embodies the simplicity and goodness of Russia itself. Sasha, like the ancient, snow-covered city of Suzdal, offers glimpses of purity and principle to the washed-up, cynical and vain writer Kim Esenin (Mikhail Ulianov), who has come to the Russian 'golden ring' for inspiration. Sasha has researched the work of Alexander Chizhikov, a poet of real talent who died in 1934. His talent will live on, whereas Esenin endures a living death of compromise and moral capitulation. Sasha may be Esenin's muse, but her boyfriend Andrei is about to leave for Israel, a frustrated writer fed up living the lie. Sasha, as a good Russian girl, cannot go with him and remains in Russia.

More mundane concerns are at the heart of Churikova's portrayal of Asia Kliachina in Andrei Konchalovskii's *The Chicken Riaba* (1994), a grimly realistic sequel to *Asia's Happiness*. No longer is Asia the embodiment of the forces of nature, as in the earlier film, but rather a symbol of the social collapse of post-Soviet Russia. She is a hardened alcoholic who succeeds in uniting the other, equally drink-sodden villagers against all attempts at modernisation and the incursions of organised crime. Still, she remains the strongest and most self-willed character in the village – even if it gets her and the rest of the village nowhere.

The films of Kira Muratova

The major female director in Russian cinema is undoubtedly Kira Muratova. She began making films in the early 1960s, initially with her husband Alexander Muratov, shortly after her graduation from The All-Union Cinematography Institute in 1959. Most of her films have been produced in Ukraine, although even early in her directorial career she suffered from the censorship apparatus: her third film *Brief Meetings* (1967), in which she also starred, about a relationship between two women loving the same man, had a troubled distribution history. The film contains some social comment about short-changing in the retail trade and especially the accommodation crisis in Soviet cities. Muratova focuses on the long wait families have to bear in order to receive an apartment, with substandard amenities, even lacking a water supply. Otherwise it is a film based on the flashbacks of two women, a village girl Nadia and the regional Party committee official Valentina (played by Muratova). Both recall their relationship with Maxim, a geologist (played by Vladimir Vysotskii), and in the end we are left with a picture of women's lonely lot, either abandoned by men or used by them.

Her next film, *Long Farewells* (1971), was banned outright and shown only in 1987. It is again about a difficult, if not impossible, relationship between a man and a woman and her teenage son caught in the middle. Subsequent films also chart the breakdown of male–female relationships. In *Getting to Know the Outside World* (1978) women can get their own way only by being dominant and forthright. Men and women may be on an equal footing at the workplace (here, a building site), but the viewer is constantly reminded that this is not the case in emotional relationships. Women are exploited in marriage, relationships and work.

Among the Grey Stones (1983) was cut so heavily that Muratova refused to be credited as writer and director, but it remains highly significant as a bridge between her early work and that of the post-Soviet period. Based on a story by Vladimir Korolenko, it contains the absurdist ensemble acting recognisable in *Enthusiasms* a decade later and motifs of madness and alienated children that characterise her later work. Children here are like dolls, they may even fall in love with dolls, while adults are unstable, too wrapped up in their own private dilemmas. The cruelty of adults towards children in this film is repaid with interest in her subsequent films, most notably when the little girl poisons her invalid grandfather at the end of *Three Stories*.

A Change of Fate (1986) is based on Somerset Maugham's story 'The Letter'. It also contains elements of the absurd, linguistic repetition and nonsensical verbal exchanges between characters that is a major feature of Muratova's work in the 1990s. People talk at cross-purposes, but generally fail to communicate. The plot, such as it is, concerns a young woman accused of killing her husband, but who is acquitted. Nevertheless, among the many flashbacks embedded in the narrative there is a shockingly violent scene when she shoots him and we know from the note her defence lawyer finds that she had intended to kill him. Still, the plot is secondary to the plethora of grotesque and absurd moments, including optical illusions and special visual effects: a man displays his skill at card tricks in front of the camera, another stands still, perfectly calm despite the burning hat on his head and a prison guard nonchalantly fondles the breasts of his female prisoner.

The Aesthenic Syndrome (1990) is a relentlessly depressing film about breakdown and decay and obviously offers an allegorical statement on the condition of the contemporary Soviet Union. The film begins with the inconsolable grief of a female doctor who has just lost her husband. She verbally abuses passers-by, refuses to tend a sick neighbour and invites a drunk into her bed, only to kick him out later in a mixture of despair and revulsion. This last episode was particularly controversial, as it was the first scene in a Soviet film to feature a full frontal male nude. Other taboos are broken regularly in the film, especially towards the end when a middle-aged woman mouths Russian obscenities at length at the screen as she travels on an underground train. Elsewhere in the film, a teacher is beaten up by his pupils and a father physically manhandles his teenage daughter.

The Aesthenic Syndrome is a disturbing film, but one which has a peculiar logic and a powerful momentum to it. This is more than a picture – and we are reminded that what we are watching is a film within a film – of a society in crisis; rather, it is facing apocalyptic meltdown. Muratova's film has affinities with the literary work of Liudmila Petrushevskaia and Valeriia Narbikova, who in the late 1980s and early 1990s specialised in pictures of dysfunctional families, moral and spiritual malaise and social decay. The film also has affinities with the postmodernist Vladimir Sorokin, whose grotesque and often repugnant novels also feature linguistic collapse, psychological breakdown and no small amount of travesty, parody and satire. More significantly, both Sorokin and Muratova mock and deconstruct all manifestations of authority and even the nature of artistic representation itself.

The Sensitive Policeman (1992) continues the Sorokin association, with its gloom, grotesque characters and absurd narrative. It is set in 1991, the last year of the Soviet Union, and revisits the themes of collapse and disintegration that became prominent in *The Aesthenic Syndrome*. Kolia Kirilliuk, a policeman, finds a baby abandoned in some bushes, rescues it and takes it to a local orphanage. He and his wife Klava then try to adopt it legally, but the court decides to give the baby Natasha to a much older woman. All forms of civic authority are here mocked: the police, the callous medical staff in the orphanage and the blindness of the court judge. The moral is clear: a society that abandons its children and treats them with an indifference bordering on contempt is irredeemable. Muratova juxtaposes images of bickering neighbours with those of their dogs fighting. These people, however, possess few human features, repeating each others' words and complaints and engaging in circular, pointless dialogues. Characters are filmed in isolation from each other, in darkness or dimly lit surroundings, perched on the edge of madness and breakdown. They do not talk, but rather shout at each other. Again, as in the earlier film, communication is absent, the lack of social cohesion threatens catastrophe.

Enthusiasms (1994) continues Muratova's increasing obsession with hospitals as chronotope. Again, by way of comparison, it is interesting to note the frequency with which Petrushevskaia visits hospitals in her fiction of the late 1980s and 1990s. The film has little plot, other than the training and performance of racehorses, and Muratova's focus is more on the behaviour of the characters, with intertextual references to other icons of Russian cultural achievement. Characters walk about, gesticulate and talk to little purpose, amid close-ups of horses. The animal world and the human world are again juxtaposed, so that there is, essentially, little difference between them.

The film opens as several seemingly crazy characters fall about to the sounds of Beethoven's Ode to Joy and this immediately reminds the viewer of the self-immolation of the apparently mad Domenico in Andrei Tarkovskii's *Nostalgia* of ten years earlier. The world of horseracing contains references to the famous scene in *Anna Karenina*, when Anna gets publicly upset and pained at Vronskii's fall, much to the anger of her husband. The horserace itself is accompanied by orgasmic, ecstatic female screaming, a parody of the scene in *The Commissar* where riderless horses race across a landscape to the sound of dying men's voices and Klavdiia Vavilova's screams of pain at giving birth. *Enthusiasms* has neither a beginning nor an end, neither a focus nor a theme, but gives us another picture of an aimless existence, where human values count for little, as measured against the spiritual legacy of some of the great works of Russian culture.

Three Stories (1996) is Muratova's most important film to date and also her most harrowing. The three stories are all concerned with murder and so

Renata Litvinova in Three Stories *(Kira Muratova, 1996)*

obviously represent a development of Muratova's concern with society's ever-expanding moral vacuum. In the first, a man confesses to a boilerhouse worker that he has murdered his neighbour simply because she accused him of stealing her soap. The boilerhouse itself is like the pit of hell, containing a horribly mutilated corpse about to be consigned to the flames, a crazed boilerman and a couple of aggressively homosexual men. The second story is entitled 'Ophelia' and thus immediately conjures up images of Shakespeare's doomed heroine. However, the nurse 'Opha' (played by Renata Litvinova, who also played a nurse in *Enthusiasms* and who wrote this part) is here no passive sufferer about to go mad and drown herself. Rather, she drowns her own mother for having given her up for adoption as a child. Ophelia is utterly amoral and unflinching, as she strangles a young mother who has abandoned her baby to the orphanage. She sleeps with a doctor in order to gain access to archives and thence the names and addresses of those who have given up their children.

The third story, 'Death and the Maiden', offers as its base another literary source (Ariel Dorfman's 1991 play of the same name, about human rights abuses in Chile in the early 1970s). The veteran and much-respected actor Oleg Tabakov plays a wheelchair-bound old man playing with his young granddaughter on the terrace of their country house. He regales her with strictures and prohibitions, she becomes increasingly irritable and resistant,

death in the Gulag. He had been arrested after the war as a former prisoner of the Germans. The end of the film sees the family come together in symbolic Christian communion as they all partake of the bread and wine on the table, overcoming the power of the lie for the sake of the future.

The late 1980s saw the production of films that offered more challenging portraits of young women. Vasilii Pichul's Vera (*Little Vera*, 1988) (played by Natalia Negoda, subsequently to become a *Playboy* centrefold and appear in American films of the early 1990s) wants something more out of life than the drudgery and low expectations that her family foist on her and to escape the dead-end industrial town where she lives. She is attracted to the nonconformist individualist Sergei and falls in love with both him and the promise of a better life. In the end she stays with her family, grudgingly aware that only love and forgiveness can lead to a better life – at home. The hard-currency prostitute Tania in Petr Todorovskii's *Intergirl* (1989) may get the life she dreams of when she marries a Swedish businessman and emigrates, but once out of Russia she feels pangs of regret and nostalgia. She is punished for her 'desertion' of her Motherland when, on her way to Stockholm airport in order to return home, she is killed in a motor accident. The message is clear: good girls stay in Russia, with their families and should not think above their (domesticated) station. This idea lives on beyond the collapse of the Soviet Union: in Alexei Balabanov's *Brother 2* (2000), the hitman hero Danila 'rescues' a Russian girl forced to work as a prostitute in the States and brings her back home to Russia.

Dmitrii Astrakhan's *You Are My Only One* (1993) is part of this recently established rejection of 'the fairytale of escape' and the new 'myth of endurance and survival' (Graffy, 1999, p. 167). Evgenii is an engineer living in a cramped flat with his doctor wife Natasha and their teenage daughter Olia when he is reintroduced to his childhood sweetheart Anna after an interval of almost 20 years. Anna is now a successful executive in Los Angeles who is in St Petersburg to oversee the takeover of the company Evgenii works for. Anna invites him to return with her to the USA and begin a new life there. He is tempted, but remains true to his Russian soul and stays with his Russian family, despite their straitened circumstances and far from ideal living conditions.

The theme of physical survival is perhaps the major one in the cinema of the post-Soviet period and, inceasingly, women can survive only if they rely on each other and not on men. Eldar Riazanov's comedy *Old Nags* (1999) relates the story of four middle-aged, unmarried women who battle against hoodlums to regain their rightful property. They have all fallen on hard times and are at the mercy of young, aggressive males who represent the testosterone-fuelled modern world of get-rich-quick entrepreneurs. Yet they take the modern world on at its own game and win, whether this be by filling a BMW car full of stinking silage, winning in a casino or seducing the head mobster.

This is a curious film in that the four women are obviously playing out Riazanov's own revenge fantasy, as he reasserts the old values and makes a mockery of the 'new Russians' seemingly demeaning society. Furthermore, the four women are played by extremely well-known and popular actresses from the Soviet period: Liudmila Gurchenko, Liia Akhedzhakova, Svetlana Kriuchkova and Irina Kupchenko. To a certain extent, they reprise the characters for which they were known a decade or so earlier: Kupchenko is the intellectual, Gurchenko the would-be flirt, Akhedzhakova the scatty and emotional one and Kriuchkova the pragmatic if put-upon type. At the end of the film Riazanov himself, as the judge who has just acquitted them of all wrongdoing, waves them away as they depart in an army truck, as if bidding farewell not only to his leading ladies (most of whom have done well by him over the years), but also to his own past glories.

Russian literature has a tradition of dangerous female sexuality that threatens masculine dominance and social stability. But characters such as Anna Karenina and Katerina Izmailova have to die for those male values to survive – and also to show other women that they must know their place. There is, however, an almost total absence of this image in film (other than literary adaptations). Women remain unthreatening, subservient, domesticated, returning to the fold or doomed to a life of loneliness. The female characters of Muratova are here an obvious and important exception.

Women in the 'golden age' were seen generally in political terms: either as willing participants in the struggle for the new world or as newly emancipated paragons of that world. In the 1930s and 1940s icons of Hollywood-like glamour were made available for the hard-working tractor driver if he fulfilled his plan. After the death of Stalin women came alive, as it were, but could not stray from the patriarchal value system of Soviet society. Even in the liberated 1980s and 1990s, where women may be shown as sexually active and independent – little Vera, for instance, who is literally 'on top' of her partner – they are still emotionally dependent on their men and can see no future without them.

A Russian Thelma and Louise do exist, however. In Valerii Todorovskii's *Land of the Deaf* (1998) women are strong because they have to be and the men are weak. Rita is a normal working girl caught up in dangerous intrigues when her boyfriend Alesha falls foul of gangsters. She even attempts to work as a prostitute in order to get money for him. Iaia ('I hate all men, they're all despicable') is deaf and works as an exotic dancer. Rita and Iaia eventually triumph over the various gangs preying on them, the mobsters kill each other and the two girls are left together with each other, in the land of the deaf where no evil is heard.[4]

Filmography

The Aesthenic Syndrome ('Astenicheskii sindrom'), dir. Kira Muratova, 1990

Among the Grey Stones ('Sredi serykh kamnei'), dir. Ivan Sidorov [Kira Muratova], 1983

Autumn Marathon ('Osennii marafon'), dir. Georgii Daneliia, 1979

Brief Meetings ('Korotkie vstrechi'), dir. Kira Muratova, 1967

Brother 2 ('Brat 2'), dir. Alexei Balabanov, 2000

By the Law ('Po zakonu'), dir. Lev Kuleshov, 1926

Carnival Night ('Karnavalnaia noch'), dir. Eldar Riazanov, 1956

The Chicken Riaba ('Kurochka Riaba'), dir. Andrei Mikhalkov-Konchalovskii, 1994

The Cigarette Girl from Mosselprom ('Papirosnitsa ot Mosselproma'), dir. Iurii Zheliabuzhskii, 1924

Cinderella ('Zolushka'), dir. Nadezhda Kosheverova, 1947

The Circus ('Tsirk'), dir. Grigorii Alexandrov, 1936

Clear Skies ('Chistoe nebo'), dir. Grigorii Chukhrai, 1961

The Commissar ('Komissar'), dir. Alexander Askoldov, 1967

The Cranes are Flying ('Letiat zhuravli'), dir. Mikhail Kalatozov, 1957

The Debut ('Nachalo'), dir. Gleb Panfilov, 1970

The Devil's Wheel ('Chertovo koleso'), dir. Grigorii Kozintsev and Leonid Trauberg, 1926

Diamond Arm ('Brilliantovaia ruka'), dir. Leonid Gaidai, 1968

Dream Flights ('Polety vo sne i naiavu'), dir. Roman Balaian, 1982

Enthusiasms ('Uvlecheniia'), dir. Kira Muratova, 1994

The Foundling ('Podkidysh'), dir. Tatiana Lukashevich, 1939

Four Loving Hearts ('Serdtsa chetyrekh'), dir. Konstantin Iudin, 1941

The General Line ('Generalnaia liniia'), dir. Sergei Eisenstein, 1929

Getting to Know the Wide World ('Poznavaia belyi svet'), dir. Kira Muratova, 1978

A Girl with Character ('Devushka s kharakterom'), dir. Konstantin Iudin, 1939

The Girl with the Hatbox ('Devushka s korobkoi'), dir. Boris Barnet, 1927

The House on Trubnaia ('Dom na Trubnoi'), dir. Boris Barnet, 1928

Intergirl ('Interdevochka'), dir. Petr Todorovskii, 1989

I Wish to Speak ('Proshu slova'), dir. Gleb Panfilov, 1976

Kinfolk ('Rodnia'), dir. Nikita Mikhalkov, 1983

Land of the Deaf ('Strana glukhikh'), dir. Valerii Todorovskii, 1998

Little Vera ('Malenkaia Vera'), dir. Vasilii Pichul, 1988

Lonely Woman Seeks Lifelong Companion ('Odinokaia zhenshchina zhelaet poznakomitsia'), dir. Viacheslav Khrishtofovich, 1986

Long Farewells ('Dolgie provody'), dir. Kira Muratova, 1971

Mama, dir. Denis Evstigneev, 1999

The Man from the Restaurant ('Chelovek iz restorana'), dir. Iakov Protazanov, 1927

A Member of the Government ('Chlen pravitelstva'), dir. Alexander Zarkhi and Iosif Kheifits, 1939

Minor People ('Vtorostepennye liudi'), dir. Kira Muratova, 2001

Moscow Doesn't Believe in Tears ('Moskva slezam ne verit'), dir. Vladimir Menshov, 1979

Mother ('Mat'), dir. Vsevolod Pudovkin, 1926

Mother and Son ('Mat i syn'), dir. Alexander Sokurov, 1997

My Only One ('Edinstvennaia . . .'), dir. Iosif Kheifits, 1975

New Babylon ('Novyi Vavilon'), dir. Grigorii Kozintsev and Leonid Trauberg, 1927

Old Nags ('Starye kliachi'), dir. Eldar Riazanov, 1999

The Personal Case of Judge Ivanova ('Lichnoe delo sudi Ivanovoi'), dir. Ilia Frez, 1985

Remember Me This Way ('Zapomnite menia takoi'), dir. Pavel Chukhrai, 1987

The School Leaving Certificate ('Attestat zrelosti'), dir. Tatiana Lukashevich, 1954

The Sensitive Policeman ('Chuvstvitelnyi militsioner'), dir. Kira Muratova, 1992

Some Interviews on Personal Matters ('Neskolko interviu po lichnym voprosam'), dir. Lana Gogoberidze, 1985

A Station for Two ('Vokzal dlia dvoikh'), dir. Eldar Riazanov, 1982

The Story of Asia Kliachina, Who Loved but Did Not Marry (Asia's Happiness) ('Istoriia Asi Kliachinoi, kotoraia liubila da ne vyshla zamuzh (Asino schaste)'), dir. Andrei Mikhalkov-Konchalovskii, 1967

The Tailor from Torzhok ('Zakroishchik iz Torzhka'), dir. Iakov Protazanov, 1926

The Theme ('Tema'), dir. Gleb Panfilov, 1979

Three Stories ('Tri istorii'), dir. Kira Muratova, 1996

Vassa, dir. Gleb Panfilov, 1983

Wings ('Krylia'), dir. Larisa Shepitko, 1966

A Word for the Defence ('Slovo dlia zashchity'), dir. Vadim Abdrashitov, 1976

You Are My Only One ('Ty u menia odna'), dir. Dmitrii Astrakhan, 1993

Notes

1. These two films served as the high points in the directorial careers of both Lukashevich and Kosheverova. Lukashevich (1905–72) did make some good films in the 1950s (especially *The School Leaving Certificate*, 1954), whereas Kosheverova (1902–89), who had worked with Kozintsev and Trauberg in Lenfilm in the 1930s, went on to make generally undistinguished films, although she continued to work well into her eighties.

2. The same theme is treated by the Georgian Lana Gogoberidze in *Some Interviews on Personal Matters*, made in Soviet Georgia in 1985. Here, too, the heroine Sofiko has a successful career (as a journalist), travelling often and widely and fails to see until too late that her husband is having an affair. Here, however, it is clear that her husband Archil finds a younger woman precisely because his wife spends too much time at her job. Furthermore, Archil dismisses her work as 'falseness' and Gogoberidze's moral stance becomes clear when Sofiko's mother, who had spent time in Stalin's camps, dies when her daughter is away on an assignment.

3. Graham Roberts observes: 'Muratova's vision [. . .] is profoundly Absurd: life is chaotic and meaningless, there is nothing that we mortals can do to avoid death, and nothing which might afford us transcendence to a higher realm. All we can do is try to distract ourselves from this "absurd" truth, by means of whatever "enthusiasm" we choose, be it telling stories, adopting lost children, riding horses, painting pictures, or even making films. Ultimately, however, there is no escape' (Roberts, 1999, p. 160).

4. It has been pointed out in an earlier chapter that Todorovskii's *Katia Izmailova* owes much to Hollywood and French *film noir*. His *Land of the Deaf* has much in common with Jean-Jacques Beineix's 1981 film *Diva*, with similar chic interiors and eccentric characters, but substitutes a rousing jazz score for the operatic extracts that distinguish the French film.

CHAPTER SIX

Film and ideology

As always in the half-century of our most recent modern history, a lofty, bright theory and creeping moral vileness somehow got naturally interwoven, and were easily transformed into one another.

(Solzhenitsyn, 1975, p. 544)

'From the very beginnings of modern Russian literature,' writes Gareth Jones, 'Russia's writers have consciously dealt with politics' (Jones, 1998, p. 63). Given their self-appointed role as teacher and moral guide, writers in nineteenth-century Russia (Pushkin, Nekrasov, Belinskii, Turgenev, Chernyshevskii, to name a few) were never far away from the burning political issues of the day and some, indeed (Tolstoi and Dostoevskii for example), sought to influence political thinking and the political process. The key historico-political moments of the nineteenth century, the Decembrist revolt of 1825 and the emancipation of the serfs in 1861, were both influenced by writers of the time and were to have a profound influence on the future of Russian literature.

Ideology entered Russian cinema with the fall of the Romanov dynasty in February 1917. A brief look at the titles of some of the films released in that year is sufficient to grasp the anti-monarchist and radical public mood: *Dark Forces: Grigorii Rasputin and his Associates*; *In the Clutches of Judas*; *Governmental Deception*; *The Revolutionary*; *The Bourgeois, Enemy of the People*. Short *agitki* released during the Civil War to blacken and ridicule the White enemy were no less tendentious, if slightly outlandish: *Proletarians of the World Unite!*; *For the Red Flag*; *The Frightened Bourgeois*; *Peace to the Huts, War to the Palaces* (Kenez, 1992, pp. 35–6). The ideological imperative was to remain with the Soviet film industry throughout its existence, although in the Soviet Union's last years ideology became distinctly muted, even subversive.

New Babylon, directed in 1929 by Grigorii Kozintsev and Leonid Trauberg of the Leningrad-based FEKS ('Factory of the Eccentric Actor') group, takes the political struggle to the streets of Paris during the Franco-Prussian War of 1871. Although ostensibly a historical film, *New Babylon* covers much of the same ideological ground as *Strike*, with class warfare waged and the eventual victory of the workers assured.

Again there is a clear differentiation between the working classes and the bourgeoisie, with the former the main victims of war and subject to exploitation at work, but bearing their wretched lot with dignity and increasing confidence in their cause. The latter are a debauched and cowardly bunch, preparing to surrender Paris to the Prussians in order to keep their way of life and privileges. For them, indeed, war is simply theatre, with tickets to be bought and applause at the final curtain.

When the workers rebel against their masters and set up the commune, their slogans could be just as apt for the workers of *Strike*: 'We will work for ourselves, and not for the bosses, the commune has decided'; 'We will not be thrown out of our houses, the commune has decided'; and, most tellingly, 'Before us is eternity, and we will be able to solve everything'. As in Eisenstein's film, the workers are crushed and the old order is reasserted, but the viewer knows that this is only a temporary setback in the historical process: 'Long live the commune' shout the workers as they die defiantly and their cause will ultimately triumph several decades later – not in France but in *Russia*.

There is one clear and important difference, however, between the films of Eisenstein and Kozintsev/Trauberg. For Eisenstein the collective is the moving force of history, the masses are the hero and so few characters are individualised. In *New Babylon*, Louise is the tragic heroine, aided by an unnamed soldier and it is through her that the audience can focus its sympathies and allegiances.

Vsevolod Pudovkin's *Storm over Asia* (1928) takes the struggle further afield, to Mongolia, where the local population is crudely exploited by American and British imperialists and their religion (Buddhism) used as a means of keeping them docile and becalmed. Against a magnificent landscape of mountains and forests, they fight back through their leader Amogolan. Once a reluctant plaything of the imperial powers but now discovering his true calling as 'the heir of Chingiz Khan', the final scenes show him leading an army of thousands of horsemen charging across the steppe, intent on driving the enemy occupier out of his country. Pudovkin's film is an anti-imperialist tract, a call to all the oppressed nations to throw off their shackles and struggle for independence.

These films of the 1920s thus followed Bolshevik policies and reflected their view of history and progress. Directors of vastly different styles and approaches, such as Pudovkin, Eisenstein, Fridrikh Ermler, Alexander Dovzhenko and Dziga Vertov were committed to the Bolshevik cause and willingly used their art to promote it. Vertov's non-fictional films *Onward, Soviet!* (1926), *The Sixth Part of the World* (1926), *The Eleventh Year* (1928) and *The Man with the Movie Camera* (1929) both celebrated the new world created in 1917 and hoped to improve it through its depiction 'caught unawares'. Vertov and his 'Cine-Eye' group (his wife and editor Elizaveta Svilova, together with his brother and cameraman Mikhail Kaufman) also sought to create a utopian vision of the new city through the medium of the camera, 'more perfect than the human eye for examining the chaos of visual phenomena that resemble space'. Here the life of man and the energy of the machine can become merged into a single consciousness: 'By revealing the souls of machines . . . we bring men closer to machines.' Vertov sought both to capture the reality of life – 'the film factory of facts' – on camera and then to remould it through editing and montage, as part of an aesthetic and political credo as stated in 1923:

> . . . I am the Cine-Eye. I am the mechanical eye.
> I the machine show you the world as only I can see it.
> I emancipate myself henceforth and forever from human immobility. I am in constant motion . . .
> My path leads towards the creation of a fresh perception of the world. I can thus decipher a world that you do not know.

> *(Christie and Taylor, 1994, p. 93)*

Vertov's utopian aesthetic ultimately came to nothing, as did his quixotic campaign against all kinds of 'fiction' and 'theatre' in film. With the adoption of socialist realism as the 'basic method of Soviet belles-lettres' in all forms of cultural production in 1934, a new political film emerged that had nothing to do with a director's personal beliefs and everything to do with the new demands imposed by a militant political hierarchy.

The 1930s was the decade of the Soviet political film par excellence. Moreover, these were films that reflected the new, increasingly tense atmosphere of suspicion and fear, where the need for vigilance and the 'unmasking' of internal and external enemies were dominant motifs. Films such as Ivan Pyrev's *The Party Card* (1936) and *Counterplan* (1932), directed by Fridrikh Ermler and Sergei Iutkevich, told of spies determined to wreck Soviet industry, suggested that enemies were everywhere, even in the bosom of one's family and called for the swift and decisive exercise of Soviet justice to deal with them. Ermler's two-part *The Great Citizen* (1937–9) more specifically reflected the campaigns against 'oppositionists' Trotskii and Bukharin. Films such as

Vitia Kartashov leads collectivisation in Bezhin Meadow *(Sergei Eisenstein, 1935–7)*

these, therefore, justified the show trials and purges and were very much transmission belts for the political leadership to convey its own suspicions, paranoia and ruthlessness.

These were also quite primitive films in terms of screenplay and style, with a predictably linear plot and obvious 'positive' and 'negative' heroes. Sergei Eisenstein attempted to sail with the prevailing wind. His *Bezhin Meadow* does not survive as a film, as filming was stopped on the orders of the Party in 1937 and the only extant version was destroyed in the bombing of the Mosfilm studios during the war. However, the stills that do survive retell the story of Pavlik Morozov, the 14-year-old boy killed by his fellow villagers after he had denounced his own father to the authorities for hoarding grain during collectivisation. Morozov was turned into a hero by the Stalinist ideological machine, with the clear message that loyalty to Stalin and socialism was more important and binding than family ties. In Eisenstein's film the boy Stepok is killed by his father, who had earlier beaten his own wife to death and who justifies his actions through reference to the Bible.

Eisenstein made the film as a means of recovering some favour lost during his time spent abroad, in Western Europe and then the USA, between 1929–32. The stills that remain show peasants destroying a church in a triumphant affirmation of official atheism, but Eisenstein's symbolism subverts his ideological message: the peasants themselves become saints, as their faces fill the icons and their bodies assume angelic features. Eisenstein's approach was attacked for showing 'biblical and mythological types rather than the images of collective farm workers', producing 'a direct slander against our Soviet countryside' and using the film 'as a pretext for harmful Formalistic exercises' (Shumiatskii, 1994, pp. 378–81). 'Formalism' was regarded as a heinous crime by Stalinist cultural watchdogs, as it was seen as preferring stylistic virtuosity to ideological content. Eisenstein was forced to apologise and the film was stopped.

'Formalist' devices were much in evidence in Vsevolod Pudovkin's *The Deserter* (1933), subsequently decried as a 'failure' but nevertheless one of the most significant and stylistically bold films of the decade. The 'deserter' is Karl Renn, a German shipyard worker who defects to the Soviet Union, becomes ideologically enlightened there and returns to Germany to carry the red flag and lead the workers as they demonstrate against their capitalist bosses. The working conditions in the capitalist West are, indeed, awful. The workers live in cramped hostel accommodation and are kept under strict control by a ruthless management that has both the police and a corrupt union in their pocket. The police, who suspiciously resemble American cops from Holly-wood films of the 1920s and 1930s, even go after children selling subversive newspapers. When they go on strike German workers starve and have to fight both the police and the strikebreakers brought in by the management in scenes of violence and brutality that shock even by today's standards. As police turn machine-guns against the strikers, the strikebreakers enter the shipyard to the sounds of the groans of the dying men.

In the Soviet Union, however, things could not be more different. Here the sun shines and everyone, including the policemen, smile. Workers from different countries can understand one another even without knowing one another's language. Karl's introduction to life in the Soviet Union is a celebration of man's harmonious relationship with the machine, he is not alienated from but united with, in accordance with Marxist-Leninist thought, the modes of production and distribution.

This is, of course, blatant propaganda of the most ferociously pro-Bolshevik kind, but Pudovkin's film is notable for its stylistic experimentation, in par-ticular its use of sound montage. Magnified sounds of grating and screeching metal, incongruous background music – a knockabout jazz score accom-panies a fight – snatches of conversations and radio broadcasts all enhance the totality of this picture of industrial strife and political struggle, while at the same time ensuring that such innovations remain in the viewer's mind long after the film's moral has been forgotten.

The 'Maxim Trilogy', directed by Grigorii Kozintsev and Leonid Trauberg between 1934 and 1938, offers a similarly prejudiced picture of proletarian power politics. There is much celebration of working-class culture and workers eagerly discuss politics against a background of billiards and guitar

109

playing in smoke-filled backrooms, which is also much of the source of the humour in these films. In *The Return of Maxim* (1937) the democracy of pre-revolutionary Russia is shown to be sham, as Duma delegates, led by priests and capitalists, shout down the workers' representative Baluev who complains of 'exploitation' and the 'hard labour' conditions workers have to endure. The speaker, with a portrait of Nicholas II behind him, calls for Baluev's arrest as the delegates bay for blood. In other words, the working class can improve its lot 'only with its own hands'.

The dominant image is that of the red flag, which unites young and old, men and women, and Maxim remains indefatigable, surviving to fight another day and agitating with Russian soldiers heading off for the trenches of the First World War. In *The Vyborg Side* (1938) the Revolution has been accomplished and Maxim is now a firm friend and ally of Iakov Sverdlov, whom history will recall as one of the most bloodthirsty Bolsheviks. In this film Sverdlov coolly faces down the derisive Constituent Assembly, whose cowering and cowardly deputies quickly disband when faced with a squad of Bolshevik sailors and soldiers armed to the teeth. In other words, the establishment of the 'dictatorship of the proletariat' and the one-party state were historically inevitable because the representatives of so-called democracy simply wanted to retain their old privileges and cared nothing about the ordinary people. Still, the justification of the forcible dissolution of a demo-cratically elected body is difficult to reconcile with the film's endorsement of the Bolshevik regime as humane and politically legitimate.

Moreover, *The Vyborg Side* is playing to the contemporary gallery, with its justification of the show trials of 1937, where bankers in 1917 are in the pay of the Germans, English, French and Japanese, a reflection of the increasingly outlandish charges laid at the door of 'enemies of the people' during the purges. Is it by accident that the barbarism of the new regime is upheld, when pogrom organisers are sentenced to death, whereas under Tsarism they would have simply been exiled? *The Vyborg Side* contains its fair share of barroom bacchanalia, but on a more fundamental level it reclaims the Revolution for the working class, which had been made by them, not intellectuals, and shows their methods of government and retribution. The 'Maxim Trilogy' suffers generically precisely because it is overtly political: the Marxist-Leninist ideological narrative dictates that there is no quick fix in the struggle for a new world and that this struggle will be long and painful. Therefore the films themselves are long – some would say painfully so – and, because the viewer knows the actual historical outcome, lack dramatic tension. Didactic intertitles are used to explain the action, as if the watching proletariat would not understand the significance of their own role and the films simply finish without narrative closure – after all, the ongoing international struggle for communism would last decades yet.

Stalin's policies in the 1930s virtually cut the country off from the outside world, so that under the banner of 'socialism in one country' foreigners knew little or nothing of what was happening in the Soviet Union – the terror famine of the early 1930s, for example – and the people of the Soviet Union knew about the West only what their official media selectively filtered through. So Mikhail Romm's *The Dream* (1941) reflected the official picture of the West as a place of gambling and degeneracy, where middle-aged lechers ogle young waitresses, exploitation is rife and all relationships are determined by money and status. Those agitating for a better life (here in Ukraine) are pursued by the police. As in *The Deserter*, the Soviet Union offers the 'dream' of a better life, and political union with Russia is the fulfilment of 'the dreams of the best people of Ukraine'. Yet the earnestness of the subject matter is undermined by its style or lack of it. It is filmed almost as a play, with few cinematic touches and no soundtrack other than the orchestral music that reaches crescendo to announce heightened emotions or a major narrative event.

Other political films were called upon to trumpet the cause of Soviet scientific achievement. Sergei Gerasimov's *The Courageous Seven* (1936) concerns a group of komsomol volunteers who spend 275 days in the Arctic circle at the 'Joyous Bay' station, braving the elements – ice storms, blizzards, the snowy expanses – and affirming that there is nothing that is impossible for Soviet scientists. Zhenia, the doctor, performs an operation on an eskimo in an igloo, thus testifying to the true internationalist spirit of Stalin's Russia, while others discover tin deposits. The new Soviet man can conquer nature in its wildest form, carrying the body of a friend across miles of snow to base, ignoring his own exhaustion. Furthermore, although the group consists of six men and one woman, there is no hint of sexual tension or frustration: this nearly-boys-own adventure is impeccably comradely.

Mikhail Kalatozov's *Valerii Chkalov* (1941) also praises the superhuman efforts of Soviet citizens to expand the horizons of science for the benefit of mankind. Chkalov (1904–38) is 'a born talent' but a maverick aviator, defying authority to go his own way: he is inspired but wilful, instinctive but brilliant. He is devoted to flying as an art, but does not lose his link with the people, as he helps a fisherman haul in his catch. Like all great men, he 'cannot get on with people', but he is appreciated by 'Sergo' Ordzhonikidze, the minister for heavy industry who has the mannerisms and gestures of Comrade Stalin himself. 'Tireless' Chkalov then conquers not only distance, flying from Moscow to Vancouver and being feted by the Western proletariat, but also height, as he refuses oxygen to fly as high as possible. We are not shown Chkalov's actual death in a flying accident; rather, the film ends with his words praising mankind's aspiration towards universal communism.

What is remarkable about this most dangerous of decades is not the abundance of uncompromisingly political films as those already mentioned, but the production of some films without any political content whatso-ever. *Lieutenant Kizhe* (1934), Alexander Faintsimmer's adaptation of Iurii Tynianov's 1928 novella, is an absurdist version of an absurdist work, an anomaly of its time. Tynianov's story is set in 1800 and dutifully caricatures Tsar Paul I, his officials and army officers. The lieutenant of the title does not actually exist, but is the creation of an army scribe based on a syntactical error. It is to everyone's advantage to persuade the tsar that Kizhe does, in fact, exist. So impressed is Paul that the lieutenant is promoted to colonel and then general, only to be demoted to the ranks on the tsar's whim. Kizhe even marries and his bemused bride is forced to go through with a farcical wedding ceremony (kissing thin air as the knot is tied).

Tynianov's novella also features the character of Siniukhaev, who does exist, although everyone around him denies it and who eventually disappears. This character is missing in Faintsimmer's film, possibly because discussion of a person whose existence is officially denied and who suddenly vanishes with-out trace was too close to home in 1930s Russia. The director concentrates on increasingly farcical situations and absurdist dialogue, with Prokofev's musical soundtrack and the diegetic use of song, adding a mock heroic tone. It is a film about the unreality of reality, where people can appear and disappear on the whim of the Tsar. It is apposite to note that Tsar Paul I was mentally unstable and was assassinated by his own guards in 1801.

Another thoroughly apolitical film from these years is Abram Room's *A Strict Youth* (1936), with a screenplay by the 'carnivalesque' writer Iurii Olesha and brimming with 'formalist' devices. There is a dream-like quality to the visual images, with parodies of famous Eisenstein moments (statues of lions content to remain lying where they are, a butcher holding a cleaver, but not actually slaughtering any bull). Nothing much happens: the surgeon Stepanov lives in an opulent house with his younger wife Masha and ward Fedor. What is more important is the way the film looks: black cars and a grand piano are contrasted with white shirts, floors and walls and muscular athletic bodies are juxtaposed with statues of Greek gods (another jibe at Eisenstein, but with Vertov also as a target).

The film, astonishingly for its time, also has a palpable erotic charge to it. Characters engage in idle talk about the nature of desire and the necessity of fulfilling it, thus mocking materialist principles. Communism will be achieved, some say, when all desires can be met. Giant flowers, a concert hall floor that is transformed into a body of water, ghostly characters filmed slightly out of focus all contribute to a sense of a cinematic phantasmagoria. *A Strict Youth* is a deliberately self-conscious work that draws attention to its own status and lineage, as intertitles explain the narrative, and the 'golden age' of Soviet cinema is gently mocked. It is a film about the totality of cultural experience, with reference made to cinema, literature, ballet and opera. It challenges the viewer to assess and reassess what is seen on screen. Decades before Tarkovskii, Room includes shots through windows and doors, with the use of mirrors and images of social exclusion/inclusion as characters are filmed behind railings or in front of them. A *Strict Youth* was quickly banned, having provoked a furious response from official critics.

The thaw and the 'stagnation': the emergence of allegory

It is axiomatic that all Stalinist culture was permeated with ideology and that no film, book or painting could be devoid of its 'socialist realist' content and message. As far as cinema is concerned, the historical film, the comedy and the war film were also political films, 'correcting' the 'mistakes' of the past and providing pointers to the 'radiant future'. After the death of Stalin the political tone was diluted in most films, with greater attention paid to the problems of everyday life and ordinary folk.

This can perhaps be most clearly seen in *Pavel Korchagin*, directed by Alexander Alov and Vladimir Naumov in 1956, an adaptation of Nikolai Ostrovskii's socialist realist classic *How the Steel Was Tempered* (1934). *Pavel Korchagin* features the self-sacrificing exploits of komsomol volunteers that are the main theme of the book, but the emphasis is here not so much on heroism and achievement, as on the personal price to be paid (loneliness, illness, blindness). In other words, the Stalinist ethic of struggle and commitment had now been replaced by the insistence on 'the human factor'.

Other films, however, still viewed the past as a time of heroism. *The House I Live In*, directed by Lev Kulidzhanov and Iakov Segel in 1957, provided both a slice-of-life drama about the occupants of a communal apartment, with political symbolism that gave few concessions to the new 'humanism' of the thaw. The film covers several decades, from the pre-war years to the 1950s. Here is a real sense of community, where everyone is respectful and caring, the collective works and everyone feels needed, even in times of difficulty. This apartment can be seen as a microcosm of a successfully functioning community under Stalin, where all conflicts are resolved with reference to the collective. Patriotic music throughout the film reinforces the feel-good subject matter. There is no explicit mention of the political background or leaders, apart from the symbolic return to 'Leninist norms' in the 1950s, for ordinary workers are the heroes. This is a politically conservative film of ordinary Soviet people on whom the whole political edifice is built. They keep themselves and the state going through thick and thin, the younger generation carries on the cause of its elders and even emotional dramas can ultimately be resolved.

The thaw and de-Stalinisation produced a dichotomy in Soviet society that was to last until the demise of the Soviet Union itself and even beyond. On the one hand, there were those who welcomed the opportunity for greater freedom and openness. On the other, there were those who yearned for the certainties of the past and the 'strong hand' of leadership. Both these tendencies can be seen in two key films of the late 1950s to early 1960s.

Nine Days of One Year was directed by Mikhail Romm in 1961 and proved both extremely popular and controversial. It is set among young nuclear physicists, one of whom becomes dangerously affected by radiation in the course of his work. The film combined both a warning of the dangers inherent in nuclear science and a fairly glamorous picture of the life and self-regard of these young Soviet upwardly mobile professionals. The film's ideological credentials are undoubteldy liberal, however, with its warnings about the dire consequences of nuclear conflict. By comparison, Viktor Ivchenko's *Emergency*, made in 1958, is a straightforward anti-capitalist Cold War tract. It is based on an actual event: the capture of a Soviet tanker in 1954 by the Chinese of Formosa, present-day Taiwan. In Ivchenko's film the Chinese are obviously in the pay of the USA, as they imprison the tanker's crew and encourage crew members to defect. This is a very long film and it details the various psychological torments and capitalist temptations to which these honest souls are subject, as well as their strategies of resistance. They are eventually returned to their homeland, living examples of the indomitability of the human spirit, but, more importantly, the inner steel of the average Soviet citizen. The anti-imperialist theme, of course, is loud and clear.

These are two films that, in their differing ways and with their widely divergent agendas, confront the issues of the day head-on. Others were more circumspect, especially given the changing political climate of the mid-1960s and the return to more repressive forms of government. *The Republic of ShKID* (1966) is one of the few feature films directed by Gennadii Poloka. It is set among the hordes of homeless children roaming Soviet cities in the early 1920s and covers much the same ground as Nikolai Ekk's *The Path to Life* (1931). Poloka's film, however, works much more on the level of political allegory.

The 'republic' is the school, named in Dostoevskii's honour, which houses young homeless boys who neither recognise nor tolerate any authority. The older boys bully the younger ones and their rebellion against teachers is a rejection of all attempts to guide and educate them. The school management may have nominal power, but the children have actual control in a curious echo of William Golding's *Lord of the Flies*. The children take over the school, as if the lunatics had taken over the asylum. Poloka explores the group dynamics of power and how it affects individuals, where in this community the strong sadistically dominate the weak and where elections to governing bodies are little more than a sham.

Only the director of the school, Viktor Nikolaevich can make any meaningful contact with the children, as he talks to them as equals. At the end of the film social cohesion is achieved, young are reconciled with old, teachers with children, but Poloka has given a brief picture of a society without values that crumbles when the strong demonstrate their will to power and are prepared to use it ruthlessly. It is, in effect, a satirical take on the politics of twentieth-century Russia, whose cultural and ethical values are shown to be largely weak and ineffective when faced with brute force.

Anything approaching critical political discourse was impossible in the years of the 'stagnation' period, yet directors such as Poloka could resort to allegory and Aesopian language to make points that would be readily understood by a generally appreciative audience. The adaptation of literary texts proved to be fertile ground for the dissemination of critical, if not actually dissident, ideas, where the hallowed pages of the classics could speak to a new generation on topics of immediate relevance.

Nikita Mikhalkov's adaptations are noted for the excellence of their period detail and the strength of the acting ensemble, but, made towards the end of the 1970s, they also reflect topical political issues. Both *An Unfinished Piece for Mechanical Piano* (1977), based on Chekhov's play *Platonov* (only published in 1923) and *Several Days in the Life of I. I. Oblomov* (1979), based on Ivan Goncharov's 1859 novel *Oblomov*, are ostensibly about the failed ideals of the Russian intelligentsia in the nineteenth century. However, it is not difficult to see that the spiritual and moral impasse in which they find themselves can equally be related to the existential dead end many members of the Soviet intelligentsia saw themselves in the late 1970s. In *An Unfinished Piece for Mechanical Piano* characters are unable to establish any lasting bonds or relationships and are unable and unwilling to change anything in their material world (the very charge laid against the Soviet intelligentsia by dissidents such as Alexander Solzhenitsyn and Andrei Amalrik). Mikhalkov's interpretation of the clinically indolent and apathetic Oblomov stresses his childlike innocence, he is an impractical dreamer unable to adapt to a modern cynical and pragmatic world (read the failure of the intelligentsia to engage meaningfully with authority).

If the intelligentsia are impotent, then ordinary people have to take matters into their own hands. Elem Klimov's *Farewell*, begun by his wife Larisa Shepitko before her death in a car accident in 1979, completed in 1982, but released only in 1984, confronts orthodox ideology much more critically and forcefully. Based on the 1976 novella *Farewell to Matera* by the Siberian writer Valentin Rasputin, it concerns the building of a hydro-electric dam on the

Maia Bulgakova leads the exodus from Matera in Farewell *(Elem Klimov, 1982)*

Angara river in Siberia and the physical, social and psychological upheavals in the lives of those directly affected.

Rasputin's novella offers strong condemnation of the official Marxist-Leninist doctrine of materialism and the Soviet state's commitment to industrial progress – the so-called 'scientific-technological revolution' – and Klimov's film makes full use of the visual possibilities of symbolism and allegory in order to reinforce this theme. His film therefore offers a sharp critique of official rationalist policy, points to a crisis of ideas in Soviet Russia and offers salvation through a rediscovery of past, pre-Soviet models of life, thought and belief.

The construction of the huge dam will entail the flooding of vast areas of land to create a reservoir and one of the casualties is Matera, a village situated on an island in the middle of the Angara river that has existed for over 300 years. Its culture will be destroyed, as well as the spiritual and moral values passed down from generation to generation, and its people are to be rehoused in an urban settlement further downstream, cut off from their roots and the land of their forebears. The manner of its destruction is also symbolic: the houses and scrub are to be razed by fire, then the whole island flooded. The Russia of old is to suffer an apocalyptic fate, the past will disappear to leave an uncertain future, the present a materialistic void.

Klimov's film therefore challenged, at the time when Brezhnev's 'developed socialism' was about to give way to perestroika, the accepted Marxist-Leninist notion that 'man is the tsar of nature' and can rule the natural world with mathematical precision and certainty. It asks the question: is the price for industrial progress too high? This may be a question posed by all developing societies, but it also cast into doubt existing ideological pieties of materialism and progress, as well as Russia's own fate in the late twentieth century.

Glasnost and beyond: the rejection of ideology

With *Farewell*, Klimov came as close as anyone in late Soviet Russia to an outright rejection of state ideology and its philosophical underpinning. Films that burst on to the Soviet screen in the late 1980s, either new films or those that were dusted down and taken 'off the shelf', could challenge communist ideology with greater assurance and consistency.

In January 1987 Tengiz Abuladze's *Repentance* was released and quickly became one of the key moments of glasnost. Keen to sway public opinion in favour of his reform programme, Mikhail Gorbachev encouraged every Soviet citizen to see it. A Georgian film, made in Soviet Georgia in Georgian, it both echoes and anticipates the treatment of Stalin in later Russian films. The film focuses on the demonic figure of Varlam Aravidze, mayor of a small Georgian town who routinely disposes of those who resist him or whom he suspects of opposition. In his physical appearance and gestures Aravidze is an amalgam of Stalin, Beria, Hitler and Mussolini: a composite image of tyranny that gives the film a universal significance. The wider allegory is suggested by shots of medieval knights pursuing their victims. One of the major motifs is father-hood, as the son is required to atone for the sins of the father. In fact, the film's Russian title suggests more 'atonement' than mere 'repentance'. The crimes of the past lead inexorably to suicide and tragedy in the present and, in the end, the son must dig up the body of his father and throw it off a cliff face for it to be devoured by carrion birds so that stability and justice may be restored.

Other films of these years explored the recent past, not from a historical angle, but rather as either exercises in the analysis of terror as a system of government or as part of a wider agenda to air the grievances of the past and put them right. Alexander Proshkin's *The Cold Summer of 1953* (1988) is, as the title suggests, set in the months following Stalin's death. Following the 'Voroshilov Amnesty' of March 1953, which, in Solzhenitsyn's words, 'seeking to win popularity with the people, flooded the whole country with a wave of murderers, bandits, and thieves' (Solzhenistyn, 1975, p. 416), a group of vicious criminals take over a remote Russian village which is the current place of exile of two political prisoners. As class enemies, they did not benefit from the amnesty. The criminals bloodily and sadistically kill the village policeman and set about terrorising the population with an eye to rape and pillage. They are opposed only by the two politicals, Bosorgin and Starobogatov, who eventually carry the day. Starobogatov, however, dies in the final gunfight. On his release later from exile, Bosorgin travels to see Starobogatov's family in Moscow and passes on to them his belongings. He is confronted by Starobogatov's eldest son and told that the family was right to have disowned their father back in the 1930s. It was, he says, their only way forward, even though it may be difficult to understand now, 20 years later.

On one level, Proshkin's film works like a good old-fashioned shoot 'em up, with clearly defined good and bad guys and is a very exciting example of that genre, indebted as it obviously is to *The Magnificent Seven* (1960). On another, more symbolic level, it is a film about Russia's rediscovery of its soul, not only in the aftermath of Stalin's death, but also in 1988, the height of glasnost. Evil needs to be purged for future generations to prosper.

It is therefore an appeal to past values: Starobogatov (literally, 'old wealth') is identified as a member of the old intelligentsia, arrested for having been to the West and whose death is the loss of this last link with a better, untarnished world. Bosorgin is a former Red Army soldier who had fought his way out of enemy encirclement during the war only to be arrested by the NKVD on suspicion of being a spy (how else, after all, could he have escaped if he hadn't been recruited?). He is the tough warrior, the *'bogatyr'* of folklore who vanquishes the enemy and restores peace. He and Starobogatov, repositories of the bravery that won the war, on the one hand, and the cultural values of a bygone age, on the other, strike a blow for the insulted and injured of recent history. However, the future remains uncertain: the only person in the village to help the bandits is the survive-at-all-costs Party representative and he remains in place and in charge after the shootout. In other words, the evil of the recent past may have been rooted out, but there is much work that still needs to be done.

Evgenii Tsymbal's *Defence Counsel Sedov* (1988) is the most powerful and outspoken attack on the evils of Stalinism from these years. Running at little more than 40 minutes, it is a concise and supremely ironic account of the lawyer Sedov, called from Moscow to defend some agronomists accused of sabotage in the small provincial town of Ensk. It is the late 1930s, when Nikolai Ezhov was head of Stalin's secret police, the NKVD. Sedov manages to convince his superior in Moscow that the men are innocent. His superior not only physically resembles Andrei Vyshinskii, Stalin's loathsome public prosecutor during the show trials, but also repeats Vyshinskii's actual phrases. They are, indeed, released, but a price has to be paid. In Stalin's Russia the fact of arrest is tantamount to proof of guilt and if these men are innocent, there must be an act of sabotage afoot. All those who helped Sedov in Ensk are themselves 'exposed', accused of spying (for Poland and Japan) and executed. Sedov is hailed as a hero, but his idealism has been abused for evil ends. Narrative closure brings with it an acute awareness of how Stalinism as a system functioned. It was not only the terror inflicted from above on an unknowing population, but rather the insidious recruitment to its ranks of thousands of otherwise decent people, involving them in crime and tyranny. The power of Tsymbal's film derives exactly from the realisation that Stalinism grew and flourished because it abused and perverted the noble intentions of ordinary people. Tsymbal skilfully knits documentary footage from the 1930s into his fictional drama, recreating the officially sponsored happy and carefree image of reality with a black and white narrative shot in winter, emphasising bleakness and gloom.

A major feature of these anti-Stalin films was the unrelenting emphasis on squalor, deprivation and brutality. Vitalii Kanevskii's *Freeze, Die, Rise Again* (1989) is probably the most extreme example of this trend. Shot in black and white and set among political prisoners in Siberia in the late 1940s, life is a struggle to survive. The everyday is sordid and filthy, the gloom reinforced by being viewed through the eyes of children, Galia and Valerka. There is not much plot, but this is a world where children are the ultimate victims: Galia and Valerka are preyed on by bandits and are little safer than the puppies that are born only to be immediately drowned. This is a world where a 15-year-old girl begs an old man to impregnate her so that she can be evacuated, and insanity is just a mud pie away, with little sign of the spiritual or religious uplift inherent in the title. Alexander Kaidanovskii's *The Kerosene Seller's Wife* (1988) is also set among the dispossessed and is a black, at times surreal comedy of sorts about two brothers – one the victim of history, the other one of its movers – amid variations of the theme of betrayal and the consequences for future generations.

Valerii Ogorodnikov's *Prishvin's Paper Eyes* (1989), whose title refers to the pieces of paper newsreaders would put over their eyelids when reading a text (before the day of the autocue) to give the impression that they were always looking at the camera, offers a more complex narrative. As the opening credits roll, the camera stays on a couple in the increasingly frenzied act of fornication on a sofa. He is a Red Army officer (still in uniform or most of it), she is obviously his much younger mistress. Ogorodnikov aims to shock the viewer with his opening images, but a greater surprise is in store shortly afterwards when it become clear that this is a film being made about the year 1949 and Stalin, referred to by the director of this film within a film as 'the bloody executioner of Russia'. The actor Prishvin decides to delve deeper into history, interviewing people from that time and finding that he is unable to play the part of the officer called upon to shoot prisoners in the back of the head. The past invades the present yet again.

The interlocking time frames are interspersed with actual newsreel footage, showing not only Stalin, Molotov, Malenkov and others, but other tyrants: Mussolini, Hitler, Mao. Thousands cheer adoringly, but it is not clear whether this mass adulation is directed at Stalin, any of the others or, which is more likely, all of them. Ogorodnikov also shows clips of music and dancing shot for the fledgling Soviet television industry in the late 1940s. Cheerful and happy faces are intercut with the dance of the *oprichniki* from part two of *Ivan the Terrible*, a witty montage that suggests the murderous nature of a regime hiding behind sanitised images of homeliness. Old men condemn Eisenstein's film as 'justification of personal tyranny' and 'a mockery of the memory of three generations of the Russian intelligentsia', quoting verbatim from Alexander Solzhenitsyn's novella *One Day in the Life of Ivan Denisovich* (1962). Stalin's smiling face looks on as the Odessa steps sequence from *Battleship Potemkin* is played, clearly a means of dealing with unruly citizens of which he would have approved.

Prishvin's Paper Eyes is an ambitious film that not only explores the tyranny of the recent past, but also attempts to place the Soviet experience of it within the context of twentieth-century history as a whole. It also plays with the viewer's perception of reality and the truthfulness of filmic representation. Prishvin finds the horror of the past too momentous to recreate in fictional form and the director's manipulation of actual footage and Eisenstein's historical montages reveals how both art and filmed reality can easily become merged into propaganda of the most odious kind.

Stalin features as the central character in Iurii Kara's *Balthazar's Feast or a Night with Stalin* (1989), a loose adaptation of Fazil Iskander's satirical novel *Sandro from Chegem* (Iskander wrote the screenplay). Although the film primarily works as a historical portrait of Stalin and his associates Beria and Kalinin (played by the character actors Valentin Gaft and Evgenii Evstigneev respectively), it also makes its political points about the trappings of power and the corruption and degradation to which this leads. The film is set in 1935 and Stalin is, of course, the central character, orchestrating the evening and forcing people to humiliate themselves for his own gratification. Stalin may be a dangerous figure, but Kara deliberately intensifies the implied menace by having the short, stooped dictator played by the towering actor Alexei Petrenko.

Other films offered an altogether more symbolic or allegorical treatment. Mark Zakharov's *To Kill the Dragon* (1988) is an adaptation of *The Dragon* (1943), Evgenii Shvarts's allegorical play about tyranny. Amid a plethora of visual effects and jokes, for which Zakharov is renowned as a theatre director, the film shows how the knight Lancelot rids the town of its tyrannical dragon. However, just killing it does not solve the problem, as a dragon has many guises and he may return later in a different form. Vadim Abdrashitov's *The*

Servant (1988) examines tyranny as psychological trauma rooted in the Russian national subconscious without which, the film suggests, Russia itself cannot exist. Abrashitov offers a study of the relationship of two men, the former party boss Andrei Gudenov and his 'servant', his former chauffeur Pavel Kliuev, now a successful choirmaster. Gudenov not only imposes his will on Kliuev, influencing even his choice of wife, but he can dominate others too, literally calling the tune as a whole football team dances for him. In the present, Gudenov wills Kliuev to carry out the murder of a political opponent. This is more than power play, however, as Kliuev willingly submits. Abrashitov's film does not offer a discourse on competing masculinities, the usual frame of reference for these films about Stalin, but one of domination and submission. The relationship between Kliuev and Gudenov is a mirror of the sado-masochistic relationship of people and power in twentieth-century Russia.

Other films made in the twilight years of Soviet power focused not on the evils of the past as the uncertainties of the present, on the potential for chaos and social breakdown. Iurii Mamin's *Sideburns* (1990) begins with rowdy youngsters running riot in a provincial town, kids without values or respect for the older generation. Depravity and lawlessness are the norm until the arrival by boat of a group of young men with sideburns, dressed in nineteenth-century garb and all Pushkin lookalikes. In the name of the much-vaunted literary values of the past, a cultural totalitarianism takes hold as muscle-bound thugs recite *The Bronze Horseman* and followers of Pushkin and Lermontov fight it out for the soul of Russia. These Pushkinists have nothing but contempt for ordinary people, but the ease with which they can assert control is shown when a sculptor remoulds a bust of Lenin into the likeness of Pushkin. The end of the film sees the Communist Party take control and shave off the sideburns of the Pushkinists, but even after this symbolic castration there seems little difference between life under cultural fascists and life under ideological tyrants.

Mamin's film is a clever mix of allegory and political satire, using the country's most revered writer as a pretext for tyranny and repression and thus mocking the intelligentsia's claim that true morality ensues from adherence to traditional cultural values. But there is also a much darker hint, to the effect that fascism and communism are not very different and the one can easily take over from the other.

It is not difficult to see in these and other films of the glasnost period a revulsion for the ideology of a state that for decades had terrorised its citizens and indulged in mass murder. Stalin may have been demonised, but what little political legitimacy the communists claimed was soon swept away in the aftermath of the August 1991 coup. Henceforth politics was rejected, other than settling accounts with the recent past and ideology became subsumed in other genres, especially the historical film. What emerges, in post-Soviet film, is a country grappling with its awesome historical legacy, struggling with an identity based more on cultural values than political or social structures and unsure of its geo-political status. Even war, the one area in which Russians could feel certain of the justness of their cause, became riddled with ambiguity and uncertainty.

Filmography

Balthazar's Feast or a Night with Stalin ('Piry Baltazara ili noch so Stalinym'), dir. Iurii Kara, 1989

Bezhin Meadow ('Bezhin lug'), dir. Sergei Eisenstein, 1935–7

The Cold Summer of 1953 ('Kholodnoe leto 53-ego goda'), dir. Alexander Proshkin, 1988

Counterplan ('Vstrechnyi'), dir. Fridrikh Ermler and Sergei Iutkevich, 1932

The Courageous Seven ('Semero smelykh'), dir. Sergei Gerasimov, 1936

The Death Ray ('Luch smerti'), dir. Lev Kuleshov, 1926

Defence Counsel Sedov ('Zashchitnik Sedov'), dir. Evgenii Tsymbal, 1988

The Deserter ('Dezertir'), dir. Vsevolod Pudovkin, 1933

The Dream ('Mechta'), dir. Mikhail Romm, 1941

The Eleventh Year ('Odinnadsatyi'), dir. Dziga Vertov, 1928

Emergency ('Ch.P.: Chrezvychainoe proisshestvie'), dir. Viktor Ivchenko, 1958

Farewell ('Proshchanie'), dir. Elem Klimov, 1982

Freeze, Die, Rise Again ('Zamri, umri, voskresni'), dir. Vitalii Kanevskii, 1989

The Great Citizen ('Velikii grazhdanin'), dir. Fridrikh Ermler, 1937–9

The House I Live In ('Dom v kotorom ia zhivu'), dir. Lev Kulidzhanov and Iakov Segel, 1957

The Kerosene Seller's Wife ('Zhena kerosinshchika'), dir. Alexander Kaidanovskii, 1988

Lieutenant Kizhe ('Poruchik Kizhe'), dir. Alexander Faintsimmer, 1934

The Magnificent Seven, dir. John Sturges, 1960

The Man With the Movie Camera ('Chelovek s kinoapparatom'), dir. Dziga Vertov, 1929

New Babylon ('Novyi Vavilon'), dir. Grigorii Kozintsev and Leonid Trauberg, 1927

Nine Days of One Year ('Deviat dnei odnogo goda'), dir. Mikhail Romm, 1961

The Path to Life ('Putevka v zhizn'), dir. Nikolai Ekk, 1931

Onward, Soviet! ('Shagai, Soviet!'), dir. Dziga Vertov, 1926

The Party Card ('Partiinyi bilet'), dir. Ivan Pyrev, 1936

Pavel Korchagin, dir. Alexander Alov and Vladimir Naumov, 1956

Prishvin's Paper Eyes ('Bumazhnye glaza Prishvina'), dir. Valerii Ogorodnikov, 1989

Repentance ('Pokaianie'), dir. Tengiz Abuladze, 1987

The Republic of ShKID ('Respublika ShKID'), dir. Gennadii Poloka, 1966

The Return of Maxim ('Vozvrashchenie Maksima'), dir. Kozintsev and Trauberg, 1937

The Servant ('Sluga'), dir. Vadim Abdrashitov, 1988

Several Days in the Life of I. I. Oblomov ('Neskolko dnei iz zhizni I. I. Oblomova'), dir. Nikita Mikhalkov, 1979

Sideburns ('Bakenbardy'), dir. Iurii Mamin, 1990

The Sixth Part of the World ('Shestaia chast mira'), dir. Dziga Vertov, 1926

Storm Over Asia ('Potomok Chingiz-Khana' = 'The Heir of Chingiz Khan'), dir. Vsevolod Pudovkin, 1928

A Strict Youth ('Strogii iunosha'), dir. Abram Room, 1936

Strike ('Stachka'), dir. Sergei Eisenstein, 1925

To Kill the Dragon ('Ubit drakona'), dir. Mark Zakharov, 1988

An Unfinished Piece for Mechanical Piano ('Neokonchennaia pesa dlia mekhanicheskogo pianino'), dir. Nikita Mikhalkov, 1977

Valerii Chkalov ('Valerii Chkalov'), dir. Mikhail Kalatozov, 1941

The Vyborg Side ('Vyborgskaia storona'), dir. Kozintsev and Trauberg, 1939

The Youth of Maxim ('Iunost Maksima'), dir. Kozintsev and Trauberg, 1936

CHAPTER SEVEN

The Russian war film

Only after we have overthrown, finally vanquished and expropriated the bourgeoisie of the whole world, and not merely of one country, will wars become impossible.

(Lenin (1916), 1981, p. 79)

It is no exaggeration to say that over seven decades the Soviet state thrived on war: it came about in the ruins of the First World War, was consolidated by Civil War, acquired its own legitimacy in the Second World War, and in the 70-odd years of its existence developed its own identity through relentless and usually ruthless class war, especially against its own citizens. As Lenin affirmed, the Bolshevik state could only be sustained and developed in conditions of such a war. Accordingly, the war film has been a staple ingredient of Soviet cinema and the years immediately following the First World War were, indeed, crucial ones for the development of Soviet cinema. This is particularly true of the Civil War, as Richard Taylor notes:

Without the challenge of the Civil War it is unlikely that the Soviet cinema would have developed the forceful, distinctive and revolutionary visual style of the 1920s, and without that style the effectiveness of the cinema in transmitting the Bolshevik world-view both within and beyond the frontiers of the USSR would have been severely restricted.

(Taylor, 1979, p. 63)

In short, Russia's twentieth-century capacity for waging war gave cinema much fertile soil, be it the First World War, the Civil War, the Great Patriotic War (as the Russians call the struggle against the Fascist German invader from 1941–5) and more recent campaigns, such as the Afghan war of 1979–89 and the Chechen conflict of the post-Soviet period. The Soviet and post-Soviet cinematic treatment of all these conflicts will be the subject of this chapter.

The Soviet Union's methods of waging war were unlike those of Western countries, with the exception of Nazi Germany. War was above all, according to Lenin, a struggle not of nation-states, but of ideologies, be it Reds against Whites or fascists against communists. In his recent book on Stalingrad, Antony Beevor notes the particular vigour with which Stalinism in particular pursued the demonisation of the enemy:

> Whatever one may think about Stalinism, there can be little doubt that its ideological preparation, through deliberately manipulated alternatives, provided ruthlessly effective arguments for total warfare. All right-thinking people had to accept that Fascism was bad and must be destroyed by any means. The Communist Party should lead the struggle because Fascism was totally devoted to its destruction.

(Beevor, 1999, p. 27)

Armed struggle, then, forged a particular Soviet political identity based on class antagonism. This rule would be observed in subsequent conflicts, most notably the Great Patriotic War. However, in post-Soviet times war and aggression have prompted film-makers to reconsider the Soviet legacy of violence and to question Russian imperialism and Russia's relationship with its Eastern, non-Christian peoples.

The First World War and the Civil War

Historians agree that the Russian Civil War (1918–20) was the most devastating cataclysm for Russia since the Mongol invasion. Literary recreations, such as Isaak Babel's *Red Cavalry* (1926), pull no punches in the graphic and unflinching portrayal of the brutality of the conflict, with families torn apart, merciless savagery and little honour.[1] Yet for the Bolsheviks it was above all a war of ideologies, a struggle for the new world of the 'dictatorship of the proletariat' and a rejection of the old world of 'capitalist exploitation'. Moreover, the methods used by the Bolsheviks, in particular the Red Terror, would have significant consequences for the future methods of government by the USSR's rulers, most obviously Stalin.

The definition of identity through conflict can be seen in some of the earliest Civil War films, such as Ivan Perestiani's *Little Red Devils* (1923) and Iakov Protazanov's *The Forty-First* (1927). Vsevolod Pudovkin's *The End of St Petersburg* (1927) showed the horror of the trenches in the First World War in convincingly gruesome detail and follows Lenin's interpretation of this war as the battle of international capital against the working classes of all countries. In *Arsenal* (1929) Alexander Dovzhenko moves from a similarly realistic picture of a war-torn landscape and the madness of human conflict, to a mythologisation of the armed struggle and the ultimate victory of the proletariat.

Films of the Stalin period such as *Chapaev* (1934), *Shchors* (1939) and *Kotovskii* (1942) helped establish the mythology of the Civil War and make its heroes into legends. Yet a much more interesting war film from these years is Boris Barnet's *Outskirts* (1933). It begins in 1914 and although the theme of workers uniting around the Bolsheviks to bring about the Tsar's abdication is in line with prevailing ideology, as is the fraternisation of ordinary Russian and German soldiers at the front, the film is permeated with a subversive irony. At the beginning of the film the sound of apparent gunfire used to disperse unruly demonstrators (a canonical motif of Eisenstein, for instance) turns out, in fact, to be the crackling sounds of a boy playing a hurdy-gurdy. Barnet also uses jolly, pseudo-patriotic ditties to undermine the solemnity of ideological statements and his use of visuals often expresses a grotesque sense of humour, as when bombs falling are juxtaposed with boots dropping to the ground. Elsewhere guns firing sound like machinery used for making shoes. There is also a parody of the famous scene in Lewis Milestone's *All Quiet on the Western Front* (1929). A German and a Russian take refuge in a fox hole, but instead of killing each other, they protect each other from the bombs.

The viewer's expectations of a straightforward narrative are constantly subverted. The clashing of church bells disturbs an otherwise melodic folk tune as a background to a romantic scene. Much of the narration is seen through the eyes of a German prisoner of war, with linguistic and psychological confusion as a result. The final, juxtaposed images are of happy faces as the masses march towards the future. The soldier Nikolai lies dying after his execution, but, like Timosh in *Arsenal*, proves to be invincible, as he revives to the sound of the people on the move. The film may end with a nod in the direction of Dovzhenko's mythologisation, but its irreverent tone suggests a more sardonic attitude on the part of the director.

Several decades later scepticism about ends and means would take root. Askoldov's *The Commissar* (1967) has been mentioned already in several contexts. It is also a film that questions the Bolsheviks' values and methods of the Civil War. Similarly, Gleb Panfilov's *No Ford in a Fire* (1967) features two types of commissar: one (with a striking resemblance to Lenin) who harangues others on the need to spread fear and shed blood and who sees people only in ideological categories, as 'enemies' of various hues; the other more humane, aware that what is at stake is not just victory, but the kind of Russia that is being created in the fire and misery of the Civil War. As if to echo that thought, the heroine Tania Tetkina asserts that in the future people will not be happy and we learn from a peasant that the Bolsheviks are robbing the local villages – hardly the behaviour of class brothers.

One of the most popular films of the 1960s, and one with enduring appeal, was Vladimir Motyl's *The White Sun of the Desert* (1969) – not least because of the diegetic performance of Bulat Okudzhava's guitar ballad 'Your Honour, Miss Separation'. The use of this song and the film's haunting woodwind score are not fortuitous, for *The White Sun of the Desert* is as close as there is to a Soviet 'Spaghetti' Western. The 'Spaghetti' credentials are there for all to see: the music, usually light hearted and eschewing grand symphonic scores that would normally go with the serious subject matter; the use of an exotic, sun-baked location (here Central Asia substituted for the Texas–Mexico border); a lone hero despatching dozens of enemies; the huge body count, with people killed by guns, machine-guns, knives and bombs; a collection of eccentric characters seemingly out of place in this location; and a general tongue-in-cheek style bordering on irreverence. There are some concrete nods to Sergio Leone's *The Good, the Bad and the Ugly* (1966): the hero Sukhov lighting his cigar with a stick of dynamite (in Leone's film Clint Eastwood lights a cannon with his cigar) and also surprising the villain by entering a room not through a door but through a window (again, slightly different in Leone's film, where the 'good' is surprised by the 'ugly' coming through the window).

The White Sun of the Desert tells the story of a Red Army officer, Sukhov, guarding the nine wives of local bandit chieftain Abdullah, and much fun is

Anatolii Kuznetsov in The White Sun of the Desert *(Vladimir Motyl, 1969)*

had at the contrast between 'civilised' European values and the 'backwardness' of Moslem Central Asia. The veiled wives would rather throw their dresses over their heads – and show off their legs and waists – than reveal their faces to a strange man. They are referred to as 'comrade women', 'free women of the East' and are urged to 'forget your accursed past'. 'A woman is also a person', reads a slogan. Their covered faces and bodies are regularly contrasted with the sensual features of Sukhov's own wife Katerina Matveevna, dressed in red and seen against a luscious rural backdrop, as Sukhov recalls her in various nostalgic moments. In the end Sukhov survives, as do eight of the wives, but virtually everyone else is killed.

Motyl's film does for the Civil War film what such directors as Sergio Leone did for the Hollywood Western: as Christopher Frayling says, 'By substituting themes and images taken from an Italian historico-cultural context for the traditional bases of the Western genre, Leone creates a fresh cinematic mythology, critical but clearly located, crude but visually sophisticated' (Frayling, 2000, p. 188). Where Leone breathed fresh life into the Western and made it popular again in the 1960s, Motyl 'updates' that most solemn of subjects, the Russian Civil War, by incorporating elements from Leone, adding a catchy theme tune and removing some of the ideological gloss. Other films from the 'stagnation' period gave the Civil War the Western treatment, such as Edmond Keosaian's *The Elusive Avengers* (1966, a remake of *Little Red Devils* with the action transferred to Soviet Ukraine) and especially Ali Khamraev's *The Bodyguard* (1980), where the loner hero Mirzo (played by Alexander Kaidanovskii) remains invincible and undefeated despite overwhelming odds, as he battles against recalcitrant tribesmen in Tadzhikistan in the early 1920s.

The Great Patriotic War

The Great Patriotic War was the Soviet Union's sternest test, a war that threatened the very existence of the state and the survival of the nation. It was viewed by the authorities as a struggle of opposing ideologies, fascism and communism, but was experienced by the people much more as a battle for survival against an enemy who had made the extinction or total subordination of the Slavs their stated aim. Stalin himself recognised the mortal threat when he chose to address the Soviet people on 3 July 1941, two weeks after the Nazi invasion, appealing to them not as ideological 'comrades', but blood-bound 'brothers and sisters'. It is no accident, then, that the Soviet film about the Great Patriotic War contains often harrowing details and life-or-death situations and does not flinch from the depiction of extreme and sadistic violence.

By way of comparison, the war has been viewed very differently in the national cinemas of Western Europe. Major films have looked at the moral issues thrown up by the war, often rejecting national stereotyping or hackneyed images. In France, another occupied country that suffered enormous blood letting, Louis Malle in *Lacombe Lucien* (1974) and *Au Revoir les Enfants* (1988) explores the fact of collaboration and tacit compliance on the part of some French citizens in the tragic fate of the Jews. The Englishman John Boorman in *Hope and Glory* (1987) views the war through the eyes of an English child during the London Blitz. The conflict is largely a backdrop for the director's reminiscences of his own childhood, not too threatening and occasionally comic. But the Russian war, after all, is deadly serious, with a more visceral immediacy. The struggle against national extinction is, as in the lines of the famous wartime song by Vasilii Lebedev-Kumach, a 'people's war', a 'holy war':

Вставай, страна огромная,
Вставай на смертный бой
С фашистской силой темною,
С проклятою ордой!

Пусть ярость благородная
Вскипает, как волна, –
Идет война народная
Священная война!

('Rise up, huge country
Rise up for a fight to the death
With the dark Fascist force,
The Accursed Horde!

'May noble fury
Boil up, like a wave, –
A people's war is waged,
A holy war!')

(Iukhtman, 2000, pp. 229–30)

The absolute hatred of the enemy is well understood in the popular poems of the time, such as Alexei Surkov's 'The Avengers' Commandment', which reaches its culmination in images of blood and death:

Мы стали беспощадней, грубей,
Полынной горечи черпнув без меры,
Во имя жизни заповедь 'Убей!'
Мы приняли как первый символ веры.

Пускай же злая сталь сечет дождем,
Летят снаряды, не минуя цели.
Лишь отомстив, мы дух переведем,
Кровь со штыка сотрем полой шинели.

(We have become more pitiless, more crude,
Having soaked up endless wormwood-like bitterness,
In the name of life the commandment 'Thou shalt kill!'
We accepted as the first symbol of faith.

So let the evil steel cut like rain
And shells fly without missing their target.
Only when we have taken our vengeance will we draw breath,
And wipe the blood from the bayonet with the hem of our greatcoat.)

(Surkov, 1965, I, 387)

Hatred of the enemy goes hand in hand with faith in the inevitable victory of the Soviet Union. In *The Lad from Our Town* (1942), one of the first war films to be made after the Nazi invasion (and shot in evacuation in Alma-Ata), the audience is reminded of how stable and peaceful life was before the war, where the sun always shone and friends got together to talk, sing and drink wine. War is a test of character and there is no room for cowards or the faint hearted. The hero is Serezha Lukonin, who goes through several trials before triumphantly returning to his tank squadron to rout a German attack. 'War changes a man, it makes him think about what is important in life and what is not,' says his doctor, as Lukonin lies wounded in hospital. The qualities required for victory are courage, self-sacrifice, resolve and the ability to inspire others and they, we are led to believe, will bring back the good days again when the war is won.

Submarine T-9, directed by Alexander Ivanov in 1943, extols the might of the Soviet navy as a single submarine crew despatches German ships and avoids depth charges and aerial bombardment. This is a low-budget flag waver designed to show the superiority of the Soviet war machine, the dedication of Russian men prepared to sacrifice themselves and, again, the inevitability of victory. The overall impression gained is that victory is indeed near, if one submarine can sink so many enemy ships, raid a German port and even land some marines ashore to blow up a strategic bridge. All this with the loss of just one man, who, of course, dies heroically.[2]

Early war films similarly emphasised the inevitability of victory and the superiority of the Soviet way of life over that of the enemy. Gerbert Rappoport's *The Courier of the Air* (1943) tells a love story between the pilot Baranov and Natasha, an opera singer, and deliberately downplays the perils of combat. As Baranov flies back to base after completing a successful mission against the Germans, Natasha's voice on the radio guides him back to safety. Another comedy of sorts, Konstantin Iudin's *Antosha Rybkin* (1942), shows how easy it is to upset the plans of the enemy, with a comic hero (Rybkin) impersonating a German soldier and leading Russian troops to rout a German foe that is cowardly, comic and utterly ineffective as a fighting force. War in both of these films is little more than farce, with caricatured, grotesque villains. Made at critical stages in the war, these and other films look forward to the day when the sun will again shine down on a victorious Red Army marching to the tune of patriotic songs, waved on by grateful womenfolk.

Young Fritz (1943), directed by Kozintsev and Trauberg, is an absurd and occasionally funny theatrical burlesque. With a cast including Mikhail Zharov, Ianina Zheimo, Vsevolod Pudovkin, Maxim Shtraukh and Konstantin Sorokin, it is a caustically satirical send-up of fascism and its supposed scientific basis, emphasising the outlandish, even grotesque appearance of the Germans. Filmed as a series of stage sketches presented to an imaginary audience, it traces the childhood and adolescence of the typically German Fritz (complete with *Lederhosen*). When he joins the Gestapo, he learns how to behead a teddy bear and hang a toy dog. Described as 'a story of how the ape was descended from man', this is a vitriolic and racist portrait of Germans as barbaric, drunken vandals without any civilising values, who come to grief at the hands of the strong and committed Russians. The film expresses total hatred of the enemy, turning the Nazis' racist agenda back on themselves. *Young Fritz* was banned for being too theatrical, for the duration of the war.

In many wartime films, Mother Russia was represented by the tortured and downtrodden female. In Fridrikh Ermler's *She Defends the Motherland* (1943), Mark Donskoi's *The Rainbow* (1943) and Leo Arnshtam's *Zoia* (1944) the central character is a female whose bravery and capacity for self-sacrifice are meant to inspire both those at the front and those in the rear. On a more visceral level, the violence directed against women (and, in *The Rainbow*, directed at the pregnant Olena Kostiuk) not only appalls the audience, but also reinforces hatred of the enemy. Martyrdom is also here not out of place, as the real-life heroine Zoia Kosmodemianskaia's execution by the Nazis at the age of 18 (powerfully re-enacted in Arnshtam's film) is meant to both embolden and inspire a whole generation.[3]

Iulii Raizman's *Mashenka* offers a fascinating exception to these films about female fighters, if only because it is set during the Finnish 'winter' war of 1939–40. Like many wartime films, it begins in the pre-war years, shown as a happy, stable time where the gathering clouds are suggested by the need to try on gas masks. This picture of a peaceful life is reinforced by an upbeat, patriotic soundtrack. Masha Stepanova is a hard-working postal worker who falls in love with Alesha Solovev (note the typical Russian names). This was one of Valentina Karavaeva's few film appearances and here, as Masha, she exudes spiritual purity and energy, an embodiment of the sincerity and inner goodness of a simple Russian girl.

With the outbreak of war – the dastardly Finns invade their humble neighbour, the Soviet Union – Masha is a frontline nurse and again meets Alesha. He is wounded in fierce hand-to-hand fighting and, as troops head off into clouds of black smoke, the film ends with the lovers promising to be together. Raizman's film does not end in promises of victory, but rather the ominous dark clouds of the greater struggle ahead with Nazi Germany. Moreover, the heroine is not a grim symbol of sacrifice and tragedy, but rather of light and innocence.

As the war progressed and eventual victory seemed near, falsification and complacency set in. Ivan Pyrev's 1944 film *At Six O'Clock in the Evening after the War* shows the war as little more than a minor inconvenience in the relationship of Vasia Kudriashov (Evgenii Samoilov) and Varia (Marina Ladynina), where they are more concerned with hitting the right notes in their numerous songs than in bringing down enemy planes. Fighting is easy: even in the chaotic months of 1941 every Soviet shell hits a German tank, Nazi forces are devastated and the viewer is entitled to ask: With this degree of inefficiency, how did the Wehrmacht ever manage to get to the gates of Moscow within three months of their invasion? Soviet soldiers can even recite poetry in the middle of a battle. The music is a mixture of triumphalist orchestrals and wartime guitar ballads sung with the diegesis. Pyrev's film shows war as musical, with a succession of songs and dances and, of course, Vasia and Varia meet up, as they had arranged at the start of the war, at six o'clock in the evening, next to Red Square as the victory celebrations begin.

The Soviet victory allowed even more gloating and the authorities were quick to enforce their own vision of the 'truth' of that victory. A major casualty of the new repression was Leonid Lukov's second part to *A Great Life*, made in 1946 but not shown until a decade later. Although it opens (by now predictably) with folk music accompanying lingering shots of the Russian sky and rolling fields, it is remarkable for its frank picture of collaborators and local police working for the Nazis amid the general destruction of war. Female chorals act as background to icon-like framed shots of women wandering through a devastated landscape, both people and buildings symbolic of a suffering Russia. As the war ends and reconstruction begins, personal relationships are also revived and the return of life is celebrated.[4]

Comedies of the early post-war years, such as Zharov's *A Troubled Household* (1947) and Semen Timoshenko's *The Silent Ace of the Skies* (1946) – both categorised as 'heroic comedies' – downplay the struggle and suffering and maintain that the war was not really hard fought at all. Timoshenko's film was one of the most popular films of 1946. The 'silent ace' is Bulochkin (a comic name that suggests 'roly-poly'), who knocks out German positions and takes on Messerschmidts in an ancient bi-plane and, after some singing in the forest and vodka and beetroot soup in the barracks, eventually gets his girl. The film is of interest because the war is shown largely as a sideshow in the personal relationships of the main characters, who proclaim at the start of the film that they will ignore girls until the war is over. Still, the war proves to be not that tough and Bulochkin does find time to flirt and woo. Furthermore, he can land his plane in an enemy minefield to pick up his girlfriend, then take off under the noses of the enemy without a scratch.

In *A Troubled Household* Commander Semibaba (another joke name, suggesting 'seven wenches') erects a false airbase to fool German bombers, plays the accordion and refuses to douse the lights during an enemy air raid. Soviet soldiers burst into song and raids against the enemy can be delayed while Soviet and French allies arrange their emotional affairs. War is here no more than an irritating interlude in the otherwise humdrum daily round of the armed forces.

This particularly whimsical approach to a horrific war still fresh in people's memories did not last long – and was subsequently criticised.[5] Other war films of the late 1940s addressed another agenda, reflecting the increasing xenophobia of the emerging Cold War. Stalin's role as the omniscient leader assumed mythological proportions. Vladimir Petrov's *The Battle of Stalingrad* (1949) and Mikhail Chiaureli's *The Vow* (1949) both unashamedly show that victory was solely due to Stalin's brilliant command of military strategy and tactics. In Chiaureli's *The Fall of Berlin* (1949–50) Stalin assumes a god-like status, Hitler as well as the Allies are in awe of him and the people adore him.[6]

The Fall of Berlin is unique in the history of the Soviet war film. Grigorii Mariamov tells us that Stalin particularly liked Chiaureli's films because of their 'unrestrained eulogizing of his personality and the creation of legends which contained no truth' and also because the dictator could find in them 'justification of his actions in historical analogies, to which Stalin attached great importance' (Mariamov, 1992, pp. 38–9). It boasts an epic sweep, taking in the pre-war years with Stalin tending his garden, a female orator offering thanks to Comrade Stalin for the happiness of this life as his portrait looks down approvingly on her. Then comes the German invasion with fire and destruction, the decisive battles of Moscow and Stalingrad and the eventual fall of Berlin.

This is a film that sets out not only to create a lasting image of Stalin as an all-seeing and wise leader, but also to rewrite recent history. Stalin can determine tactics without looking at a map because he grasps intuitively what the enemy will do and so understands strategy better than his generals. Even Hitler's generals fear Stalin and Churchill and Roosevelt plot against him in Yalta. The culmination of the film is Stalin's arrival in Berlin in an aeroplane,

Mikhail Gelovani and Maxim Shtraukh in The Fall of Berlin *(Mikhail Chiaureli, 1949–50)*

flanked by angel-like fighter aircraft, to celebrate the victory. As he descends from the heavens, the people of the world salute him in the languages of the world. Homage is paid to him as he gets out of his aircraft in cinematic images startlingly similar to those that celebrate Hitler's arrival in Nuremberg in Leni Riefenstahl's *Triumph of the Will* (1936). Stalin's heroic profile assumes the dimensions of that of Ivan the Terrible gazing out at his people stretched across a snowy landscape, acclaimed as the leader of the world.[7]

In contrast is the picture of an increasingly unhinged Hitler, furious that Stalin holds the 7 November military parade on Red Square as the battle for Moscow rages in 1941 and finally, cowering in his bunker as the end approaches, waiting to be rescued by the Americans. All the resources of Europe, as well as American business, are at his disposal, but he cannot win. 'Washington should realize that I am doing their business, their business!' he cries hoarsely, but no one outside his bunker is listening.

The rewriting of war history is foregrounded. The Germans are in league with the British, who deliberately delay the start of the second front in order to keep the Bolshevik barbarians from entering Europe. Hitler is aided by the Spanish and the Japanese, as well as the Vatican, whose cardinals should, he quips, be dressed in stormtrooper uniforms. The inhumanity of the Nazi machine reaches its most shocking point as the end approaches, when Berlin citizens in underground shelters are deliberately drowned as Nazi leaders flood them in a desperate attempt to gain a few hours for the wedding of Hitler and Eva Braun.

This is the new history, with the war not as a colossal conflict claiming tens of millions of lives, but as the great leader moulding a new world order. Chiaureli is careful to observe strict verisimilitude, with visually accurate portraits of Stalin, Churchill, Roosevelt, Molotov, Kalinin, Hitler, Goebbels, Goering and Zhukov and a clear message that a new era in world history has begun.

Vladimir Braun's *In Peaceful Days* (1950), the title of which is itself ironic, takes as its subject matter the Cold War. Here the Soviet enemy is spied on by an unnamed capitalist country which is probably Great Britain, judging by the costumes and manners, desperate to learn the secrets of the Soviet submarine. One such submarine hits a mine and sinks to the bottom of the sea.[8] The Cold War is but a continuation of the world war and to reinforce this message the enemy captain is a former Nazi U-Boat captain and one of the crew has the bespectacled look and toothy grin of a caricatured Japanese. The nefarious plans of the imperialist enemy, however, are thwarted by the bravery and resourcefulness of Soviet sailors, who manage to save themselves and the honour of the Soviet fleet.

In Peaceful Days is also a colour film – like *The Fall of Berlin* – but is otherwise dogged by poor production values. Model boats bob up and down in a tub of swirling water in emulation of a storm, while water, presumably from a bucket by the out-of-shot assistant director, is thrown over the protagonists in close-up. The film is a triumphalist affirmation of the superiority of the Soviet armed forces and way of life in general over that of the capitalist enemy and a warning to Soviet citizens to be vigilant.[9] Soviet sailors are well groomed and well dressed in clean white uniforms, musically gifted and with a courteous and chivalrous attitude to the girls on shore. The quarters they live in are very clean, the walls hung with portraits of Lenin and Stalin and they are looked after by a caring and paternalistic officer class. Political education takes place under a banner that proclaims, 'We will win the great battle for peace'. The foreigners are correspondingly furtive and dastardly. In other words, there is little substantial difference between the 'cold' war and the 'hot' one of a few years before. And, as in the last one, the motherland they are fighting for is a sun-blessed land of blossoming parks, shy and demure young women and fit, athletic young men.

With Stalin's death in 1953 political and cultural life generally moved away from the 'big' issues of politics and history to return to the 'little man' so beloved of nineteenth-century writers. In the treatment of the war, the shift was away from showing the decisive battles won by epic heroes, to small-scale skirmishes and the real fears and emotions of ordinary soldiers. Indeed, the geographical shift went further, away from the frontline and to the rear and the tribulations of the civilian population.

The Cranes Are Flying (1957) marks an important shift in the de-ideologisation of the war. Similarly, Grigorii Chukhrai's *The Ballad of a Soldier* (1959), in which Alesha Skvortsov is given a few days' leave for destroying two German tanks, removes the false heroism from military achievement. In the brief opening combat scene Alesha is clearly vulnerable and terrified, hardly the redoubtable and fearless fighter of a decade earlier, he rather 'performs his feat precisely because of his fear' (Woll, 2000, p. 98). He travels home by train, but, because of a string of adventures and mishaps, he finally has only a few minutes with his mother before he has to return to the front – never to return, as the viewer knows. Alesha's mother, filmed against a vast expanse of sky and amid fields of wheat blowing in the breeze, with rising orchestral strings as sentimental backdrop, is the symbol of Mother Russia being defended by her true sons. Yet Chukhrai's *Clear Skies* a few years later (1961) eschews abstraction and affirms the raw human reality of pain and loss caused by the war. Moreover, in the fate of Alexei Arbatov, it brought out into the open, during one of the key years of de-Stalinisation, the fate of Soviet prisoners of war who were regarded with suspicion and even contempt by their fellow citizens after they were liberated.[10]

A key film in the thaw period is Sergei Bondarchuk's *The Fate of a Man* (1959), based on the Sholokhov novella of the same name. The Civil War veteran Andrei Sokolov begins the film as a contented peasant, married with three children, filmed against a sunny rural backdrop complete with happy, singing peasants. The clichés do not stop there. Maximum emotional potential is realised as we see this ordinary man pitted against the inhuman Nazi machine once the war breaks out.

Andrei is captured and is forced into a vodka drinking match with the German commandant Müller, a match which he wins through sheer force of will. The bread he wins as a prize he dutifully shares among his fellow prisoners. No punches are pulled in showing the privations Russian prisoners of war endure, the arbitrary cruelties of the Nazis who summarily execute communists and Jews and the conditions in an extermination camp, where women are separated from their children. The film is also candid in showing the human scale of the German victories in the early months of the war and the willingness of some Soviet citizens to denounce communists in the camps.

The film's theme is the strength of spirit of the average Russian and the rather typical name of the hero is here not accidental. Sokolov tries to escape from the camp and is hunted down by dogs. The second time he is successful and even manages to bring a German officer with him as a prize. He is welcomed back into the ranks of the Red Army, with no hint of an NKVD interrogation, and is sent home to recuperate for a month. There he grieves for his wife and daughters who have been killed, only to be brusquely reminded by his father that others have also lost loved ones and he should show greater resilience. He finds his son Vasilii, now an officer, but Vasilii is soon also killed. Sokolov's reintegration into society occurs when he adopts the orphan Vania (an intense and moving portrayal by Pavlik Boriskin), who offers him a new beginning and a new life, even though he remains haunted by the past.

The Fate of a Man is a straightforward and realistic war film with characteristically harrowing details and a candour that is surprising even for its relatively liberal time. It is, however, a film that emphasises not so much the horrors of war and the perfidy of the enemy, but the inner strength and fortitude of the Soviet man. The film is remarkable in that it shows a soldier who, 'by the end of the War, [. . .] is plagued by anxiety and self-doubt' and who knows that 'as a survivor he has to face more uncertain times ahead' (Haynes, 2000, p. 166). In looking to the post-war challenges ahead, Andrei's ordeal may be only just beginning.

The Fate of a Man can be directly compared to *The Story of a Real Man*, directed a decade earlier in 1948, at the height of Stalin's 'cult of personality', by Alexander Stolper. Alexei Meresev is a much more straightforward hero who typifies the superhuman personal exploits of Soviet soldiers. Both the novel by Boris Polevoi and the film contain easily resolvable conflicts (or none at all) and a strictly two-dimensional approach to the war. Meresev is a fighter pilot whose plane is brought down in a wintry forest and with incredible physical strength and inner will he crawls through snow, forests and storms for 18 days to safety. In doing so he loses both his legs. Nevertheless, he must return to the fray, complete with artificial legs and he inspires others in the hospital where he recuperates through his sheer determination and dedication. As his commanding officer says at the end: 'With such people we can win any war.'

Meresev, then, does not suffer from self-doubt and his physical disability only hardens his inner steel. He is a perfect example of the socialist realist positive hero – all political will and no human weakness, and he provides a counterpoint to the pained figure of Sokolov a decade later. Not for him a lifetime ahead of coping with personal loss and the responsibility for a young orphan; rather, he wants only to play a part in the coming victory. In this respect he is a double for Vasia Kudriashov in *At Six O'Clock in the Evening after the War*, who also loses a leg. In the films of the thaw period and in particular the despairing legless soldier (Evgenii Urbanskii) in *The Ballad of a Soldier*, we are allowed to see the real suffering of the war: physical disability does not lead to greater inner resolve, but pain and loneliness.

There was, especially during the 1960s and 1970s, a certain triumphalism evident in the depiction of the war. Iurii Ozerov's impressively massive *Liberation* (1968–71) is told in five parts, beginning with the Nazi invasion and culminating in the Soviet and Allied victory in May 1945. It is also a co-production with East Germany, Italy and Romania, it runs to almost eight hours and its claim to epic status is reinforced with its inclusion of actual historical personages such as Winston Churchill alongside fictional characters. Ozerov went on to make other similar large-scale international co-productions, such as *The Battle for Moscow* in 1985 and *Stalingrad* in 1989.

Those 'uncertain times' of *The Fate of a Man* nevertheless spread to the depiction of the war in the 'stagnation' period and none better than Alexei German's *Trial on the Roads*. This is a controversial and long-banned film – it was released only in 1986 – about Lazarev, a former Red Army soldier turned Nazi collaborator, who returns to the fold (note the motif of resurrection in the name) and eventually dies in a heroic single-handed action. However, attention is rather paid to the callous disregard for life, as the unit's commissar is prepared to blow up a bridge even though a column of Russian POWs is travelling beneath it. Partisans are not viewed in a heroic light, but rather as a threat to the peasant community which is resentful that demands for food will lead to reprisals from the Nazis. In the film's finale we see that human values nevertheless count for nothing, as, in the final push for Berlin, those commissars who care nothing for human life are promoted to high rank. Despite the film's stereotypical portrayal of the Nazi enemy as evil – collaborators, even teenagers, are irredeemable – it asks uncomfortable questions about the Soviet conduct of the war and the dehumanising impact of ideology.

Andrei Smirnov's *Belorussia Station* (1970) offers a dispiriting picture of the contemporary Soviet environment, with the present unfavourably compared to the past. This elegiac tale of four wartime friends reuniting in 1970 for the first time since 1946 offers a rejection of the modern world, where the generation that won the war is not understood by the youth of a quarter of a century later. This is an unashamed lament for past certainties. The modern world of television addiction, restaurant culture and tinny pop music should not be the sum of the victory achieved by these heroes (two of whom are played by perennial favourites Evgenii Leonov and Anatolii Papanov), as they see families falling apart and an alienated younger generation generally obsessed with materialistic cares. A rather reactionary film, it tells us that only those who have experienced true loss and grief can really understand the values of comradeship and share a sense of belonging.

Other war films of the 'stagnation' period offered more uncomfortable visions of the war and its later implications for Soviet society. Larisa Shepitko's *The Ascent* (1976) is perhaps the most important war film of the

1970s and one of the key films of the entire Brezhnev period. It is based on *Sotnikov*, a controversial 1970 novella by the Belarusian writer Vasil Bykov, generally acknowledged as the greatest Soviet writer on war themes. Bykov was, ironically, tolerated and even rewarded by the Soviet government, but was hounded out of post-Soviet Belarus and into exile in Finland.

In Bykov's story, two partisans in Nazi-occupied Belorussia are captured by the Germans while hiding in the house of a peasant woman. Sotnikov is physically the weaker, ill with pneumonia and wounded, while his companion Rybak, at least initially, both talks and acts tough. Sotnikov is tortured but refuses to say where his unit is encamped, while Rybak baulks at the very threat of torture and goes over to the enemy. Unbroken and unbowed, despite his frail condition, Sotnikov climbs the gallows and Rybak is forced to kick the stool away from under him.

In Shepitko's film the physical details are harrowing. Shot in black and white, it dwells on the bleak, wintry landscape – a symbol of the nation's suffering – and the privations of the partisans. When Sotnikov is wounded, Rybak carries him on his back in a tortuous journey through the snow. Bykov's finale focuses on the inspiration Sotnikov's bravery provides to a younger generation; Shepitko includes Bykov's scene of the young boy staring in adoration into Sotnikov's eyes as he is about to be executed, but she also adds a touch of her own. As he is about to die, Sotnikov's head is wreathed in an aura of saintly light. This is the ascent into heaven not only of one implacable and courageous patriot, but of the country as a whole. Through self-sacrifice and enormous suffering, the country can achieve victory and everlasting greatness.

There is a third character in this tale of heroism and purgatory: Portnov (played by Anatolii Solonitsyn, a Tarkovskii stalwart). Dressed all in black, Portnov is a former communist now turned cynical Nazi interrogator, the worst kind of collaborator who preys on Rybak's insecurities, but whose wiles are rejected by the physically weaker Sotnikov. Portnov would have served as the typical 'positive hero' in Stalinist fiction, the centre of resistance to Nazism, yet here he is its evil embodiment. Is Shepitko here suggesting that there is little difference between serving Nazi or communist masters?

The equation of Communists and Nazis is made again in another Bykov adaptation. Mikhail Ptashuk's *Sign of Disaster* (1986) bears the hallmarks of an emerging greater openness about the war. Made in the early perestroika years, it is an unremittingly grim and downbeat tale of Nazi occupation and particularly the eagerness of some citizens to collaborate with the enemy and terrorise the local population, their former peacetime neighbours. More significantly, it features several flashbacks to collectivisation a decade or so previously, where the Party activists enforcing a blatantly unjust policy are little different from the wartime collaborators expropriating vodka and food.

Significantly, Potap, one of the former 'poor' peasants enforcing the expropriation of richer farmers ten years before, is now a Nazi thug. Others collaborate out of a need for revenge for injustices served on them under collectivisation, such as the confiscation of property, or out of a self-confessed need to feed a large family.

The Germans are stereotypically depicted as evil, sadistic and barbaric – but so are the Party activists terrorising the rural community in the flashbacks. Suicide and self-sacrifice are the only means of escape from the remorseless cycle of coercion and brutality. Violence is employed against helpless peasants frequently and without motivation, both by the Germans and the Bolsheviks. This is powerful, visceral stuff, offering no salvation, with no indication of an eventual victory. Victims such as Stepanida and her husband Petrok can only be seen in symbolic terms as Christian martyrs. Significantly, Petrok is filmed carrying a cross uphill, rather like Tarkovskii's Christ in *Andrei Rublev*, and Stepanida's face is bathed in ethereal light as she lies in bed after another physical beating. The cinematic treatment of war does not get much bleaker than this.

Fifteen or so years later Ptashuk revisits the War in Belorussia in his *In August 1944* (2000), his adaptation of Vladimir Bogomolov's powerful novel of the same name, also called *The Moment of Truth*, which appeared in 1973.[11] The film boasts an impressive cast (Evgenii Mironov, Alexei Petrenko and Alexander Baluev, among others), but, as a post-Soviet treatment of the war that could have delved into truths once deemed unacceptable, it disappoints. We may have expected more criticism of the Party and Stalin and some visual flair, but all of this is missing. In fact, *In August 1944* is a surprisingly traditional war film that would not have been out of place in the 1970s, with a committed central hero Alekhin (played by Mironov) searching for dastardly German spies in the Belorussian countryside and towns. A solemn voice-over, orchestral music reaching crescendo and rushing camera shots all add to the impression of earnestness. Bogomolov's story criticises Stalin's demand for results at any price and the intrusive role of the commissars in military decision making, and Ptashuk includes these motifs. Otherwise this is a standard tale of cat and mouse, although undeniably tense as the final shootout approaches. Even in more liberal times, Russian attitudes to the Great Patriotic War remain entrenched and determinedly one sided.

Probably the most harrowing film about the war, however, also dates back to the 1980s. Elem Klimov's *Come and See* (1985) is an invitation to the audience to witness an unflinching and relentless trawl through the Nazi atrocities in occupied Belorussia, as experienced by the adolescent boy Flera. Flera is no 'son of the regiment', but rather a survivor and eyewitness to some of the most shocking images ever to have been set on film about the war: German soldiers herding villagers into a church and then setting it on fire, and tossing back inside the young boy who attempts to escape; dozens of corpses of recently executed villagers heaped at the back of houses, caught on camera as if by chance. Klimov piles on the horror with an attention to minute detail which emphasises just how mundane massacre can be: a German soldier dragging a girl by the hair suddenly stops to ask a comrade for a light. These Germans are merciless and barbaric and there is no quarter asked here. Klimov manipulates his audience to applaud the subsequent execution of the Germans – in cold blood – by a band of partisans. Flera shoots at a photograph of Hitler, an image that goes back in time so that the last picture we see is a photograph of the Führer as a young child: the seemingly innocent and pure origin of this evil.

Vladimir Rogovoi's *Officers*, made in 1971, attempts to glamourise army life and reflect the power of the Soviet state through the might of its army. It is otherwise an awkwardly handled would-be epic spanning the years 1919 to 1970 and the parallel lives of two soldiers whose first taste of action is in the Civil War and whom we last see as elderly generals benevolently overseeing the military exploits of another generation. We are shown brief glimpses of conflicts on the Chinese border, the Spanish Civil War, the Great Patriotic War and – it is at least suggested – the Soviet crackdown in Czechoslovakia, with tales of heroism and sacrifice all underpinned by the film's motto: 'There is such a profession as defending the Motherland.' The army is here the defender of the state and an embodiment of its greatness.

Recent conflicts

This 'greatness' was steadily eroded in subsequent decades. The ten-year engagement of the Soviet Union in Afghanistan received scant attention in the cultural media before the advent of glasnost. Documentaries and films, appearing in the late 1980s, showed, often in grim detail, the human cost of the war.

It was in the post-Soviet period that the emerging post-imperialist trauma could be more fully explored. Vladimir Khotinenko's *The Muslim* (1995) used the conflict as a basis of exploring Russia's relationship with its non-Christian Eastern neighbours. Kolia Ivanov is a Russian soldier who has spent eight years in captivity in Afghanistan and has converted to Islam. He returns to his native village to find wholesale drunkenness, crime and corruption, the locals fed on a diet of vodka and foreign sex films, and alienation within his own family. His loutish brother Fedka tries to bring him back to Orthodoxy by forcing him to drink vodka and kiss an icon, but Kolia stands firm. Such a model of honesty and moderation cannot thrive in such a community and Kolia is eventually killed by a former comrade from his Afghan days.

This is a confrontation between Russia and the 'other' world beyond its borders. The name of the hero is significant, approximating to 'Nick Johnson'. The Russian Everyman returns home to the village, for centuries seen as the repository of spirituality and the Russian 'soul' and his own high moral stock is a stark contrast to the degradation and venality all around. The film offers a sad commentary on the moral and spiritual crisis of post-Soviet Russia, shorn of any values or identity, its own traditions and culture hopelessly compromised.

Sergei Bodrov's *Prisoner of the Mountains* (1996) has already been discussed (Chapter Two) as an updated literary adaptation that denounces Russian imperialism. A companion piece is Alexander Rogozhkin's *Checkpoint* (1998), which concerns a group of soldiers stationed somewhere in the Caucasus (probably also Chechnya) and their troubled relationship with the local population. Their superiors care little for them and look to cover their own backs, as the soldiers are blamed for the death of a young village boy during a routine patrol. These young soldiers are treated with undisguised contempt by the locals, they themselves use local women for paid sex and make no attempt to understand the local culture. The contempt eventually becomes deadly serious, as a young female sniper picks them off in the finale (shades of Kubrick's 1987 film *Full Metal Jacket* here). Rogozhkin has made a film that questions Russia's role in the troubled Caucasus region in the late 1990s, with corruption and self-serving in the military hierarchy, a media circus looking only for sensation and not truth, a dangerous and resentful local population and a handful of decent Russian boys at the mercy of them all.

The war film offers some useful clues as to the changing nature of Soviet and then post-Soviet Russian national identity over the decades. In films about the Civil War the war theme is embedded in, but secondary to, the ideological certainties demanded of the genre. The Great Patriotic War provides many films that profess hatred of the enemy and depict the awful nature of armed combat, but also gives film-makers the opportunity to explore the shifting thematic and aesthetic possibilities allowed by successive regimes. Conflict, nevertheless, remains a constant necessity, whether in wartime or the 'peaceful days' of the Cold War. Post-Soviet directors show war as the painful consequence of failed imperial ambition, a reflection of an uncertain, crisis-stricken national psyche numbed by decades of ideology-driven struggle.

Filmography

All Quiet on the Western Front, dir. Lewis Milestone, 1929
Antosha Rybkin, dir. Konstantin Iudin, 1942

Arsenal, dir. Alexander Dovzhenko, 1929

The Ascent ('Voskhozhdenie'), dir. Larisa Shepitko, 1976

At Six O'Clock in the Evening after the War ('V shest chasov vechera posle voiny'), dir. Ivan Pyrev, 1944

Au Revoir Les Enfants, dir. Louis Malle, 1988

The Ballad of a Soldier ('Ballada o soldate'), dir. Grigorii Chukhrai, 1959

The Battle for Moscow ('Bitva za Moskvu'), dir. Iurii Ozerov, 1985

The Battle of Stalingrad ('Stalingradskaia bitva'), dir. Vladimir Petrov, 1949

Belorussia Station ('Belorusskii vokzal'), dir. Andrei Smirnov, 1970

The Bodyguard ('Telokhranitel'), dir. Ali Khamraev, 1980

Chapaev, dir. Vasilev Brothers, 1934

Checkpoint ('Blokpost'), dir. Alexander Rogozhkin, 1998

Clear Skies ('Chistoe nebo'), dir. Grigorii Chukhrai, 1961

Come and See ('Idi i smotri'), dir. Elem Klimov, 1985

The Commissar ('Komissar'), dir. Alexander Askoldov, 1967

The Courier of the Air ('Vozdushnyi izvozchik'), dir. Gerbert Rapoport, 1943

The Cranes Are Flying ('Letiat zhuravli'), dir. Mikhail Kalatozov, 1957

The Elusive Avengers ('Neulovimye mstiteli'), dir. Edmond Keosaian, 1966

The End of St Petersburg ('Konets Sankt-Peterburga'), dir. Vsevolod Pudovkin, 1927

The Fall of Berlin ('Padenie Berlina'), dir. Mikhail Chiaureli, 1949–50

The Fate of a Man ('Sudba cheloveka'), dir. Sergei Bondarchuk, 1959

The Forty-First ('Sorok pervyi'), dir. Iakov Protazanov, 1927

The Good, the Bad and the Ugly, dir. Sergio Leone, 1966

A Great Life ('Bolshaia zhizn'), dir. Leonid Lukov, 1946 (released 1957)

Hope and Glory, dir. John Boorman, 1987

In August 1944 ('V avguste 1944-ogo'), dir. Mikhail Ptashuk, 2000

In Peaceful Days ('V mirnye dni'), dir. Vladimir Braun, 1950

Kotovskii, dir. Alexander Faintsimmer, 1942

Lacombe Lucien, dir. Louis Malle, 1974

The Lad from our Town ('Paren iz nashego goroda'), dir. Alexander Stolper and Boris Ivanov, 1942

Liberation ('Osvobozhdenie'), dir. Iurii Ozerov, 1968–71

Little Red Devils ('Krasnye diavoliata'), dir. Ivan Perestiani, 1923

Mashenka, dir. Iulii Raizman, 1942

The Muslim ('Musulmanin'), dir. Vladimir Khotinenko, 1995

No Ford in a Fire ('V ogne broda net'), dir. Gleb Panfilov, 1967

Officers ('Ofitsery'), dir. Vladimir Rogovoi, 1971

Outskirts ('Okraina'), dir. Boris Barnet, 1933

Prisoner of the Mountains ('Kavkazskii plennik'), dir. Sergei Bodrov Sr., 1996

The Rainbow ('Raduga'), dir. Mark Donskoi, 1943

The Red Danube, dir. George Sidney, 1950

The Red Menace, dir. R. G. Springsteen, 1949

Shchors, dir. Alexander Dovzhenko, 1939

She Defends the Motherland ('Ona zashchishchaet rodinu'), dir. Fridrikh Ermler, 1943

Sign of Disaster ('Znak bedy'), dir. Mikhail Ptashuk, 1986

The Silent Ace of the Skies ('Nebesnyi tikhokhod'), dir. Semen Timoshenko, 1946

Stalingrad, dir. Iurii Ozerov, 1989

The Story of a Real Man ('Povest o nastoiashchem cheloveke'), dir. Alexander Stolper, 1948

Submarine T-9 ('Podvodnaia lodka T-9'), dir. Alexander Ivanov, 1943

Trial on the Roads ('Proverka na dorogakh'), dir. Alexei German, 1971

A Troubled Household ('Bespokoinoe khoziaistvo'), dir. Mikhail Zharov, 1947

The Vow ('Kliatva'), dir. Mikhail Chiaureli, 1949

The Whip Hand, dir. William Cameron Menzies, 1951

The White Sun of the Desert ('Beloe solntse pustyni'), dir. Vladimir Motyl, 1969

The Woman on Pier 13, dir. Robert Stevenson, 1949

Young Fritz ('Iunyi Frits'), dir. Grigorii Kozintsev and Leonid Trauberg, 1943

Zoia, dir. Leo Arnshtam, 1944

Notes

1. Evan Mawdsley, in his preface to his major study of the Civil War (1987), writes: 'If the term "apocalyptic" fits any event in recent world history, it fits the Russian Civil War. This is not to suggest that the events of 1917–20 were the end of the world. The revolutionaries saw what was happening as the *beginning* of a new human order, and if they did not in fact found a new Jerusalem, we can see, seventy years later, that they certainly created in Russia something remarkable and enduring. But their hold on power was bought at the price of great suffering and an unknown but terrible number of deaths – perhaps seven to ten million in all. War and strife, famine and pestilence – the Four Horsemen of the Apocalypse – devastated the largest country in Europe for three years.'

2. The influential film scholar and critic Rostislav Iurenev nevertheless admired the fact that *Submarine T-9* and other such films 'met the patriotic feelings of the audience, and truthfully and interestingly showed separate events of the war', but were flawed artistically: 'The film-makers' efforts were directed at the verisimilitude of recreating events, and not at processes, thoughts and feelings.' (See R. N. Iurenev, 'Kinoiskusstvo voennykh let', in Kim, 1976, pp. 235–51 (p. 245).)

3. *The Rainbow* was made by the Kiev film studio, evacuated to Central Asia, and shot in Alma-Ata. It is regarded as the best Ukrainian film about the war and has won prizes in the United States. Soviet appreciation of *The Rainbow* makes the all-important symbolic link explicit: 'Olena [Kostiuk] is a woman of few words and gestures, all of her exists inwardly, she listens to the life that is beating inside her.

And how expressive are her eyes, her face, how spiritually rich and noble is this simple peasant women, who merges in our consciousness with the image of the Motherland.' (See Kornienko, 1975, p. 135.)

4.   Stalin's cultural henchman Andrei Zhdanov called the film 'ideologically and artistically false' and complained that it 'points our people in the wrong direction and cultivates bad morals'. He was especially outraged by the drinking scenes. (See Mariamov, 1992, p. 79.)

5.   In his mammoth history of the Soviet film comedy, Rostislav Iurenev rails: 'Is this war? Are these people at war, at the heroic and severe events of the War? What does *The Silent Ace of the Skies* and similar films tell us? That being at war is pleasant and simple? That our victory was easy?' (See Iurenev, 1964, pp. 400–1.) Iurenev also admits that *A Troubled Household* gives a 'false and distorted' picture of the War (p. 402).

6.   Peter Kenez discusses in some detail the portrayal of Stalin's 'cult of personality' in these and other films of the last years of the dictator's rule. Stalin was played by several actors, but there was no room for the actor to express himself: 'However, aside from some mannerisms of speech and gesture, it mattered little who was the actor. Playing the Supreme Leader imposed severe limitations on the work of the artist. Given the need to calculate carefully every gesture, given the pompous, wooden lines they had to utter, it is impossible to blame the actors for not portraying a believable character.' (See Kenez, 1992, p. 235.)

7.   Grigorii Mariamov states that Stalin personally approved of the invented flight to Berlin: 'He was flattered to see himself descending "from the heavens" in a sparkling white and gold tunic, slowly making his way towards the crowd rapturously greeting him.' (See Mariamov, 1992, p. 110.)

8.   This film offers an eerie anticipation of the disaster that befell the *Kursk* atomic submarine in the Barings Sea in July 2000. The submarine was lost with all hands (more than 100 men) and the Russian authorities insisted it had hit a Western submarine or mine, in the absence of any evidence. It seems clear now that the submarine went down as a result of a botched attempt to launch a missile during a military exercise.

9.   There was also a string of Hollywood Red-baiting pictures at the time, the very titles of some of which tried to convince the viewer of the danger lurking 'under the beds': *The Red Menace* (1949), *The Woman on Pier 13* (1949), *The Red Danube* (1950) and *The Whip Hand* (1951) are among the most prominent. Needless to say, as with the Soviet counterpart, the quality of these films is very poor.

10.   Geoffrey Hosking notes: 'Perhaps the most unfortunate Soviet citizens of all were those soldiers and civilians who fell into German captivity. The Germans regarded them as "subhuman" and herded them together in what were essentially concentration camps where they slowly died of starvation and disease while performing manual labour. The Soviet government's attitude towards them was no more solicitous: it equated surrender with treason and had refused to sign the Geneva Convention on prisoners of war, which meant that the Red Cross could not forward letters or food parcels to them from their families at home. Furthermore, those who managed to escape – and this included those who made their way out of military encirclement – were promptly subjected to intensive NKVD interrogation, and many of them were sent to labour camps, or even executed as spies, (Hosking, 1985, pp. 288–9).

11.   Bogomolov is also the author of the 1958 short story *Ivan*, which forms the basis of Tarkovskii's film *Ivan's Childhood* (1962).

CHAPTER EIGHT

Private life and public morality

All happy families are alike but an unhappy family is unhappy after its own fashion.

(Tolstoi, 1977, p. 13)

Thus famously begins Lev Tolstoi's *Anna Karenina*, arguably the greatest Russian novel of the nineteenth century, published in serial form in the years 1875–7 and in its entirety in 1878. *Anna Karenina* is also the first Russian novel to focus on the mundane and apparently trivial crises of family life, as opposed to the 'greater questions' of God, Russia and the West, and history, that occupied other writers. The novel demonstrates magnificently that the tiny, seemingly insignificant details of life are of enormous importance to individuals, showing not only the disintegration of the Karenins' marriage, but the highs and lows of other family relationships, such as that of Levin and Kitty and Anna's brother, Stiva Obolenskii. In its depiction of some uncomfortable home truths, the pressures of domestic everyday life and its refusal to give any easy answers, *Anna Karenina* ranks as a truly modern piece of fiction.

Another, associated theme – the yawning gulf between public persona and private morality – is explored in the plays of Alexander Ostrovskii in the 1850s through to the 1870s and then again by Anton Chekhov towards the end of the century.

One of the key nineteenth-century preoccupations was the theme of 'fathers and sons', after Turgenev's novel about the changes in radical values within the generations of one family, but a theme also stretching to Dostoevskii (*The Brothers Karamazov*). Everyday life as experienced in town and village is another theme that runs throughout the classical Russian literary tradition, beginning with Pushkin and continuing well into the twentieth century.

These three themes – family life and the seeming irreconcilability of the public and private spheres, the contrast of town and country and youth and the 'generation gap' – are of major importance in the way Russian cinema has treated the theme of *byt*: the melodramatic twists and turns of everyday life.

Family life

Pre-revolutionary Russian cinema revelled in the dramas and (usually) tragedies of everyday life, as they reflected current concerns and trends, in particular Russia's belated industrialisation and urbanisation and the tensions in gender and class relations that ensued. Directors such as Iakov Protazanov in *The Keys to Happiness*, co-directed with Vladimir Gardin (1913), and *The Maidservant Jenny* (1917), and Evgenii Bauer in *Twilight of a Woman's Soul* (1913), *Child of the Big City* (1914), *Daydreams* (1915), *A Life for a Life* (1916) and *The Dying Swan* (1916), showed 'a world of shadows darkening even the sunniest days, a world in which nothing is permanent' (Youngblood, 1999, p. 143). After the Revolution, directors such as Abram Room, Boris Barnet, Protazanov and in particular Fridrikh Ermler also chose the everyday realities of the 'new' society as their favoured locale, in contrast to the technically more innovative and seemingly more significant historical and political epics of Eisenstein and Pudovkin.

One of the most important films of the 1920s was Room's drama *Bed and Sofa* (1927), about a *ménage-à-trois* brought about by the chronic housing shortage in Soviet cities in the years following the Civil War. The film shows Moscow growing and moving, shot from roof level and the street, the expansive public spaces acting as counterpoint to the stifling confines of the one-room apartment that serves as the main locale for the action. Volodia moves to Moscow in search of work and moves in with his Civil War buddy Kolia and Kolia's wife Liuda. Volodia sleeps on the sofa while Kolia and Liuda share a tiny bed behind a tactfully erected screen. Kolia is suddenly called away on a business trip and Volodia sets about seducing his friend's wife, who shows herself far from unwilling to be wooed. Kolia is relegated to the sofa when he returns, but then he regains Liuda's affections. She gets pregnant and is urged by the two men to seek an abortion. She refuses and leaves them both. The last image we have is her leaving on a train, just as the first image of the film had been of Volodia arriving in Moscow on a train. Kolia and Volodia remain in the apartment, Kolia on the bed and Volodia on the sofa.

There are some genuinely funny moments in what is in any event a fairly black comedy of adultery and betrayal, and none of the three characters emerges with any credit. Both Kolia and Volodia are selfish and manipulative ('we are both scoundrels' is their common insight at the end of the film), Liuda seems weak and malleable until her sudden decision to have her baby regardless. Private tribulations are contrasted with public duty and the new

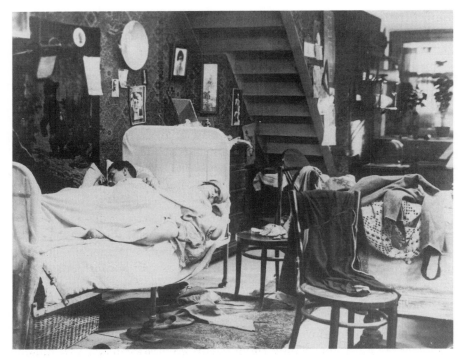

Nikolai Batalov and Liudmila Semenova in Bed and Sofa *(Abram Room, 1927)*

life of the Soviet city is shown in very prosaic terms: the abortion clinic works like a conveyor belt, with women queuing up with their tickets to be next in line for the doctor. It is an ironic portrayal of the life of the new working class, deprived of decent living accommodation and devoid of moral values other than their own gratification.

Room's film was remade by Petr Todorovskii in post-Soviet times under the title *Retro in Three* (1998) (in English it is called *Ménage-à-Trois*), transferring the action from NEP Russia to the equally uncertain early post-Soviet years. There are hints of civil strife (Chechnya?) in the early part of the film, as Sergei leaves his cockroach-infested flat, with bombs exploding outside, to travel to Moscow. There he eventually moves in with his friend Kostia and girlfriend Rita, a photographer specialising in pictures evoking the past. Her special interest is in costumes from the 1920s, which establishes the film's 'retro' relationship to *Bed and Sofa*. The role of Rita as active 1990s career woman is very different from the passive character of Liuda in Room's film.

Sergei graduates from sleeping on the sofa to sharing Rita's bed and Rita becomes pregnant, although, as with Liuda, it is not clear who the father is. The film contains many references to the times – a loutish *nouveau riche* Russian in his Mercedes-as-status-symbol, Sergei's initial grinding poverty and feigned madness that he adopts to beg some money from passers-by – but it also reflects the lack of certainties in a new age where individuals have to look to themselves for advancement and what is here today may be gone tomorrow. *Retro in Three* takes Room's basic plot and updates it in whimsical fashion, but the clear references to the unstable and unpredictable nature of the times link the two films.

One of the peculiar features of Soviet films about everyday life in the 'golden age' of the 1920s was the plot's dependence on chance to enable characters to get out of the daily grind. In Zheliabuzhskii's film *The Cigarette Girl from Mosselprom* (1924), Zina sells cigarettes on street corners until she is suddenly spotted by a film company and offered a glamorous life in the movies. The film provides a satirical look at the film industry, but it is this stroke of initial good fortune that introduces Zina to her future love and so provides for her future happiness. Natasha, the milliner in Boris Barnet's *The Girl with the Hatbox* (1927), wins 25,000 rubles on the lottery. The film manages to satirise NEP types, such as the the exploitative hatshop manager Irène and her grasping husband Tager, but in the end Natasha (sensually played by Anna Sten) proves able to rise above circumstance and win the day only with a large slice of luck. Iakov Protazanov's *The Tailor from Torzhok* (1926) also concerns a lucky lottery ticket (this one worth 100,000 rubles) and closes with another happy ending, with the hero Petelkin (the 'tailor') getting his girl and fortune. Protazanov's film also contrasts the old with the new and has a gallery of negative NEP characters – a priest, a fortune teller, a shopowner who thinks nothing of beating his drudge Katia – but also has to rely on the fairytale outcome for its closure. Protazanov's darker melodrama *The Man from the Restaurant* (1927), by way of contrast, offers no easy solutions and is a fairly grim tale of exploitation in the immediate pre-revolutionary years, amid general vileness and debauchery.

The subsequent decades saw little attention paid to individual or family lives, with emphasis more on the 'larger' themes of socialist construction and the perceived need to create historical or political heroes. Families existed, but the private family was subsumed into the greater Soviet family and conflicts were to be resolved only with reference to the collective. A typically Stalinist film in this respect is Iosif Kheifits' *The Big Family*, released in 1954 (i.e. a year after Stalin's death) and based on a notorious novel by diehard Stalinist Vsevolod Kochetov, published in 1952. The 'family', of course, is not just the Zhurbins, four generations of the Leningrad shipyard workers led and dominated by the fearsome patriarch Ilia, replete in Stalinesque moustache and tunic, but also the larger Soviet family to which all members of society belong. Thus, there are no problems that cannot be solved through the collective and wisdom filters down from the older generation, represented by 77-year-old Matvei, upholder of the values of October, to the younger members. The shipyard honours old Matvei by naming its latest ship after him, just as his family do so by naming the youngest great-grandchild Matvei. Only the inconstancy of women threatens the social fabric, as one is tempted away by the lure of greater affluence.

The Big Family also reinforces the Leninist myth of the power of the working class (and it is specifically a *Russian* working class, with surnames such as Zhurbin, Basmanov, Ivanov and Skobelev). If you work hard, the factory will give you your own separate accommodation so that you do not have to live with your parents or in a communal apartment. These workers are also highly cultured and are treated to a Rakhmaninov concert in the shipyard. The soundtrack also reinforces the political message, with triumphant orchestral music expressing positive emotions and a folkloric male voice choir to provide the patriotic ardour. Needless to say, the film is shot in the summer, as the sun always shines on Soviet workers. A few years later Alexander Zarkhi's *Heights* (1957), although demonstrably a film of the thaw period with its closer attention to individuals, similarly championed working-class values, showing Soviet workers building a blast furnace, finding time to organise their love lives and urged on by genuine ideological commitment.

The disparity between the public image and the private person could not be expressed in the repressive years of the 'stagnation period', but towards the end of Brezhnev's gerontocracy some bold statements could be heard. In his last films the veteran director Iulii Raizman, who began working during the years of the 'golden age' (he played a small part in Pudovkin's 1925 classic *Chess Fever*), turned his attention to the private family dramas of individuals. In *Private Life* (1982) a high-ranking bureaucrat Abrikosov (played by Mikhail Ulianov) is forced into early retirement and, as he is obliged to spend more time at home, finds himself a stranger within his own family. This is an old man's film, slow moving and reflective, with everyone around Abrikosov unable to understand that he feels cast on the scrapheap with nothing more to look forward to in life. Only when the family finally pulls together in the face of a crisis (the death of his first wife and mother to his eldest daughter), does Abrikosov realise what true values are. He is then suddenly summoned to the ministry with the possibility of returning to work, and as he dresses he looks in the mirror – and there the film leaves us. Like the middle-aged Gurov at the end of Chekhov's story *The Lady with the Lapdog* (1899), Abrikosov has perhaps really seen himself for the first time. The viewer is left unsure whether Abrikosov will return to his former bureaucratic self or whether, like Gurov, he has become a better person.

In Raizman's *A Time of Wishes* (1984) Vladimir Dmitrievich Lobanov (Anatolii Papanov) is a middle-aged widower who weds the much younger Svetlana (Vera Alentova). He is a thoroughly decent and unassuming man, she is well connected and unafraid of using her talent for getting things done to her advantage. Svetlana, indeed, is tough and self-reliant and even when she is raped by her former partner she copes with it firmly, discreetly, privately. She is a figure recognisable from the Moscow stories of Iurii Trifonov written in the 1970s, which exposed the acquisitiveness and materialistic lifestyles of the so-called urban intelligentsia. She is powerless, however, when Lobanov has a fatal heart attack. 'Do something!' she yells to the doctor and the cry could be that of a whole society in terminal decline. As in *Private Life*, happiness is elusive and public posturing merely hides private anguish and failure.

Family happiness, or the lack of it, is also one of the major themes of post-Soviet cinema. Eldar Riazanov's *Prediction* (1992), despite its topical references to civil strife, such as street shootings, muggings, troops on the streets, is nevertheless a sentimental tale of how love will win through despite hardships on the way – significantly, again the love of an older man for a much younger woman – and the child they conceive is the well-worn symbol of hope for the future. The melodramas of Dmitrii Astrakhan, such as *You Are My Only One* (1993) and *Everything Will Be OK* (1995) also serve to remind Russians that, despite the hardships and the struggle to survive in the new Russia, life can still be lived and even enjoyed.

The security and stability of family life in the cinema of the 1990s have been endangered above all by the threat of violent crime, and the urban crime thriller has become the dominant popular genre for domestic audiences. Stanislav Govorukhin's *The Voroshilov Sniper* (1999) stars the veteran classical actor Mikhail Ulianov in a sensational role, that of vigilante avenger. He is a former wartime sharpshooter forced to take up arms again in the modern age when his teenage granddaughter is brutally gang raped. The rape itself is shown in uncomfortable detail, a clear attempt to manipulate the audience in rooting for vengeance. The police are either powerless or indifferent – the father of one of the rapists is a police colonel who stops the investigation – and so old Ivan Fedorovich has to rely on his own resources to exact justice. One of the rapists is shot in the groin and loses his manhood (just deserts), another is badly burned when his BMW car is blown up (symbolic castration) and the other loses his sanity as he waits for the ever-expected bullet (psychological emasculation).

This is more than *Death Wish* for a new Russia, however. The targets are not just the three brazen, self-confident young men who think that they are 'unpunishable', but rather the trappings of post-Soviet Russia itself: a hopeless police force, the symbols of affluence from cars to ostentatious personal jewellery to imported whisky and the perceived alienation of parents and their children. Ivan Fedorovich points his high-powered rifle at not only the villains of the piece, but symbolically at the whole social edifice of modern Russia. The film carries the hallmarks of Govorukhin's yearning for past absolutes that he exhibited in his 1992 documentary *The Russia We Have Lost*.

Sergei Bodrov Jr. in Brother *(Alexei Balabanov, 1997)*

Crime and killing can actually bring families together, as in Alexei Balabanov's popular and controversial *Brother* (1997), and its sequel, *Brother 2* (2000). Both films do not shrink from showing callous and brutal violence, as they follow the amoral and deadly efficient hitman Danila as he cleans up St Petersburg of Chechen and Russian gangsters, all the while helping the destitute and the powerless, as well as a damsel in distress.

The motif of family unity is there from the start of the first film, as Danila takes up his gun in order to help out his brother, also a professional killer. In the sequel he takes his trade to Moscow and then Chicago, blowing away not only Russian gangsters but also assorted blacks and American villains. His brother, meanwhile, takes on the Ukrainian mafia single handedly. Balabanov's films are interesting as a cinematic development that turns away from the traditions of Soviet cinema and borrows heavily from modern Western films. In particular, they exhibit the influence of Quentin Tarantino, with a rock music soundtrack, moments of extreme violence, quirky humour and an absence of any moral stance. Danila kills without mercy or remorse, but his victims are all bad guys and so deserve what they get. There is no condemnation of Danila's chosen profession, learned, we are led to believe, in the killing fields of Chechnya; indeed, the films offer a glorification of it. The job of hitman, these films say, is as valid as any other means of earning money in the new Russia. At the end of both films, Danila is not so much interested in money as in dispensing justice and his saving grace is his concern for those at the harsh end of everyday life. In the end, he is just a decent Russian country lad getting by the best way he can.

Bodrov Jr. has tried himself to get in on the directorial act, with his film *Sisters* (2000). This is also a film about crime and hitmen threatening the integrity of a family, as two half-sisters go on the run from the mafia and survive on their own wits and ingenuity. Against a background of general squalor, police corruption, the apathy of relatives and passers-by, they are saved by their gangster father, who just happens to be tougher and more ruthless than the bandits on their trail. *Sisters* also has a rock soundtrack and is obviously heavily influenced by the *Brother* films. The only way to survive in the crime-infested Russia of the post-Soviet period, these films tell us, is to take up the gun.

Town and country

Life in the countryside has always been a popular topic with film-makers, as it offered fertile ground for reflections on Russia's past, present and future. In the 1920s the countryside was seen as a place where life was tough and full of 'class contradictions'. In Fedor Otsep's *The Land Imprisoned* (1927) the common folk are seen at one with the natural world, a couple's kiss is framed against wheat blowing and undulating in the wind and a mother bringing in the hay is a clear image of Mother Nature providing for her people. The landowners, however, laugh at the misery of the peasants and Mariia (another evocative portrayal by Anna Sten) has to travel to the town to earn enough for her family. She is the object of a landowner's lustful attention, at the same time as further misery is heaped on her family when they are evicted from their home. The poverty of life in the village, where Mariia's baby dies, is matched only by the misery in the city – Mariia is arrested as a prostitute and can only get work in a brothel. She goes back to the family on hearing that her husband Iakov has had an accident at work in a quarry. She returns as spring bursts out all around and the story is resolved as the tale of a fallen woman redeemed through the love of her family, against a background of nature regenerated.

Sergei Eisenstein's *The General Line* (1929) captures in memorable images the struggle of the peasantry against the kulaks in the 1920s and ends with the triumphant arrival of technology to help work the land, much to the despair of the 'exploiters' who see their power and source of income being eroded. At the start of the film a house is sawn in two as a visual symbol of the destruction of the family through commercial exploitation, and peasants starve as fat kulaks treat them with disdain. These peasants are too poor even to own a horse and a cow has to pull the plough. When the cow dies of exhaustion, people take up the yoke. Salvation comes not through the church

vibrant city, symbol of the industrial future, growing and developing on a massive scale. Dziga Vertov's revolutionary documentary *The Man with the Movie Camera* (1929) is a celebration of 'the power of Soviet Communism in the machine and the city' (Roberts, 2000, p. 92). The city is observed from sunrise to sunset and the seemingly unobtrusive camera follows events as they happen: a road accident, a baby being born, a couple getting married as another sign for a divorce. The camera does not make things happen, as in a fictional film, but rather records life 'caught unawares', whether this be a woman rousing herself from bed in the morning, crowds of people in public transport, miners working in dark and confined conditions or people sunning themselves on a Ukrainian beach. Streets in the centre of Moscow thrive with movement and people, while punters enjoy a glass of beer in a smoke-filled bar. All of this is captured by the cameraman, literally dominating his real-life material as he films from the roof of one of Moscow's tall buildings. Ultimate control of this reality is maintained by the editor, who remakes these images with bold, self-conscious and modernist strokes. Freeze-frame and split screen, slow motion and super-imposed shots and even animation are all used to create the impression of dynamism, the city seen in utopian terms as the ideal locus for the merging of man and machine in the new industrial age.

The political idealism at the heart of Vertov's film is absent in films about city life from later decades, where the harshness of urban reality can no longer be ignored. True, in the films of Grigorii Alexandrov in the 1930s, Moscow is the place where dreams can come true and life can become a fairytale. In later decades, though, reality would set in. In Pavel Lungin's *Taxi Blues* (1990) and the same director's mafia thriller *Line of Life* (1995) the city is dark and dangerous, with lethal traps for the unwary. Karen Shakhnazarov captures one day in the life of the city in *Day of the Full Moon* (1998), a series of vignettes of daily life, dreams, fantasies and violent and sudden death in Moscow in the 1990s. Since the collapse of the Soviet Union the city has become the symbol for everything that has gone wrong, it is no longer a synecdoche for the building of a great new world, but rather a sordid and dangerous place that has disowned its past and has no future.

Alexander Zeldovich's *Moscow* (2000) is a gangster thriller that portrays not the people pulling the triggers, but those who give the orders, the men and women who are both gangster bosses and legitimate business dealers in a Moscow marked by conspicuous consumption and a desire to live life to the full in the here and now. With a screenplay by Vladimir Sorokin, a writer who deconstructs the symbols of totalitarianism in the most grotesque and brutal way, post-Soviet Moscow is seen as a metaphorical hell on earth, with food, alcohol, drugs and sex all available on demand. Culture has no value and is not spared the excess, as a gangland hit is carried out at a ballet performance. The ballerina's white dress is soaked in the blood of the murdered man, a clear metaphor for the besmirching of innocence and purity in a deadly world devoted entirely to indulgence and pleasure.

Youth

Fridrikh Ermler had attacked the apparent sexual hypocrisy of young komsomol members in his film *The Parisian Cobbler* (1928), and the issue of Soviet youth in the 1920s attracted much critical comment and debate. The first Soviet sound film was also a film about youth. Nikolai Ekk's *The Path to Life* (1931) is set in 1923, in the aftermath of the Civil War, when there are gangs of homeless and orphaned children on the streets of major cities. They are a constant source of petty crime, as they must pilfer and pickpocket in order to survive. The film's motto is loudly proclaimed: 'In the Soviet Republic there should not be any deprived and homeless children. Let there be young and happy citizens.'

The rehabilitation and reintegration of these children into society is accomplished through respect and affection, rather than military-like regimentation. Despite the temptation to return to their illegal ways through provocation by prostitutes and the hardened gangster Zhigan, the boys remain true to their new vocation – manufacturing rails for the railway – although a price has to be paid: their leader Mustafa is killed, a sacrifice for the greater cause.

In Stalinist cinema, however, problems of youth or for that matter any other social malaise did not exist. The problems of the homeless children in the aftermath of the Civil War (*besprizorshchina*) were deemed to have been solved through the collective work ethic and now society was united in its drive to industrialise and modernise. As we have seen, fathers and their children belonged to one happy family and were united in their ideals and values. 'Youth' would resurface only during the thaw, both in the literature of the period ('youth prose', roughly from 1956 to 1964) and cinema.

In Georgii Daneliia's *I Walk Around Moscow* (1963) the young cast (including a baby-faced Nikita Mikhalkov and a teenage Inna Churikova) get up to nothing much except have fun in the course of a day in Moscow, where they have an altercation with the police, consult an established writer, but still look up to their fathers for moral guidance. The 'fathers' are not foregrounded and the focus is very much on the ebullience of youth. This is a society opening up to the world, with foreign tourists in Moscow and the promise of greater freedom for the younger generation.

It is in this context that Iulii Raizman's *And What If It Is Love?* (1962) can be regarded as very much the ground breaker. The puppy-love romance between Kseniia and Boris is condemned by parents and teachers and Raizman makes clear the stifling conservatism of the collective, dominated by the older generation. Not for Boris and Kseniia the wise counsel of older heads; rather, the two young lovers face condemnation and intimidation.

The film begins with roving shots of courtyards and streets filled with people going about their business and children heading for school. But the vivacity and energy of young people is checked by the regimentation of the school as embodied in the unforgiving sternness of Mariia Pavlovna, the teacher of German whose instruction in German grammar stifles all imagination and initiative. We see the destructive power of the collective as the gossip of adults in the courtyard condemns Boris and Kseniia and she is even beaten by her mother in front of the assembled grown-ups. All because of a love letter found in school.

All that is left for the youngsters are stolen kisses in an abandoned church, lit up by a shaft of sunlight. They are both threatened with expulsion and Kseniia attempts to kill herself in despair. She and Boris part and she leaves to restart her life in Novosibirsk. Thus a young, sincere relationship is destroyed by the collective and in particular the representatives of authority. This is not just a generation gap melodrama, but an allegory, set during de-Stalinisation, of the continuing dominance of Stalinist oppression and intolerance (as personified in Mariia Pavlovna) and the pressure of intimidation. The film goes further, however, as it clearly condemns the right of the collective to interfere in the lives of individuals. Josephine Woll comments on the film's significance:

> And What If It's Love? *broke major taboos. It has no positive hero. It regards the 'collective, that eternally wise buttress of the typical', as neither irreproachable nor wise. It not only insisted that audiences judge for themselves but that they judge themselves.*
>
> *(Woll, 2000, p. 136)*[3]

Raizman's film aroused much comment in the press of the time and remains one of the most controversial Soviet films about youth. The Party's Central Committee was annoyed, noting the 'opposed' images of young and old, the latter being characterised as 'petit bourgeois and philistine [. . .] or people who are indifferent and not capable of understanding younger people'. The Cultural Section of the Central Committee wanted the film banned: 'This film is an ideologically erroneous work. Concentrating the viewer's attention only on the shady aspects, the depiction of abnormal, negative phenomena that eclipse everything bright and pure in our life, the film *And What If It Is Love?* creates a one-sided and distorted picture of Soviet reality.'[4]

However, this was nothing compared to the furore around another youth film made at the time, Marlen Khutsiev's *Ilich's Gate*, completed in 1962 but reworked and finally released in an altered form only in 1965. Khutsiev's film, to be sure, was radical in just about every respect, not only in its subject matter, but also its stylistic approach and even its soundtrack. *Ilich's Gate* follows three male friends around Moscow in the course of a year. It has no real plot, but aims for a documentary authenticity akin to that of Italian post-war neo-realism, taking in the real public spaces of streets and courtyards, as well as private apartments. Crowds are filmed moving and jostling and it is unclear where the 'real people' end and the actors begin. These young Russians want fun, enjoy jazz and attend poetry readings by Evgenii Evtushenko and other young Turks of the day. But they also take part in May Day parades and celebrate Iurii Gagarin's recent space flight. Students from Third World countries also testify to the opening up of society to the outside world.

But all is not as innocent as it may seem. Casual sex may be taken for granted in Western cinema, but 'amorality' can, under the strict ideological guidelines of Soviet cinema, have its dark political side. Nikita Khrushchev attacked the 'heroes' for not knowing how to live and what to aspire for in life: 'No, society cannot count on such people – they are not fighters and not people who change the world. They are morally sick people, old despite their youth, bereft of any lofty aims or calling in life.'[5]

Khrushchev, as well as Mosfilm dignitaries who discussed the film, were outraged by the film's 'fathers and sons' conflict, the failure to set up the older generation as moral teachers for the young. Sergei engages in a long dialogue with the father of his girlfriend Ania, who attacks the youth of today for their 'protest' and their lack of faith, railing against their presumption and lack of experience. Rather, in line with the writers of 'youth prose' (Vasilii Aksenov, Anatolii Gladilin, Andrei Bitov, Vladimir Voinovich and others), these young men were rejecting the hypocrisy and the compromises of their elders, even if they were far from rejecting the tenets of Marxism-Leninism. They wanted to be individuals in a new world, but were hardly storming the ramparts.[6] In purely cinematic terms, these films took the camera on to the streets and into courtyards, showing the far from glamorous life of ordinary people.

In the late 1960s and early 1970s there was no shortage of films for and about young people – Stanislav Rostotskii's *We'll Survive Till Monday* (1968) and Sergei Solovev's *A Hundred Days After Childhood* (1974) are among the most significant – but it was in the late Brezhnev period that films appeared where the cracks really did start to show. Dinara Asanova's *Tough Kids* (1983) resembles *The Path to Life* in that it shows a team of delinquents learning respect and trust in order to be reintegrated into society. But these are not orphans, as in the earlier film, and their plight cannot be blamed on some social cataclysm such as the Civil War. Rather, they are children who have been abused at home by alcoholic parents or else abandoned. The film also has an open ending, as it remains unclear whether love and respect will ever turn these emotionally bruised kids into responsible citizens.

Of an altogether different caste is Rolan Bykov's *Scarecrow* (1984) and it is also far removed from the realistic depiction of youth angst of 20 years before. Bykov's film is about the victimisation and persecution of Lena, a 12-year-old girl living in a provincial Russian town, by her schoolmates. This is a disturbing film not only because it is about innocence under attack. Lena confesses to a 'crime' she did not commit, to be ostracised by her classmates for her 'betrayal', who then burn an effigy of her. Moreover, the film shows, like Gennadii Poloka's *The Republic of ShKID*, the true malevolence of an unchecked collective. The adults are shown as weak, uncaring or indifferent. Yet the collective, on the surface, is peaceful and eminently presentable: the town is visited by tourists and the wooden buildings are seen as great monuments to Russian timber architecture. Beneath the surface, however, these kids are involved in petty crime and victimisation. There is no happy ending, justice does not triumph, as Lena and her old grandfather are forced to leave the town. The children finally learn of their mistake, but their call for forgiveness is too little too late. *Scarecrow*, therefore, may focus on young people but its theme strikes at the very essence of totalitarianism and tyranny.

The film also has a nationalistic and spiritual resonance. Lena and her grandfather live in an apartment bedecked with paintings that her grandfather (the 'one in patches', as the kids cruelly call him) avidly collects. Most of these paintings are by the family's own ancestors. Their home is therefore a centre of culture and identity within an otherwise philistine environment. Lena is often filmed against the backdrop of a church, she covers her head in a shawl like the Old Believers who suffered for the cause under Peter the Great and her face is bathed in light like an iconic image. Her act of self-sacrifice accords with Orthodox belief and she achieves a moral victory when her innocence is confirmed at the end of the film. Lena the 'scarecrow', therefore, represents innocence under attack from an implacable evil, culture destroyed by modern-day philistinism and Mother Russia herself suffering in a secular and materialistic age.[7]

A few years later and Gorbachev's glasnost allowed these pent-up or barely concealed feelings of repression and alienation full expression. The late 1980s saw films such as the hard-hitting documentary *Is It Easy to be Young?* (1986), made by the Latvian Iuris Podnieks, Karen Shakhnazarov's *The Courier* (1987), Vadim Abdrashitov's *Pliumbum or A Dangerous Game* (1987), Vasilii Pichul's *Little Vera* (1988), Rashid Nugmanov's *The Needle* (1988), Valerii Ogorodnikov's *The Burglar* (1988) and Sergei Solovev's *Assa* (1988). Within a few years the Soviet cinema-going public had confirmed what it had probably known privately all along; namely, that young people suffered from aimlessness, frustration and alienation, that drug taking, alcoholism and casual sex were rife and that the children of the 1980s had little faith in the values and expectations of their fathers.

The Needle not only starred 1980s rock legend Viktor Tsoi, who was killed in a car crash in 1990, but also contained graphic images of drug abuse (and how to go about it). However, *Little Vera* was the most controversial of these films, with its affirmation of youth culture and its relatively frank portrayal of sex. At the same time the director gives us an unflinching portrait of juvenile delinquency and gang warfare in a Soviet industrial backwater, the us versus them stand-off between young people and the police and alcoholic and abusive fathers. Despite a sentimental attempt to reconcile abusive father with wayward daughter, this is a film about breakdown and collapse. If ever a film showed the end of the Soviet dream and just how far away was 'advanced socialism', this was it.

Valerii Ogorodnikov was in his mid-thirties when he made his first film, *The Burglar*, with a script by Valerii Priemykhov, the actor who had played the understanding and idealistic youth welfare worker in *Tough Kids*. It is also a much more subversive film than others of this period. *The Burglar* is a film of protest more radical than Pichul's film, for the heroes of these young people are violent revolutionaries and would-be assassins. The older generation offers little support or understanding and seems out of touch.

The film has little plot, other than the theft of a synthesiser by Semen, a 13-year-old boy, so that his elder brother Kostia can use it in his pop group. There is lots of footage of rock and punk concerts, Russian punks are arrested by the police simply because of the way they look and Kostia sings 'I need air'. The film is a call to young people to express themselves, to assert their right to their own culture (markedly similar to that in Western Europe a decade earlier) and it is also a rejection of all that has gone before. Ogorodnikov's film is angry and pointed, pouring scorn on society's attempts to regulate its young people's musical tastes through regimented ballet classes or brass bands. The nihilism of these punks is also shocking, as it offers a fundamental challenge to a strict and intolerant society.

The end of the film sees the old hierarchies re-established, a sign that this society cannot be changed, but must be replaced. Semen is arrested for theft and his father arranges his release only through the Soviet time-honoured way of calling an important friend for a favour. A folk song sung by an appropriately demure young girl accompanies the end of the film, but this is artificial closure. The visceral energy of these young people and the depth of their rejection of the norm make *The Burglar* the most important youth film of the Soviet period and a clear pointer to the need for fundamental change.

These films locked into a youth subculture that had never before been paraded on the Soviet cinema screen and also affirmed the right of young people to live as they wished to live. Parents – especially fathers – hardly set an example to their children and have little positive experience to pass on to them. Spiritual successors to *Ilich's Gate*, these films tell of the absence of any link between the generations and the irrelevance of ideology. Young people just want to have fun, and why can't boys wear earrings?

This theme is continued and developed in post-Soviet film. Sergei Solovev returns to his favourite topic of youth in his *A Tender Age* (2000) and it is interesting to compare this film with his *Assa*, made in 1988 at the height of Gorbachev's campaign of glasnost. *Assa* may be a celebration of late Soviet youth culture, with its dance halls, flashing disco lights and rock music, but it is also very much a film of its time; that is, not so much about the problems of youth as the need to transform society generally.

Assa combines its youth theme with the gangland thriller motif, through the involvement of Sergei with a criminal Krymov (played by Stanislav Govorukhin). This eventually leads to his death at the hands of Krymov's thugs, although Krymov is then despatched by his own moll Alika, who had had a relationship with Sergei. *Assa* has a gritty and naturalistic feel to it, with a meandering plot and much use of youth slang – rather innovatively explained in various subtitled 'footnotes' along the way. Govorukhin's character, however, holds the film together. He is an older man, born in the 1930s, a representative of a discredited order now trying to corrupt and control the younger generation. The fact that he fails is of little comfort, for young people remain confined within a stifling social atmosphere that restricts their movements and regards initiative with suspicion. The closing credits feature Viktor Tsoi and his group Kino, as they hammer home the message of the film in the singer's customarily pained but forthright delivery:

Мы ждем перемен
Перемен требуют наши сердца
Перемен требуют наши глаза.

(We await change
Change is demanded by our hearts
Change is demanded by our eyes.)

Assa is an exposé of a subculture that was not meant to exist in the Soviet Union, part of a reality that flourished independently of the generation of the 'fathers', whose pernicious influence as embodied by Krymov continues to make itself felt.

A Tender Age is a film from a different time and one which is not content with merely highlighting a problem, but that also analyses it. The later film also has claims for artistic status, with a classical musical score, surreal flights of fantasy and guest slots for established character actors such as Liudmila Saveleva (Natasha Rostova in *War and Peace*), Valentin Gaft and Kirill Lavrov.

That is not to say that *A Tender Age* does not have its faults. It is diffuse, with many digressions and irrelevancies, but these oversights are part of an (over)ambitious plan to make sense of Russian history in the last couple of decades of the twentieth century. Solovev explicitly sets his film within a Russian cultural continuum, as the three parts all have literary headings: 'The Idiot', 'Fathers and Sons' and 'War and Peace'.

The film offers a mixture of reality and fantasy, comedy and tragedy, war (Chechnya) and peace in an attempt to account for the resigned madness of today. Only in Russia can a monkey with the name Prokhor beat up a 'new Russian' in his BMW car, only in Russia can hoodlums machine-gun a kiosk for the sake of some chewing gum and only someone as unfortunate as Gromov can survive ambush and bombardment in Chechnya to be then hit on the head by the canister of supplies parachuted in to him. Happiness, in the end, is only a dream marriage in Paris.

Absurdities abound in this film. The pupil Dagaev strips naked in class to provoke the glamorous new chemistry teacher, whom he then seduces in the laboratory, a flaming Bunsen burner in the foreground. Decades later, when Dagaev is in a mental hospital with a drugs problem, she is his only visitor. The stuttering military instructor Bespalchikov (literally 'fingerless') sounds off demagogically before his class of pupils about the dangers of American imperialism and performs a brilliantly sustained lament on why the Soviet Union lost the Cold War, culminating in him smashing his head in a kung-fu attempt to break a pile of bricks. He dies a futile death in Chechnya.

The solemnity of the Soviet Union's adherence to military values is debunked when schoolboys release a white dove in the hall where a military celebration is taking place, causing the bird to fly into the lights, resulting in electrical failure and general chaos. The central character Gromov has relatives who are linked to the perceived glorious Soviet past, be it the war or the space programme, but Gromov himself is interested only in girls.

A Tender Age makes a series of telling points about the problems of youth in the post-Soviet age, tracing the roots of the malaise to preceding decades. The Chechen war may be terrible, but peace is also unpredictable, with the ever-present worries about money and debt. The film explores the wounds of the present through reference to the past, showing a generation crippled both physically and morally by the cataclysms it has had to live through and the attitudes that informed the official value systems of the past.

When the Soviet state was established it proclaimed its aim to create the 'new' Soviet man, one freed from the commercial pressures and exploitation of capitalism and devoted to the ideology of building socialism and communism. The future lay in the electrified city, the village represented the darkness and ignorance of the past. The present could be sacrificed for the sake of the future, youth was the natural supporter of the new regime, older generations could be treated with circumspection. As the decades went by, the larger Soviet 'family' came to be more important than the nuclear one and at least in visual images and the written word the countryside had caught up with the town in material terms. What post-Stalin film tells us, increasingly, is of the failure of authority to regulate private life and the subsequent attempts to make sense of reality beyond ideology. By the time we get to the late Soviet and post-Soviet periods, it is clear that the dream has failed, both the city and the village are both desperate and gloomy places, prospects for young people are bleak and there is little hope.

But there are also continuities with the pre-1917 period. If Tolstoi and Chekhov speak of the hypocrisy of society and its intolerance of any defiance of perceived morality, then in the cinema of the 1970s and 1980s there is also a yawning gap between public stance and private morality, between word and deed. The films of Iakov Protazanov and Evgenii Bauer usually offered bleak endings to personal problems (murder or suicide), and the films of the post-Soviet period also eschew the often artificial and ideologically crafted happy endings of the majority of Soviet melodramas. In Soviet times resistance to the collective ended with the individual leaving its embrace; since then, in the absence of social ethics or accepted spiritual values, individuals must face up to social breakdown and injustice alone, by calling on their own wits and resources, even if that involves 'tooling up' with high-powered rifles and sawn-off shotguns.

Filmography

Alien Kin ('Chuzhaia rodnia'), dir. Mikhail Shveitser, 1954

And What If It Is Love? ('A esli eto liubov?'), dir. Iulii Raizman, 1962

Asia's Happiness ('Asino schaste'), dir. Andrei Mikhalkov-Konchalovskii, 1967

Assa, dir. Sergei Solovev, 1988

Bed and Sofa ('Tretia Meshchanskaia'), dir. Abram Room, 1927

The Big Family ('Bolshaia semia'), dir. Iosif Kheifits, 1954

Brother ('Brat'), dir. Alexei Balabanov, 1997

Brother 2 ('Brat 2'), dir. Alexei Balabanov, 2000

The Burglar ('Vzlomshchik'), dir. Valerii Ogorodnikov, 1988

Chess Fever ('Shakhmatnaia goriachka'), dir. Vsevolod Pudovkin, 1925

The Chicken Riaba ('Kuritsa Riaba'), dir. Andrei Mikhalkov-Konchalovskii, 1994

Child of the Big City ('Ditia bolshogo goroda'), dir. Evgenii Bauer, 1914

The Cigarette Girl from Mosselprom ('Papirosnitsa ot Mosselproma'), dir. Iurii Zheliabuzhskii, 1924

The Courier ('Kurer'), dir. Karen Shakhnazarov, 1987

Daydreams ('Grezy'), dir. Evgenii Bauer, 1915

Day of the Full Moon ('Den polnoluniia'), dir. Karen Shakhnazarov, 1998

The Dying Swan ('Umiraiushchii lebed'), dir. Evgenii Bauer, 1916

Everything Will Be OK ('Vse budet khorosho'), dir. Dmitrii Astrakhan, 1995

The General Line ('Generalnaia liniia', subsequently released as *The Old and the New*: 'Staroe i novoe'), dir. Sergei Eisenstein, 1929

The Girl with the Hatbox ('Devushka s korobkoi'), dir. Boris Barnet, 1927

Happy Go Lucky ('Pechki-lavochki'), dir. Vasilii Shukshin, 1972

Heights ('Vysota'), dir. Alexander Zarkhi, 1957

A Hundred Days After Childhood ('Sto dnei posle detstva'), dir. Sergei Solovev, 1974

Ilich's Gate ('Zastava Ilicha'), dir. Marlen Khutsiev, 1962–65

Is It Easy to be Young? ('Legko li byt molodym?'), dir. Iuris Podnieks, 1986

It Happened in Penkovo ('Delo bylo v Penkove'), dir. Stanislav Rostotskii, 1957

I Walk Around Moscow ('Ia shagaiu po Moskve'), dir. Georgii Daneliia, 1963

The Keys to Happiness ('Kliuchi schastia'), dir. Iakov Protazanov and Vladimir Gardin, 1913

The Kuban Cossacks ('Kubanskie kazaki'), dir. Ivan Pyrev, 1949

The Land Imprisoned ('Zemlia v plenu'), dir. Fedor Otsep, 1927

A Life for a Life ('Zhizn za zhizn'), dir. Evgenii Bauer, 1916

Line of Life ('Liniia zhizni'), dir. Pavel Lungin, 1995

Little Vera ('Malenkaia Vera'), dir. Vasilii Pichul, 1988

The Maidservant Jenny ('Gornichnaia Dzhenni'), dir. Iakov Protazanov, 1917

The Man from the Restaurant ('Chelovek iz restorana'), dir. Iakov Protazanov, 1927

The Man with the Movie Camera ('Chelovek s kinoapparatom'), dir. Dziga Vertov, 1929

Ménage-à-Trois ('Retro vtroem'), dir. Petr Todorovskii, 1998

Moscow ('Moskva'), dir. Alexander Zeldovich, 2000

The Needle ('Igla'), dir. Rashid Nugmanov, 1988

The Parisian Cobbler ('Parizhskii sapozhnik'), dir. Fridrikh Ermler, 1928

The Path to Life ('Putevka v zhizn'), dir. Nikolai Ekk, 1931

Pliumbum or A Dangerous Game ('Pliumbum, ili opasnaia igra'), dir. Vadim Abdrashitov, 1987

Prediction ('Predskazanie'), dir. Eldar Riazanov, 1992

Private Life ('Chastnaia zhizn'), dir. Iulii Raizman, 1982

Red Guelder Rose ('Kalina krasnaia'), dir. Vasilii Shukshin, 1973

The Republic of ShKID ('Respublika ShKID'), dir. Gennadii Poloka, 1966

The Russia We Have Lost ('Rossiia, kotoruiu my poteriali'), dir. Stanislav Govorukhin, 1992

Scarecrow ('Chuchelo'), dir. Rolan Bykov, 1984

The Tailor from Torzhok ('Zakroishchik iz Torzhka'), dir. Iakov Protazanov, 1926

Taxi Blues ('Taksi-bliuz'), dir. Pavel Lungin, 1990

A Tender Age ('Nezhnyi vozrast'), dir. Sergei Solovev, 2000

There Lives Such a Lad ('Zhivet takoi paren'), dir. Vasilii Shukshin, 1964

A Time of Wishes ('Vremia zhelanii'), dir. Iulii Raizman, 1984

Tough Kids ('Patsany'), dir. Dinara Asanova, 1983

Tractor Drivers ('Traktoristy'), dir. Ivan Pyrev, 1939

Twilight of a Woman's Soul ('Sumerki zhenskoi dushi'), dir. Evgenii Bauer, 1913

The Voroshilov Sniper ('Voroshilovskii strelok'), dir. Stanislav Govorukhin, 1999

We'll Survive Till Monday ('Dozhivem do ponedelnika'), dir. Stanislav Rostotskii, 1968

The Wedding ('Svadba'), dir. Pavel Lungin, 2000

You Are My Only One ('Ty u menia odna'), dir. Dmitrii Astrakhan, 1993

Notes

1. It is estimated that dekulakisation, the collectivisation of agriculture, and the resulting famine had killed about fourteen million people between 1930 and 1937. (See Conquest (1986), pp. 306–7.)

2. Geoffrey Hosking notes: 'A prominent feature of the life of the Soviet people in the last generation or two has been sheer uprootedness. People have been torn from their moorings by war, urbanization, political oppression and the creation of a modern industry and a collectivized agriculture. In their millions they have been swept into factories, building sites, army barracks, labour camps, and then often pushed back out again into a world ill prepared to receive them. Their education has been scrappy, their work experience harsh, and little in the way of culture or settled family life has cushioned them against the bewildering peripetia of this existence. These are the people for whom Vasily Shukshin (1929–74) speaks.' (See Hosking, 1980, p. 162.)

3. Irina Shilova recalls her own response to this film on its release: 'This was a film about fear and the cost of disobedience. It was a film about the national genetic type as formed in socialist reality.' (See Shilova, 1993, p. 72.)

4. 'Dokladnaia zapiska Otdela Kultury TsK KPSS o filme Iu. Raizmana "A esli eto liubov?"', in Fomin, 1998, pp. 130–1.

5. 'Iz rechi N. S. Khrushcheva na vstreche rukovoditelei partii i pravitelstva s deiateliami literatury i iskusstva', in Fomin, 1998, p. 130.

6. In his otherwise rather self-congratulatory memoirs Anatolii Gladilin admits to the limited ambitions of 'youth prose' up to the key moment in 1962: 'It wasn't just Khrushchev's reforms, but the literary revolt of the youth that provoked the appearance in print of Solzhenitsyn's *One Day in the Life of Ivan Denisovich*. However, after *Ivan Denisovich*, the atmosphere changed abruptly. We were calling for a revolution in literature, but Solzhenitsyn in fact called for a revolutionary transformation of society. True, there were no direct revolutionary appeals in Solzhenitsyn's novella, but *Ivan Denisovich* transferred the emphasis of the struggle from literature to politics. And, of course, the foundations really started shaking then' (Gladilin, 1979, p. 102).

7. Benjamin Rifkin asserts the religious dimension: 'Lena's symbolic death and resurrection, her sacrifice in imitation of Christ, and her identification with Russia's cultural legacy and historical spiritual values – its medieval churches – are among the most important elements of the film's Christian subtext.' (See Rifkin, 1993, p. 191.)

CHAPTER NINE

Autobiography, memory and identity: the films of Andrei Tarkovskii

'Truth is in memory. He who has no memory has no life.'

(*Rasputin*, 1990, II, 351)

With the political imperative so dominant in Russian cinema of the Soviet period, the persistence of a personal, private sphere may seem incongruous. Sergei Eisenstein, perhaps the greatest film director in the Soviet Union, was interested above all in the 'big' themes of history, revolution and social progress. Andrei Tarkovskii, who can easily claim second place (and some would say first), has, more than any other Russian film-maker, empowered the personal, investing his images and symbols – although he himself would deny that they were as such – with an individual and intensely private significance that nevertheless spoke to millions of his fellow Russians. After all, his films are about those essentials that everyone has in common:

In all my pictures the theme of roots was always of great importance: links with family house, childhood, country, Earth. I always felt it important to establish that I myself belong to a particular tradition, culture, circle of people or ideas.

(*Tarkovsky*, 1991, p. 193)

Although his films concern themselves with issues dealt with in separate chapters in this book – the war, images of women, history and politics – it seems entirely appropriate to discuss them all collectively as the work of Russia's greatest *auteur* director.

Tarkovskii's favourite device is the mirror: the individual reflects his times and the times reflect upon the individual. After the release of *Mirror* (1974), which did not have much public discussion other than hostile criticism in the official media, Tarkovskii records how he received mail from people across the country, generally positive. He quotes a woman from Gorkii: 'Thank you

Oleg Iankovskii and Ignat Daniltsev in Mirror *(Andrei Tarkovskii, 1974)*

for *Mirror*. My childhood was like that . . . Only how did you know about it?' This reciprocation spurs him on:

> *One surely couldn't hope for greater acknowledgement of what one is doing. My most fervent wish has always been to be able to speak out in my films, to say everything with total sincerity and without imposing my own point of view on others. But if the vision of the world that has gone into the film turns out to be one that other people recognise as a part of themselves that up till now has never been given expression, what better motivation could there be for one's work?*

> *(Tarkovsky, 1991, p. 12)*

In other words, in a totalitarian culture the private assumes a social function, as it provides the forum for discussion and debate that could not be publicly envisaged.

Tarkovskii's films are autobiographical not only in that they are about his own life and ideas about art, but also because they are part of a peculiar Russian cultural tradition. It is generally accepted that autobiography traces not only the development of a creative consciousness, but also the interaction of that individual with the times. In Russia, however, the autobiography has assumed an additional function: it offers a comment on the times and shows how the life of the individual encapsulates and even symbolises the fate of a whole nation. We can trace this theme back to Alexander Herzen and his monumental *Past and Thoughts* (1852–69) and Maxim Gorkii's trilogy *My Childhood; My Apprenticeship; My Universities* (1913–23), which is acknowledged as a classic of the genre. Also, not for nothing does Anna Akhmatova claim in her epic poem *Requiem* (1935–40) to represent all the grieving women of Russia whose husbands have been devoured by the Gulag:

> О них вспоминаю всегда и везде,
> О них не забуду и в новой беде,
> И если зажмут мой измученный рот,
> Которым кричит стомильонный народ,
> Пусть так же они поминают меня
> В канун моего погребального дня.

> (Of them I recall always and everywhere,
> Of them I will not forget even in my new woe,
> Even if they gag my tortured mouth,
> Through which a hundred million people cry,
> Let them then so remember me,
> On the eve of my funeral.)

> *(Akhmatova, 1998, III, 29)*[1]

Andrei Tarkovskii was born in 1932 and his childhood coincided with the war. His childhood is one of the major motifs in *Mirror*. In 1951 he finished his schooling and enrolled in university to study Arabic. He gave up, however, after one year and, after a period of time working with geologists in Siberia, was accepted in 1954 to study under the director Mikhail Romm in the State Cinematography Institute in Moscow. His graduation film, *The Steamroller and the Violin*, was made in 1960, and this was followed in 1962 by his first feature film, *Ivan's Childhood*. In the next two decades, up to his death in 1986, Tarkovskii made another six feature films. *Andrei Rublev* was made in 1966, but only released in the USSR in 1971, followed by *Solaris* in 1972, *Mirror* in 1975 and *Stalker*, his last film made in the Soviet Union in 1979. He travelled to Italy several times between 1979 and 1983 to make *Nostalgia* (1983) and a documentary, *Time of Travels* (1982). In 1985 he was diagnosed with terminal cancer, and he died in December 1986, shortly after the completion (in Sweden) and release of his last film, *The Sacrifice*.

Ivan's Childhood depicts the war through the eyes of a child, the orphaned Ivan Bondarev, and is part of a tradition exemplified by Elem Klimov's *Come and See* (1985). Moreover, it can more readily be seen as a remake of – and riposte to – Vasilii Pronin's 1946 socialist realist *Son of the Regiment*, based on the novella of the same name by Valentin Kataev. In Pronin's film Vania is a young orphan boy nicknamed 'little shepherd' by the regiment that adopts him. He becomes not only their mascot, but the adopted son of Captain Enakiev, who lost his son at approximately the same age as Vania is now. Enakiev is killed in action and this event serves as Vania's rite of passage as he is accepted as an officer cadet and is finally seen as part of the victory parade on Red Square.

Son of the Regiment shows the war as a straightforward battle of good and evil, where even the German women are cruel and sadistic. Red Army soldiers are heroes all, as the medals festooning their tunics show. The Russian countryside is bathed in moonlight and heavily romanticised. Tarkovskii's film debunks all these images and the associated heroic symbolism.

Tarkovskii's title is, of course, ironic, as Ivan's childhood has, in effect, ended with him as an orphan. Ivan works on the front line as a spy, gathering information on German troop movements for Captain Kholin of the Red Army. The landscape he works in is blasted and wretched and despite the assumed inevitability of the Soviet victory, there is no upbeat ending. The narrative is also broken up into different strands, the most vivid being Ivan's dreams/memories of a sun-drenched idyllic time before the war, gazing down a well with his mother or gathering apples in a rainstorm.

The film observes the conventions of the war film genre only to a certain extent. The patriotic theme of sacrifice for the Motherland is observed: Kholin is killed, as is the old retainer Katasonych, and we learn at the very end, when

Lieutenant Galtsev finds Ivan's photograph among military files in Berlin, that Ivan has been hanged. The sufferings of the people are paraded before us, as a crazed old peasant mourns the loss of his family in his bombed-out house, with only the stove (a symbol of domesticity and spiritual strength) remaining upright. 'Lord, when will this all end?' he asks.

Similarly, the music of the film – which is sparsely used – is Russian folk music, a clear patriotic motif, right down to the singing of the popular song 'Katiusha' that signifies the end of the war and the Soviet victory. Elsewhere there are church bells – abandoned religious icons are part of the collateral damage littering the landscape – and a gently cascading harp melody signals Ivan's 'return' to his childhood memories/dreams.

Otherwise, this is not a typical Soviet war film. There are no great battles, although this is in line with the trend during the thaw, and we see no Germans other than ghostly figures passing Ivan in the forest at night. War is above all an eerie, almost abstract spectacle, as we see flares burst and bullets sing through the air, bombs tear holes in the earth and trees collapse. There are some startling images, such as a plane that has nose-dived into the ground sticking out upright.

Rather, seeming opposites come together. We are never quite sure whether the sunlit images of childhood we see are Ivan's memories or his dreams. The natural setting of trees, fields and water – we first see Ivan's face through a spider's web in a forest – is grotesquely juxtaposed with a picture of Ivan wading through a flooded wintry forest as he moves between the German and Russian lines. Kholin carries on a romantic liaison with the nurse Masha in a birch forest and their relationship is a symbol of the unity of the country in its war effort: he is from Krasnoiarsk in Siberia, where the artist Surikov lived for a while, as he maintains, she from Peredelkino just outside Moscow, where the writer Alexei Tolstoi, she says, can be seen taking his walks. Fire and water are placed not in opposition, but apposition, as Ivan takes a bath with a fire burning in the background. Water and fire are soon to become among Tarkovskii's favourite images. Contrary to the conventions of the genre, Germans are not demonised, as Ivan reads through some captured art books and dwells particularly on Dürer's disturbing engraving *The Four Horsemen of the Apocalypse* of 1498.

But the film is remarkable above all for its sheer stylistic virtuosity and the director's evocation of images that offer evidence of great cinematic vision and imagination. When Ivan's mother is killed by the well, water splashes on to her body like a grotesque parody of gushing blood, an image that looks forward to one in *Andrei Rublev* when a saw pulsates in rhythm to the cut artery of a dying man. When Ivan collects apples in a storm, the trees are lit up by lightning and rain patters on the apples that are then munched by horses. The horse will also feature in Tarkovskii's later work, as a symbol of both artistic freedom and apocalyptic death. The final image is of a dead tree on a beach, as Ivan basks in his sun-kissed, carefree childhood, a reminder of the devastated trees of wartime and a future pointer to the end of Ivan's innocence.

After *Ivan's Childhood* Tarkovskii attempted a historical epic, the three-hour *Andrei Rublev*. This film, however, although it observes the conventions of the historical film, is not solely about the life of Russia's most famous icon painter (1360–1430). In films about artists we are accustomed to seeing how great canvases are created, the inspiration behind them and the development of the artist's personality. In Tarkovskii's film we get none of this, we never see him paint, neither do we get to know much about his life. Rather, the director focuses on the interaction of the artist and his repressive, brutal age.

Rublev is not the only artist on show, and when the film begins we see another man taking off in a home-made balloon. Thus, in the very beginning of the film we are presented with a metaphor for the impetus and drive of the creative imagination. The (literally) uplifting experience is short lived, however, as the balloon crashes to earth after a few exhilarating moments in the air, with horses stampeding on the ground. When the balloon falls, the camera turns to a horse thrashing about in pain, a metaphor for thwarted artistic ambition. Other artists in the film are summarily dealt with by the powers that be. Stonemasons are blinded so that they can no longer create images of beauty and a bawdy jester has half his tongue cut out as punishment for singing ditties poking fun at the Grand Prince.

For Andrei, as for the jester, art should give the people, oppressed and brutalised as they are, images that counter the fear in their lives, whereas his teacher Theophanes the Greek insists that the people are ignorant and primitive and should be forever reminded of the Last Judgement. For Theophanes, the purpose of art is to keep people in their place before God and remind them of their subservience to a higher authority. Andrei is unable to paint sinners boiling in pitch and, as the vivid and startling technicolor epilogue makes clear, revels in clear and bright splashes of colour that celebrate the beauty of God's world.

Tarkovskii's film not only shows the trials and tribulations of the artist, but also his triumph. In order to achieve true inner freedom, the artist must sacrifice part or all of himself, in line with Orthodox theology. The artist is a Christ figure, giving of himself so that the people become free and the Saviour we see is a demonstrably Russian Christ, crucified in a wintry landscape on a hillside that seems to run with blood. Images of mock crucifixion abound, as when Andrei is tied up on a post by the pagans whose celebrations he disturbs, and the jester is knocked unconscious by two soldiers, holding him by each arm, who throw him head first against a tree trunk. Andrei takes a vow of silence after killing a man and has his faith in God's world restored by a miracle: the creation of a huge bell ('a festival for the people') by a young boy with no experience or prior knowledge of how to build one.

Andrei Rublev, however, is more than a parable about the artist, his sufferings and his creativity in repressive times. It is also about Rublev's place in Russian culture and Russia's place in the world. As Rublev and the 'master' bellmaker Boriska create things of beauty for the people and Russia emerges from the dark ages with the victory over the Tartars at Kulikovo in 1380 – significantly, an event of enormous importance in Russian history not even hinted at in the film – so it opens out to the outside world, as Italian ambassadors arrive to inspect the bell at the end of the film.

The problems inherent in making a historical film, especially one based on an individual vision of history that has little to do with the Party's insistence on class antagonism and economic determinism, can be seen in the 'review' of the film by the Party's Central Committee. The film, it announced, had a 'misguided conception', it was 'anti-historical' in that not enough was shown about the people's struggle against the Mongol yoke, there is no mention of the 'high level of culture', the development of manufacturing and industry or the growth of major cities such as Vladimir, Suzdal, Tver and Moscow. In other words, if facts (suitably tailored, of course) were missing, it could not be history: 'The film's ideological erroneousness is not open to doubt' (Fomin, 1998, p. 147), concluded the Party.

Tarkovskii's next film, strange as it may sound, is also very much about earth, roots and belonging. Touted as the Soviet Union's reply to Kubrick's 1968 film *2001: A Space Odyssey*, *Solaris* has the trappings of a science fiction film. It is set on a space station above the planet Solaris, but it features few special effects or dramatic episodes. Rather, outer space is simply the backdrop to a philosophical reflection on man's relationship with the earth, his home and his family. As in *Andrei Rublev*, a central role in man's life and ambitions is assigned to art.

Solaris is also a film about love and emotional contact, about the qualities of human life that can only be experienced and not explained by science or rational thought. Kris Kelvin is a psychologist travelling to the Solaris space station to investigate abnormalities in the crew's behaviour. He finds that one of them (Gibarian) has committed suicide, while the other two (Snout and Sartorius) seem to be mentally unbalanced. The ocean of Solaris is responsible for this disorientation, as it brings to life aspects or characters from the individual's past life or subconscious. Kelvin sees his ex-wife Hari, who committed suicide ten years previously, again by his side. He can return to Earth only when he has confronted his past, his conscience and become whole again.

So although ostensibly a sci-fi rumination on the impact of scientific discovery on human life, *Solaris* is, in fact, an anti-science film, asserting the superiority of art and poetry. Brueghel, Bach, Leonardo da Vinci, Cervantes,

Dostoevskii are all cited in detail throughout the film. Sartorius argues for the need to acquire knowledge in order to dominate nature, echoing official Soviet ideology of 'the greatness of science' (and repeated here). However, his fellow scientist Snout renounces his calling, as he says: 'We don't need other worlds, we need a mirror, man needs man.' The conflict in the film is between the soul and the mind, the spirit and the intellect. Man will destroy what he does not understand, as the scientists on Earth argue for the termination of the Solaris project. Culture provides the link between past and present and it is significant that the only soundtrack in the entire film is Bach's Choral Prelude in F Minor, used sparingly in moments when Kelvin's past comes alive.

The film has its own symmetry. The present can only be experienced if the past is integrated into it and so the beginning and end of the film both depict tentacle-like reeds under water, both a premonition and a reminder of the flowing locks of Hari's hair. So, too, at the end of the film we see the same images as at the beginning: Kelvin's house in the country, his garden and pond, his father and faithful dog. Tarkovskii gives nature human form, the Solaris ocean moves and ripples like a living body and is regarded by the scientists as a brain. Elsewhere visual similes create a natural symmetry: the folds of a duvet move and ripple as if they are composed of water and strips of paper tied to a ventilator rustle like leaves at night. Kelvin can return to Earth only when he has confronted his own conscience and feeling of guilt for Hari's drug overdose. Images of the two women he has loved – Hari and his mother – converge, just as the islands in the Solaris ocean are seen to come together towards the end of the film. But the home Kelvin returns to remains an island, cut off from the rest of humanity.

The unity of mankind is served by art, as Tarkovskii has himself affirmed:

Moreover, the great function of art is communication, since mutual understanding is a force to unite people, and the spirit of communion is one of the most important aspects of artistic creativity. Works of art, unlike those of science, have no practical goals in any material sense. Art is a meta-language, with the help of which people try to communicate with one other; to impart information about themselves and assimilate the experience of others. Again, this has nothing to do with practical advantage but with realising the idea of love, the meaning of which is sacrifice: the very antithesis of pragmatism.

(*Tarkovsky, 1991, pp. 39–40*)

Solaris is Tarkovskii's warning of the dangers for humanity when contact between individuals breaks down. It is ironic, of course, that man in the space age has to travel beyond his own planet in order to understand himself and confront his own inner being. Kelvin makes emotional contact with the planet when Hari is 'resurrected', whereas both Snout and Sartorius seek to make intellectual contact and fail. The very possibility of such contact spurs Gibarian to suicide even before the film starts. The importance of the soul and the danger of pure reason are the twin interlocking concepts at the heart of Tarkovskii's other 'science fiction' film, *Stalker*.

Stalker also features the confrontation of soul and intellect, art and science. The stalker of the title is a man with the ability to negotiate 'the zone', a place supposedly irradiated and made uninhabitable after being visited by extra-terrestrials years before. He is commissioned by two men, the unnamed scientist and writer, to take them through the zone and into its centre, a room where one's deepest wishes can come true. We learn that a previous stalker called Dikobraz ('Porcupine') committed suicide when he encountered the room, as he had understood his innermost desire to see the death of his brother in order to inherit his wealth. The writer hopes for artistic inspiration, the scientist expects the knowledge he gains will enable him to make great discoveries. In the end, we understand that he is preparing to destroy the room, a reminder of the scientists who wish to destroy the Solaris project in the earlier film.

The film's theme, of course, lends itself to various allegorical interpreta-tions. The zone could be one of radiation contamination after a nuclear holocaust, a view supported by the stalker's genetically defective daughter called Martyshka ('Monkey'), who cannot walk but can move objects telekinetically. The 'zone' also is used to denote the territory of a Russian labour camp in the Gulag and, by analogy, the Soviet Union itself. The tortuous efforts of the trio to get through the barbed wire and machine-guns and reach the room can be taken as the difficult path to truth and reason in a totalitarian society. However, the film's virtues are above all in its visual style.

As the three pass through into the zone they leave behind the black and white dreariness of an industrial wasteland and enter a green and vibrant landscape of trees, bushes and fields, scarred by man's hand but nevertheless recognisable as a natural wilderness. As the stalker rests, he has a dream where water flows over artefacts of twentieth-century strife, including cartridge shells, guns, icons, syringes. The stalker is guarded by a mysterious black dog that watches over him as he sleeps. He lies on a tiny island of earth surrounded by water, temporarily cut off from his companions and the rest of humanity – another throwback to the central image of *Solaris*.

The stalker has a profound, emotional feeling for the land and topography of the zone, so much that it often takes him away from the wife who clearly adores him. He breathes in its air and smells and embraces the earth as if his bride. He worships its contours and deeply respects its abilities to confuse and endanger the unwary (although we see nothing of its supposed dangers in the film). He is an embodiment of sheer spirituality, scorning material wealth and with only the barest of home comforts. The writer at one point pours scorn on him by donning a mock crown of thorns fashioned out of barbed wire. The scientist and the writer remain rationalistic and sceptical and their lack of faith prevents them from gaining any self-knowledge in their encounter with the room. In the end the three go their separate ways, the stalker disappointed that his companions have gained no enlightenment, the other two left cold by the experience, for them it has been a waste of time.

Mirror is also about the need for faith and communication, as the film's prologue makes explicit: a boy with a terrible stutter is, through therapy, returned to normal speech: 'I can speak,' he announces proudly and fluently. The film was criticised as 'elitist' by the official media and allowed only a limited release. It is in places esoteric and some knowledge on the viewer's part of Tarkovskii's own childhood and youth, and of contemporary Soviet history, is helpful. Tarkovskii accompanies his personal odyssey with documentary signposts of the times: Russian troops crossing the Sivash river during the war; the explosion of the first atomic bomb in 1945; the Cultural Revolution in China and border clashes between Soviet and Chinese troops in the late 1960s. But it is a film that is accessible to viewers (the previously mentioned woman from Gorkii is a perfect example) not on an intellectual level, but an emotional, even subconscious one, with its themes of childhood, roots and identity. What the director is offering is his own life as a 'mirror' of the age, a reflection of the national experience.

But Tarkovskii is not content here simply to contribute a somewhat self-indulgent if erudite essay on the nature of autobiography. Through his use of images and a multi-layered narrative and the constant interplay of dream and reality, he is reinventing the genre and asserting an individual vision of art and reality fundamentally at odds with the requirements of culture in a totalitarian society.

It is, of course, a profoundly personal film. Not only does it revolve around the director's own childhood, complete with a reconstruction of the rural home he shared with his mother and sister when he was a boy, but it also features his mother playing herself and the poems of his father Arsenii Tarkovskii inserted into the 'text' of the film at several key moments. Margarita Terekhova plays both the wife of the director (here called Alexei) and his mother as she is recalled in the past and Ignat Daniltsev plays both Ignat, Alexei's son in the present, and the young Alexei (Alesha) in one important scene.

The symmetry is not just in the casting, but also in the director's sensuous depiction of his rural childhood. A rustic scene is introduced by the sounds of a dog barking and a distant railway engine. The same sounds occur in the film's finale, set in the same rural location, Tarkovskii's country house. Here nature breathes and moves as air rustles through foliage and sudden gusts of wind signal the beginning of a storm. At the beginning of the film the doctor, played by Anatolii Solonitsyn, wonders whether nature can 'understand' and 'feel'. There are ghostly images where dream and reality overlap, of Terekhova's zombie-like appearance with her wet hair covering her face and arms outstretched. Water drips from a roof in the foreground as a barn blazes away in the background. We will be reminded of this startling image in the 'present' when, later in the film Ignat lights a fire in the yard outside his feuding parents' apartment during a rainshower.

This symmetry stretches also to the film's thematic motifs. The Leningrad boy Asafev has lost both his parents in the blockade, a mirror image of the Spanish children in newsreel footage about to be separated from their parents in the Spanish Civil War. Terekhova as Alexei's wife Natalia looks through some old photographs and notes how much she resembles Alexei's mother. She looks in the mirror and sees the director's own mother, Mariia Tarkovskaia, staring back at her. Past and present are not so easily separated, as the Spanish exiles feel nostalgia and pain for the homeland they will never see again and Alexei's past and present constantly interrupt each other. His mother's anxious telephone call to him, announcing the death of her former work colleague Elizaveta Pavlovna, abruptly plunges us into her memories of the 1930s, when a supposed typographical error in a state publication could have disastrous consequences for the whole printing house. As the foreman says: 'Some people will work, some people will be afraid.' Tarkovskii uses light and shadow to suggest the evil of the time, the near-hysterical fear it could provoke and the sense of elation when the all clear is given.

The historical past is also relevant today. The quickly disappearing stain on the table from a tea cup reminds Ignat that perhaps he has not read Pushkin's letter to Petr Chaadaev to a ghost. Pushkin's letter (written in October 1836) offers a meditation on Russia's place and role within Europe, as a reply to Chaadaev who believed that the way forward for Russia to become a modern European state was to adopt Roman Catholicism. Pushkin's letter contains a fierce assertion of Russia's strength and 'mission':

Of course the schism separated us from the rest of Europe and we took no part in any of the great events which stirred her; but we have had our own mission. It was Russia who contained the Mongol conquest within her vast expanses. The Tartars did not dare cross our western frontiers and so leave us in their rear. They retreated towards their deserts, and Christian civilization was saved. To this end we were obliged to lead a completely separate existence which, while it left us Christian, also made us complete strangers in the Christian world, so that our martyrdom never impinged upon the energetic development of Catholic Europe.

(Tarkovsky, 1991, p. 195)

In the more recent past, Tarkovskii's use of newsreel footage suggests that Russia also saved twentieth-century Western Europe and the world from, first, the Nazis and, second, the Chinese, Russian soldiers literally keeping back the tide of screaming Red Guards with interlocked arms. For Tarkovskii, Russia and Europe may be separated by history, but culturally they have much in common, as images of his childhood are accompanied by Bach's organ and choral music and he creates on film a Brueghel landscape out of a scene of children playing on a snowy hillside, with moving figures caught in the foreground and richly detailed background.

The symmetry, and potential unity, ends there, however, for Tarkovskii cannot reconcile some elements in his life and work. His father will not return to his mother, however much he may have dreamed of this, and Alexei will not return to Natalia. Human affairs are not as easily managed as historical patterns or aesthetic criteria.

The desire to reconcile the irreconcilable lies at the heart of *Nostalgia*, where the writer Gorchakov – another cipher for the director – brings Russia to Italy, but is unable, like the composer Sosnovskii, whose life he is researching, to take Italy back to Russia. The sense of melancholy announced in the title is present from the start of the film. If in *Mirror* Tarkovskii films the Russian countryside of his childhood memories as a living and breathing organism, where the camera – the viewer's eye – ultimately returns to the depths of the primordial forest, the Tuscan countryside of *Nostalgia* is grey and lifeless, enveloped in mists which obscure any sense of visual scale or perspective. Indeed, Gorchakov's memories of his rural Russian home, always in black and white, are full of people, vibrant sounds and heartfelt folk song, whereas this Tuscany is austere, bereft of the beauty with which it is usually associated. Gorchakov himself says half-jokingly that he is tired of 'beautiful landscapes'. Shots of the Italian landscape are accompanied by the metallic grating sounds of a distant buzz saw. The only perspectives we see are in private places, such as in rooms and through doors and windows, but not in the public space.

Almost everything in Italy is superficial and empty, including Gorchakov's beautiful intepreter Eugenia. She speaks little Russian in the film, as Gorchakov insists that she speak Italian to him and she even admits to reading Russian poetry in translation. The poems are by Arsenii Tarkovskii, one of the Soviet Union's foremost poets and the director's father. Gorchakov counters that poetry can only be understood in the original language and this exchange serves as a metonym for the overlying theme, as articulated by these two characters: the West does not understand Russia and Russia cannot be accommodated in the West. Eugenia tries to seduce him, but is unable to understand why she is rejected; to her, all men are just 'pigs'. The director consciously makes fun of her when, in Rome, she is dressed as a solemn office executive (emancipated, in the Western way) and she proudly says that her

Oleg Iankovskii and Erland Josephson in Nostalgia *(Andrei Tarkovskii, 1983)*

boyfriend Vittorio, of an affluent family, is interested in 'spiritual matters' and is leaving with her for a tour of India. Tarkovskii equates her aspirations and lifestyle as the symptom of a materialistic society that has lost sight of true ideals and spiritual values.

It is not just Eugenia who is mocked. Tarkovskii even has a local denigrate Italian music with its 'false sentimental wails', preferring Chinese music. The West is viewed from an alienated and thus negative viewpoint (Tarkovskii's own), so that images of Catholicism have an ironic meaning. Birds fly from the womb of a statue of the Madonna of Childbirth, Gorchakov's Russian wife is called Maria and the Italian girl he speaks to in the half-submerged house is called Angela. But even this 'angel' cannot keep him from his (demon) bottle of vodka.

Yet Russia and Italy merge in Gorchakov's increasingly dislocated consciousness and he begins to confuse images of Eugenia and his wife. As Eugenia and Gorchakov talk in a hotel corridor, a lady with a dog – right out of Chekhov's story set in Yalta – walks past. Another dog, an Alsatian, appears both in Tuscany and in Gorchakov's memories of his home. Bird feathers fall from the sky at the start of the film and one falls again as Gorchakov wakes up after drinking some vodka; in the film's final scene snow falls gently to the ground and the viewer always wonders what Gorchakov's own 'white feather patch' on his otherwise auburn head 'signifies'. What does bring the two cultures closer together, in Gorchakov's mind, is the character of the recluse Domenico.

The locals think Domenico is mad and we see in flashback the moment when his children were forcibly removed from him. He had kept them and his wife imprisoned in their house for seven years, fearing a nuclear catastrophe and the end of the world. But to Gorchakov he is one of God's 'holy fools' who divines the truth of the world and tries to save it. Before he wanted only to save his family, now he is preparing a sacrifice to save mankind. This martyrdom is the manifestation of a spirituality Gorchakov can understand and identify with, and it is not long before he dreams of looking in a mirror and seeing not his own reflection, but that of Domenico. Gorchakov in Russian thinks (as 'I') the thoughts of Domenico, as he regrets locking his family up for so long. Domenico owns an Alsatian dog identical to the one Gorchakov recalls in his memories of Russia.

The interior of Domenico's house speaks to Gorchakov of a Russian landscape, with mounds of earth resembling hills and trees and the dripping water seen and heard in *Mirror* accompanying their conversation. The fire–water motif of the earlier film again comes into play, as Domenico had tried to carry a lighted candle through the waters of the Bagno Vignoni as an act of faith. Domenico displays the total disregard for material wealth that we saw in the stalker's home.

He sacrifices himself to bring people together, but his words that 'society should be united and not fragmented' are not heeded by the Italian public, standing in isolated and static poses, and they gaze on indifferently as he plunges to the ground ablaze. Only his imbecile surrogate mirror image and his Alsatian affect any pain at the sight, accompanied by the distorted and halting strings of Beethoven's Ode to Joy. At about the same time, when Gorchakov carries the lighted candle across the now dried-up pool, the locals remain totally dispassionate when he falls dead to the ground. This is his sacrifice – but for what?

Gorchakov had come to Italy in order to research the life of the Russian serf musician Pavel Sosnovskii, who in the eighteenth century had committed suicide when he returned to Russia. Gorchakov finds his 'mirror' in Domenico, who gives him a spiritual dimension to a soulless society and Gorchakov's death 'mirrors' that of Sosnovskii. We also know that Sosnovskii took to drinking heavily just before he died, an action that Gorchakov emulates. Neither Domenico nor Gorchakov achieves anything other than a symbolic act of sacrifice. Only in death can Gorchakov merge Italy and Russia, as his rural Russian home is gradually embraced by the huge walls of a Catholic cathedral in the final scene.[2]

We should also note here the apparent tension in Tarkovskii's theories and his actual method. In *Sculpting in Time* Tarkovskii consistently rejects any notion of symbolism, yet his films are full of symbols and allegorical narratives. Similarly, he dismisses 'montage cinema' – 'that editing brings together two concepts and thus engenders a new, third one' – as 'incompatible with the nature of cinema' (Tarkovsky, 1991, p. 114). Yet both *Mirror* and especially *Nostalgia* rely heavily not on narrative development, let alone a 'plot', but on the visual and emotional associations aroused in the viewer. This is particularly evident in the intellectual montage where juxtapositions suggest ideas, such as the closing shot of the *izba*-in-cathedral, but also in the images of animals: horses and dogs to suggest death, freedom or loyalty.

Style, therefore, is almost everything. In *Nostalgia* there are several very long takes, culminating in the uninterrupted eight-minute sequence when Gorchakov carries the lighted candle across the pool of Bagno Vignoni. Light and shadow often frame the mise-en-scène, alluding to Gorchakov's split consciousness as he lies in bed in Italy, recollecting Russia. Certain motifs hark back to Tarkovskii's previous films, such as the bicycle lying under water like the many objects viewed in the Stalker's dream or the image of Gorchakov wading waist deep in water, rather like the boy spy in *Ivan's Childhood*. The barking of dogs in the Russian rustic background also reminds us of the beginning and end of *Mirror*.

There is some confusion in Tarkovskii's more important motifs, especially death and suicide. Domenico's suicide is the supreme sacrifice that is meant to save the world; examples of martyrdom are numerous in *Andrei Rublev*. Yet elsewhere suicide is shorn of its positive spiritual dimension, for Dikobraz's suicide in *Stalker* is an act of sheer desperation born of self-disgust. In *Solaris*, Hari overdoses because she thinks Kris no longer loves her and Gibarian kills himself as he is afraid of confronting the inner demons the planet may unleash. The notion of sacrifice, so important in Orthodox religion, reaches its fullest development in Tarkovskii's final film, aptly entitled *The Sacrifice*.

The 'sacrifice' is what Alexander, the central character, must perform in order to save the world. He prays to the Lord, accepting the need to sacrifice his home and his relationship with the boy, Little Man, if it can save his family and friends. This he does, by burning down his beloved home at the end of the film (amid a landscape of puddles and pools that reflect the blaze). Alexander is a former actor who has played Dostoevskii's Prince Myshkin (Tarkovskii made no secret of the fact that he wished to film *The Idiot*), as well as Shakespeare's Richard III. Both of these characters are tragic heroes, doomed and unable to escape their historical destiny. The world, as we become aware, is on the brink of nuclear conflagration and the distant thunderstorm in the early part of the film is a harbinger of the deafening roar of passing jet fighters that will later rock the house.

Erland Josephson in The Sacrifice *(Andrei Tarkovskii, 1986)*

Alexander is another version of the 'holy fool' Domenico in *Nostalgia* and, significantly, is also played by the same actor, Erland Josephson. His monologues are diatribes against the materialism of the modern world and its lack of spirituality. He finds beauty only in art, be it pictures of Russian icons or Leonardo da Vinci's 'Adoration of the Magi', for here there is real 'spirituality'. He is regarded as mentally ill by his friends and family, who, after he has set his house ablaze, finally have him taken away in an ambulance. Yet Alexander, like Domenico, can only be understood on a spiritual, even metaphysical plane, one again informed by Russian Orthodox thought. Alexander is a seer, a man who understands the truth of the world and is pained by what he sees around him. When he hears news of the nuclear stand-off that will threaten civilisation, it is his chance to act, it is the moment he has been waiting for all his life. Words are no longer needed, only deeds.

Alexander, like Domenico, neither understands nor is understood by the people around him. His wife Adelaide may be having an affair with the doctor, Victor, and his stepdaughter Marta and housekeeper Julia ignore him. His only human contacts are with the postman Otto, with whom he engages in meaningless pseudo-philosophical debates, Little Man, with whom he plants and waters a dead tree and the 'witch' Maria, the family maid, who can 'heal' his pain with her own body and soul.

As elsewhere in Tarkovskii's work, the style of the film is self-consciously elaborate. The opening shot is over ten minutes long, as it follows Alexander and Little Man planting and watering a dead tree on the coast and then moving inland. The film has little soundtrack, other than flutes, Japanese and Russian folk music heard as if in the distance, but it is framed at the beginning and end by Bach's 'Ebarme Dich' from the St Matthew Passion. There is one long tracking shot, similar to one in *Stalker*, of discarded items in an apocalyptic landscape, with running water, an abandoned and smashed-up car and debris. Most of the film is, indeed, shot indoors and there is hardly any of the perspective through doors and windows that are a feature of, say, *Mirror* or *Nostalgia*.

This sense of enclosed space is heightened when the characters are cut off from the outside world, when the television and telephone no longer work. They begin to confront the truth of their own lives, Adelaide has a nervous fit reminiscent of the one experienced by the stalker's wife and a feeling of approaching doom increases. Otto collapses and seems dead, but then revives, like Hari in *Solaris*. Other motifs suggest a breakdown in human communication, such as a telephone ringing in another room but being unanswered.

Tarkovskii also includes dream sequences, as when Alexander dreams that he flies over the heads of panic-stricken, fleeing people, or when he sleeps with Maria and they are both lifted in the air, like Kris and Hari in their gravity-free 'dance' in *Solaris*. Alexander also dreams of a wintry landscape, with bare trees and sodden earth that is then blasted by heat and fire. Significantly, when he wakes from his last dream he sees himself full length in a mirror, as if for the first time.

Tarkovskii's themes here remain consistent with those of *Stalker*. Man is faced with his own destruction because he has lost his link with nature. Alexander tells Maria how he visited his ageing mother and tidied up her garden, but then cried when he saw that he had taken away its natural beauty and made it artificial. Such, it would seem, is the fate of Europe, as nuclear powers face up to each other. Escape is possible for Viktor, who has been offered a post in Australia (the significance of the name Adelaide is obvious here) and Alexander himself prefers Japanese clothing and music.

But there is hope at the end of this film about despondency and the end of things. Little Man continues to water the tree of life and he closes the film by citing and questioning Genesis: 'In the beginning was the Word. Why is that, papa?' Dialogue and communication can bring about understanding and acceptance, and, as Dostoevskii said: 'Beauty will save the world.'

The films of Andrei Tarkovskii are to be appreciated not only on the level of aesthetic perception, but on a deeper, emotional plane and in the light of Christian ideas of moral duty and commitment. His cinema is fundamentally at odds with the requirements of an avowedly atheistic and totalitarian state and his achievement remains not only a cinematic one, but also one of moral resistance.

Tarkovskii rejects his times, he is a film-maker researching his own past as a means of understanding the present, using his own memory to gauge the national experience. As a profoundly Russian artist and thinker, he attempts to reconcile seemingly disparate strands, to seek a metaphysical unity of idea and action: 'In the end Tarkovsky demonstrates the need for both word and image in the unique, organic combination that only the cinema can achieve' (Johnson and Petrie, 1994, p. 261).

Filmography

Andrei Rublev, dir. Andrei Tarkovskii, 1966 (released in USSR 1971)
Ivan's Childhood ('Ivanovo detstvo'), dir. Andrei Tarkovskii, 1962
Mirror ('Zerkalo'), dir. Andrei Tarkovskii, 1974
Nostalgia ('Nostalgiia'), dir. Andrei Tarkovskii, 1983
The Sacrifice ('Zhertvoprinoshenie'), dir. Andrei Tarkovskii, 1986
Solaris ('Soliaris'), dir. Andrei Tarkovskii, 1972
Son of the Regiment ('Syn polka'), dir. Vasilii Pronin, 1946
Stalker ('Stalker'), dir. Andrei Tarkovskii, 1979
The Steamroller and the Violin ('Katok i skripka'), dir. Andrei Tarkovskii, 1960
Time of Travels ('Vremia puteshestvii'), dir. Andrei Tarkovskii, 1982
2001: A Space Odyssey, dir. Stanley Kubrick, 1968

Notes

1. David Wells comments: '[. . .] Akhmatova remained keenly aware of her responsibility as a poet in the long tradition of Russian poetry, to speak out on social, moral and political issues. By the 1930s she felt more than ever that she was one of the few people still able and willing to chronicle the era through which she was living, and to keep alive the literary traditions of the past.' (See Wells, 1996, p. 64.)
2. Tarkovskii himself seemed unsure as to the 'meaning' of this metaphor, rejecting any notion of 'vulgar symbolism': 'I would concede that the final shot of *Nostalgia* has an element of metaphor, when I bring the Russian house inside the Italian cathedral. It is a constructed image which smacks of literariness: a model of the hero's state, of the division within him which prevents him from living as he has up till now. Or perhaps, on the contrary, it is his new wholeness in which the Tuscan hills and the Russian countryside come together indissolubly; he is conscious of them as his own, merged into his being and his blood, but at the same time reality is enjoining him to separate these things by returning to Russia' (Tarkovsky, 1991, pp. 213–16).

It remains to be said, of course, that some films fall outside the domain of genre and, even in the confined spaces of Soviet film production, gems of individual non-conformism were made. One of the very first oddities to hit the Soviet screen was Iakov Protazanov's 1924 science fiction film *Aelita*. Ostensibly about a radio message received from Mars and the efforts of earthmen to bring about revolution and social justice in outer space, it turns out, in fact, to be nothing more than the dream of the main character. Social progress is subverted, but the film's real interest lies in the massive sets designed by the Constructivist Alexander Rodchenko and the exotic, out-landish costumes by Alexandra Exter, used for the scenes set on Mars. Indeed, the flight of imagination that takes the hero away from Earth leads to imagery that is in stark contrast to the grim and impoverished police state on Earth. *Aelita* was attacked by the critics at the time and it is outspoken in its criticism of NEP society and its rulers. Like Tarkovskii's excursions into science fiction, *Aelita* remains defiantly above and beyond genre and way ahead of its time, with its blend of satire, comedy, dream, adventure and erotica. But it serves another function: in the earliest years of Soviet power, it suggested that revolution and fundamental change were illusory, simply dream and fantasy. Of course, Protazanov was not to know that it would, in fact, become the stuff of nightmare.

So much for those films that were actually made, in whatever difficult circumstances and whatever their post-production, distribution and censor-ship problems. A final word should be reserved for those films that were *not* made, given the documentation that has recently been made publicly available. We can therefore define Soviet cinema not only by what it was, but by what it was not. Thus, Goskino refused to allow adaptations of Lev Tolstoi's *Hadji Murad* (written between 1896 and 1904 and published posthumously), about a Caucasian tribesman working for the Russian army, because it was too bloody and Gogol's *Taras Bulba* (1842), about Polish–Ukrainian rivalry, because it was anti-Polish. A film project about the life of Ghenghiz Khan was scrapped because it was feared to be anti-Russian (Fomin, 1996, p. 334). In other words, complex films about inter-ethnic relations were playing on too raw a nerve. The Central Committee of the Party reacted negatively to a Soviet–Rumanian project to film the life of the Moldovian aristocrat Dmitrii Kantemir:

> *The images of Kantemir and Peter I essentially serve as simply a pretext for an adventure film, the pseudo-historical core of which only discredits an important theme. Moreover, the screenplay expresses a groundless concept echoed in the current policy of the leaders of Rumania, to the effect that the great powers, including Russia, toyed with the destiny of Moldova regardless of the interests of its people. If this film was done only by a Rumanian film studio then we would at least be able to understand how they are inspired by the ideas of profaning Moldovan history and Moldova's traditional links with Russia. But in the case of a joint production such an approach is inadmissible.*
>
> *(Fomin, 1998, pp. 152–3)*

But perhaps the greatest loss to Soviet Russian cinema was the refusal to film Vasilii Shukshin's project on the Cossack leader Stepan Razin in the late 1960s. The script contained too much violence and the figure of Razin himself was too elemental and spontaneous, not the 'full-blooded image of a national hero' that was required (Fomin, 1996, p. 332). Although no film was made, the irony is that Shukshin's script was published in journal form and then as a separate book (Shukshin, 1971).

The history of Russian cinema shows continuities as well as breaks, just as the advent of cinema itself saw many of the cultural, aesthetic and moral indices of the nineteenth-century literary heritage absorbed and integrated. Soviet cinema is no more and the Soviet state, as foreseen in *Aelita*, failed in its experiment to refashion man and society. As George Faraday has demonstrated, Soviet and post-Soviet Russian film-makers continue to see themselves as standard bearers of the intelligentsia, whose roots go back to the nineteenth century, where 'the true artist is defined as someone who refuses to pander to the powers-that-be, but is inspired, rather, by selfless concern for "the people"' (Faraday, 2000, p. 22). Post-Soviet cinema will undoubtedly carry on and develop many, if not most, of the traditions, motifs and themes of its twentieth-century predecessor, as it maintains its search for its true audience.

Filmography

Aelita ('Aelita'), dir. Iakov Protazanov, 1924

FURTHER READING

Beumers, B. (ed.) (1999) *Russia on Reels: The Russian Idea in Post-Soviet Cinema* (I. B. Tauris, London).
A collection of essays, speeches and documentary materials on post-1991 Russian cinema. Some articles discuss individual directors (Astrakhan, Muratova, Sokurov), some look at trends and themes (adaptations, images of leaders, landscape myths).

Christie, I. and Taylor, R. (eds) (1994) *The Film Factory: Russian and Soviet Cinema in Documents, 1896–1939* (Routledge, London and New York).
Invaluable collection of documents on pre-Soviet and the first two decades of Soviet film, presented in a year-by-year layout, richly illustrated with clips from films of the time. It is especially useful for tracing the often fragile relationship of politics and cinema in the Soviet period, with articles and excerpts from speeches and books by directors, cultural figures, critics and politicians. It also contains appendices with factual information of film production and distribution and the films mentioned in the text.

Fomin, V. I. (1996) *Kino i vlast: Sovetskoe kino, 1965–1985 gody* (Materik, Moscow).
Very interesting collection of archival documents, letters, Party resolutions and telegrams relating to the prohibition or restricted distribution of such films as Tarkovskii's *Andrei Rublev* and *Mirror*, Shepitko's *The Ascent*, Klimov's *Agony* and Panfilov's *The Theme*.

Fomin, V. I. (comp.) (1998) *Kinematograf ottepeli. Dokumenty i svidetelstva* (Materik, Moscow).
Of major interest as a collection of documents relating to the Party's generally heavy-handed attitude towards the cinema in the years from the death of Stalin in 1953 to the early 1970s. Worthy of particular attention are the recorded discussions of Tarkovskii's *Andrei Rublev*, Raizman's *And If This Is Love?*, Khutsiev's *Ilich's Gate* and Ermler's *Before the Judgement of History*.

Kenez, P. (1992) *Cinema and Soviet Society, 1917–1953* (Cambridge University Press, Cambridge and New York).
Authoritative and pertinent analysis of the development of Soviet cinema, especially under Stalin, with attention paid to individual films and directors, as well as an overview of the industry itself and how the Party and Stalin used and controlled it.

Lawton, A. (1992) *Kinoglasnost: Soviet Cinema in Our Time* (Cambridge University Press, Cambridge and New York).
Focusing on the intense film activity of the glasnost years, with reference to the late 1980s in particular, this is a richly detailed examination of both the cinema

industry and its audience in late Soviet Russia, with discussion of almost 200 films.

Leyda, J. (1973) *Kino: A History of the Russian and Soviet Film* (George Allen & Unwin, London).
Second edition of the classic account of the history of Russian cinema first published in 1960. Particularly strong on the 1920s and 1930s, it is enlivened by the author's personal insights and observations dating from his own experiences in Soviet Russia in those years.

Taylor, R. (1979) *The Politics of the Soviet Cinema, 1917–1929* (Cambridge University Press, Cambridge and New York).
Seminal account of the relationship between politics and cinema in the early years of Soviet power, culminating in the establishment of Party control.

Woll, J. (2000) *Real Images: Soviet Cinema and the Thaw* (I. B. Tauris, London and New York).
Chronological examination of Soviet film from the death of Stalin to the late 1960s, relating how films reacted to political change and how they reflected changing mores.

Youngblood, D. J. (1992) *Movies for the Masses: Popular Cinema and Soviet Society in the 1920s* (Cambridge University Press, Cambridge and New York).
Analysis of Soviet cinema in its early years that examines the work of otherwise little-known directors, such as Iakov Protazanov and Boris Barnet, with emphasis on films that were intended not as vehicles for political enlightenment, but as entertainment.

Youngblood, D. J. (1999) *The Magic Mirror: Moviemaking in Russia, 1908–1918* (University of Wisconsin Press, Madison and London).
The first real attempt to examine in detail the film industry of the pre-Soviet period, with a detailed analysis of some key films. The book succeeds in locating cinema as a signifier of social change and an indication of the incursions of modernity into what was still a relatively backward-looking society, before the Bolshevik Revolution turned cinema on its head.

BIBLIOGRAPHY

Akhmatova, A. (1998) *Sobranie sochinenii v shesti tomakh* (Ellis Lak, Moscow).

Andrews, M. (1999) *Landscape and Western Art* (Oxford University Press, Oxford and New York).

Attwood, L. (1998) 'Gender Angst in Russian Society and Cinema in the Post-Stalin Era', in Kelly, C. and Shepherd, D. (eds) *Russian Cultural Studies: An Introduction* (Oxford University Press, Oxford and New York), pp. 352–67.

Bakhtin, M. (1981) 'Forms of Time and of the Chronotope in the Novel', in *The Dialogic Imagination. Four Essays*, translated by Caryl Emerson and Michael Holquist (University of Texas Press, Austin).

Bakhtin, M. (1984) *Rabelais and his World*, translated by Hélène Iswolsky (Indiana University Press, Bloomington).

Barthes, R. (1977) *Image, Music, Text*, translated by Stephen Heath (Fontana, London).

Beardow, F. (1997a) 'Soviet Cinema – War Revisited (Part 1)', *Rusistika*, 15, 19–34.

Beardow, F. (1997b) 'Soviet Cinema – War Revisited (Part 2)', *Rusistika*, 16, 8–21.

Beardow, F. (1998) 'Soviet Cinema – War Revisited (Part 3)', *Rusistika*, 17, 11–24.

Beardow, F. (2000a) 'Soviet-Russian Cinema: From Adolescence to Alienation – The Representation of Youth (Part 2)', *Rusistika*, 21, 19–25.

Beardow, F. (2000b), 'Soviet-Russian Cinema: From Adolescence to Alienation – The Representation of Youth (Part 3)', *Rusistika*, 22, 13–26.

Beevor, A. (1999) *Stalingrad* (Penguin Books, London and New York).

Beja, M. (1979) *Film and Literature: An Introduction* (Longman, London and New York).

Bergan, R. (1997) *Eisenstein: A Life in Conflict* (Little, Brown and Company, London).

Bergson, H. (1999) *Laughter: An Essay on the Meaning of the Comic*, translated by Cloudesley Brereton and Fred Rothwell (Green Integer, Copenhagen and Los Angeles).

Bethea, D. (1989) *The Shape of Apocalypse in Modern Russian Literature* (Princeton University Press, Princeton).

Beumers, B. (2000) *Burnt By the Sun* (I. B. Tauris, London and New York).

Boardman, J. (1986) 'Greek Art and Architecture', in Boardman, J., Murray, O. and Griffin, J. (eds), *The Oxford History of the Classical World* (Oxford University Press, Oxford).

Bodrov, S. (1996a) 'Ne tolko o chechenskoi voine', *Literaturnaia gazeta*, 7 August, p. 8.

Bodrov, S. (1996b) '"Govoriat, my sdelali anti-russkuiu kartinu"', *Obshchaia gazeta*, 3 July, p. 8.

Brown, Royal S. (1994) *Overtones and Undertones: Reading Film Music* (University of California Press, Berkeley, Los Angeles and London).

Christie, I. and Taylor, R. (eds) (1991) *Inside the Film Factory: New Approaches to Russian and Soviet Cinema* (Routledge, London and New York).

Christie, I. and Taylor, R. (eds) (1994) *The Film Factory: Russian and Soviet Cinema in Documents, 1896–1939* (Routledge, London and New York).

Clark, K. (2000) *The Soviet Novel: History as Ritual*, 3rd edn (Indiana University Press, Bloomington and Indianapolis).

Conquest, R. (1986) *The Harvest of Sorrow: Soviet Collectivization and the Terror–Famine* (Oxford University Press, Oxford and New York).

Dolinskii, I. L. (1969) 'Tridsatye gody', in Zhdan, V. (ed.) *Kratkaia istoriia sovetskogo kino, 1917–1967* (Iskusstvo, Moscow).

Dovzhenko, A. (1967) *Ia prinadlezhu k lageriu poeticheskomu . . .* (Sovetskii pisatel, Moscow).

Eremin, Dm. (1948) 'O konflikte v kinokomedii', *Iskusstvo kino*, 5, 9–12.

Everett, W. (2000) 'Singing our Song: Music, Memory and Myth in Contemporary European Cinema', in Holmes, D. and Smith, A. (eds) *100 years of European Cinema: Entertainment or Ideology?* (Manchester University Press, Manchester and New York).

Faraday, G. (2000) *Revolt of the Filmmakers: The Struggle for Artistic Autonomy and the Fall of the Soviet Film Industry* (Pennsylvania State University Press, University Park, Pennsylvania).

Fomin, V. I. (comp.) (1998) *Kinematograf ottepeli. Dokumenty i svidetelstva* (Materik, Moscow).

Forbes, J. and Street, S. (2000) *European Cinema: An Introduction* (Palgrave, Basingstoke and New York).

Frayling, C. (2000) *Spaghetti Westerns: Cowboys and Europeans from Karl May to Sergio Leone* (I. B. Tauris, London and New York).

Furmanov, D. (1966) *Chapaev* (Detskaia Literatura, Moscow).

Genis, A. (1999) *Dovlatov i okrestnosti* (Vagrius, Moscow).

Gillespie, D. (2000) *Early Soviet Cinema: Innovation, Ideology and Propaganda* (Wallflower Press, London).

Gillespie, D. and Zhuravkina, N. (1996) 'Sergei Bodrov's *A Prisoner in the Caucasus*', *Rusistika*, 14, 56–9.

Givens, J. (1999) 'Vasilii Shukshin and the "Audience of Millions": "Kalina Krasnaia" and the Power of Popular Cinema', *The Russian Review*, 58, 2, 268–85.

Gladilin, A. (1979) *The Making and Unmaking of a Soviet Writer: My Story of the 'Young Prose' of the Sixties and After*, translated by David Lapeza (Ardis, Ann Arbor).

Graffy, J. (1998) 'Soldier, Soldier', *Sight and Sound*, 3, 34–5.

Graffy, J. (1999) 'Dmitri Astrakhan: A Popular Cinema for a Time of Uncertainty', in Beumers (1999).

Gray, C. (1986) *The Russian Experiment in Art, 1863–1922*, revised and enlarged edition (Thames & Hudson, London).

Haynes, J. (2000) 'Brothers in Arms: The Changing Face of the Soviet Soldier in Stalinist Cinema', *Modern Language Review*, 95, 1, 154–67.

Heldt, B. (1987) *Terrible Perfection: Women and Russian Literature* (Indiana University Press, Bloomington and Indianapolis).

Holmes, D. and Smith, A. (eds) (2000) *100 Years of European Cinema: Entertainment or Ideology?* (Manchester University Press, Manchester and New York).

Hosking, G. (1980) *Beyond Socialist Realism: Soviet Fiction since 'Ivan Denisovich'* (Paul Elek and Granada, London).

Hosking, G. (1985) *A History of the Soviet Union* (Fontana/Collins, London).

Hutchings, S. C. (2000) 'Word and Image in El'dar Riazanov's "S legkim parom". Or, The Irony of (Cinematic) Fate', *Essays in Poetics*, 25, 236–55.

Iukhtman, A. S. (comp.) (2000) *Ia khochu, chtoby pesni zvuchali: Zastolnye pesni* (Folio, Feniks and Abris, Kharkov, Rostov-on-Don, Kiev).

Iurenev, R. (1964) *Sovetskaia kinokomediia* (Nauka, Moscow).

Iurenev, R. (1976) 'Kinoiskusstvo voennykh let', in M.P. Kim (ed.) *Sovetskaia kultura v gody velikoi otechestvennoi voiny* (Nauka, Moscow), 235–51.

Johnson, V. T. and Petrie, D. (1994) *The Films of Andrei Tarkovsky: A Visual Fugue* (Indiana University Press, Bloomington and Indianapolis).

Jones, W. G. (1998) 'Politics', in Jones, M. and Feuer Miller, R. (eds) *The Cambridge Companion to the Classic Russian Novel*, (Cambridge University Press, Cambridge and New York), 63–85.

Kenez, P. (1992) *Cinema and Soviet Society, 1917–1953* (Cambridge University Press, Cambridge and New York).

Kheifits, I. (1966) *O kino* (Iskusstvo, Leningrad and Moscow).

Khrushchev, N. S. (1957) *Za tesnuiu sviaz iskusstva s zhizniu naroda* (Politizdat, Moscow).

Kim, M. P. (ed.) (1976) *Sovetskaia kultura v gody velikoi otechestvennoi voiny* (Nauka, Moscow).

Kornienko, N. (1975) *Kino sovetskoi Ukrainy: Stranitsy istorii* (Iskusstvo, Moscow).

Kozintsev, G. (1983) *Sobranie sochinenii v piati tomakh* (Iskusstvo, Leningrad).

Kuleshov, L. and Khokhlova, A. (1975) *50 let v kino* (Iskusstvo, Moscow).

Lawton, A. (1992) *Kinoglasnost: Soviet Cinema in Our Time* (Cambridge University Press, Cambridge and New York).

Layton, S. (1994) *Russian Literature and Empire: Conquest of the Caucasus from Pushkin to Tolstoy* (Cambridge University Press, Cambridge and New York).

Lenin, V. I. (1981) 'The Military Programme of the Proletarian Revolution', in *Collected Works: Volume 23, August 1916–March 1917* (Progress and Lawrence & Wishart, Moscow and London).

Likhachev, D. (1987) 'Smekh v drevnei Rusi', in *Izbrannye raboty v trekh tomakh* (Khudozhestvennaia Literatura, Leningrad), III, 343–417.

Lipatov, V. (1978) 'Povest bez nazvaniia, siuzheta i kontsa', *Novyi mir*, 4–6, 4–55, 118–85, 153–92.

Lunacharskii, A. (1924) *Teatr i revoliutsiia* (Moscow).

McFarlane, B. (1996) *Novel to Film: An Introduction to the Theory of Adaptation* (Clarendon Press, Oxford).

Mariamov, G. (1992) *Kremlevskii tsenzor: Stalin smotrit kino* (Kinotsentr, Moscow).

Mawdsley, E. (1987) *The Russian Civil War* (Allen & Unwin, Boston).

Mayne, J. (1989) *Kino and the Woman Question: Feminism and Soviet Silent Film* (Ohio State University Press, Columbus).

Mitta, A. (2000) *Kino mezhdu adom i raem (kino po Eizenshteinu, Chekhovu, Shekspiru, Kurosave, Fellini, Khichkoku, Tarkovskomu . . .)* (Podkova, Moscow).

Mordiukova, N. (1998) *Ne plach, kazachka!* (Olimp, Moscow).

Nove, A. (1982) *An Economic History of the USSR*, revised edition (Penguin, Harmondsworth).

Orwell, G. (1954) *Nineteen Eight-Four* (Penguin, Harmondsworth).

Parfenov, L. A. (comp.) (1999) *Zhivye golosa kino: Govoriat vydaiushchiesia mastera otechestvennogo kinoiskusstva (30-e–40-e gody). Iz neopublikovannogo* (Belyi bereg, Moscow).

Parthé, K. (1992) *Russian Village Prose: The Radiant Past* (Princeton University Press, Princeton).

Pasternak, B. (1992) *Doctor Zhivago*, translated by Max Hayward and Manya Harari (Harvill Press, London).

Pritulenko, V. (1996) 'Svoimi slovami', *Iskusstvo kino*, 9, 65–71.

Rasputin, V. (1984) 'Proshchanie s Materoi', in *Izbrannye proizvedeniia v dvukh tomakh* (Molodaia Gvardiia, Moscow), II, 201–380.

Richardson, R. (1969) *Literature and Film* (University of Indiana Press, Bloomington and Indianapolis).

Rifkin, B. (1993) 'The Christian Subtext in Bykov's *Čučelo*', *Slavic and East European Journal*, 37, 2, 178–93.

Roberts, G. (1991) 'Esfir Shub: A Suitable Case for Treatment', *Historical Journal of Film, Radio and Television*, 11, 2, 149–59.

Roberts, G. (1999) 'The Meaning of Death: Kira Muratova's Cinema of the Absurd', in Beumers, B. (ed.) (1999), 44–60.

Roberts, G. (2000) *The Man with the Movie Camera* (I. B. Tauris, London and New York).

Room, A. (1994) 'Cinema and Theatre', in Christie and Taylor (1994).

Schama, S. (1995) *Landscape and Memory* (Fontana, London).

Shilova, I. (1993) . . . *I moe kino* (Kinovedcheskie Zapiski, Moscow).

Shukshin, V. (1971) 'Ia prishel dat vam voliu', *Sibirskie ogni*, 1–2, 3–95, 3–122; (1974); *Ia prishel dat vam voliu* (Sovetskii Pisatel, Moscow).

Shumiatskii, B. (1994) 'A Cinema for the Millions', in Christie and Taylor (1994).

Solzhenitsyn, A. I. (1975) *The Gulag Archipelago 2. 1918–1956. Parts III–IV*, translated by Thomas P. Whitney (Collins/Fontana, London).

Sorlin, P. (1980) *The Film in History: Restaging the Past* (Barnes & Noble, Totowa, New Jersey).

Stites, R. (1991) 'Soviet Movies for the Masses and for Historians', *Historical Journal of Film, Radio and Television*, 11, 3, 243–52.

Surkov A. (1965) *Sobranie sochinenii v chetyrekh tomakh* (Khudozhestvennaia Literatura, Moscow).

Synessios, N. (2001) *Mirror* (I. B. Tauris, London and New York).

Tarkovsky, A. (1991) *Sculpting in Time: Reflections on the Cinema*, translated by Kitty Hunter-Blair (University of Texas Press, Austin).

Taylor, R. (1979) *The Politics of the Soviet Cinema, 1917–1929* (Cambridge University Press, Cambridge and New York).

Taylor, R. (1999) 'Singing on the Steppes for Stalin: Ivan Pyr'ev and the Kolkhoz Musical in Soviet Cinema', *Slavic Review*, 58, 143–59.

Taylor, R. (2000) *The Battleship Potemkin* (I. B. Tauris, London and New York).

Taylor, R. (ed.) (1998) *The Eisenstein Reader* (BFI, London).

Taylor, R. and Spring, D. (eds) (1993) *Stalinism and Soviet Cinema* (Routledge, London and New York).

Taylor, R., Wood, N., Graffy, J. and Iordanova, D. (eds) (2000) *The BFI Companion to Eastern European and Russian Cinema* (BFI, London).

Tolstoi, L. (1960) *The Cossacks; Happy Ever After; The Death of Ivan Ilyich*, translated by Rosemary Edmonds (Penguin, Harmondsworth).

Tolstoi, L. (1977) *Anna Karenina*, translated by Rosemary Edmonds (Penguin, Harmondsworth).

Troianovskii, V. (ed.) (1996) *Kinematograf ottepeli. Kniga pervaia* (Materik, Moscow).

Turovskaya, M. (1993) 'The Tastes of Soviet Moviegoers during the 1930s', in Lahusen, T. and Kuperman, G. (eds) *Late Soviet Culture: From Perestroika to Novostroika* (Duke University Press, Durham and London), 95–107.

Vlasov, M. P. (1970) *Sovetskaia kinokomediia segodnia* (Znanie, Moscow).

Wells, D. N. (1996) *Anna Akhmatova: Her Poetry* (Berg, Oxford and Washington).

Youngblood, D. J. (1999) *The Magic Mirror: Moviemaking in Russia, 1908–1918* (University of Wisconsin Press, Madison and London).

Zemlianukhin, S. and Segida, M. (1996) *Domashniaia sinematika. Otechestvennoe kino, 1918–1996* (Dubl-D, Moscow).

Zemlianukhin, S. and Segida, M. (2001) *Filmy Rossii: Igrovoe kino, 1995–2000* (Dubl-D, Moscow).

Websites

The websites listed here are available in both Russian and English, with the exception of the last one.

www.museikino.ru
A large site about the Moscow Cinema Museum, with an account of its manuscript holdings, library facilities and exhibitions.

www.film.ru
A large site with lots of links, containing film news and reviews of the latest films. Tends to favour foreign films, especially those from Hollywood.

www.miff.ru
Contains the programme of the annual Moscow Film Festival.

www.ntvprofit.ru
The largest and best site for news of the latest Russian films, with an archive going back to 1997. Also contains detailed filmographies of the leading actors, actresses and directors, with reports of films currently under production.

www.kinoizm.ru
Interesting site that provides an insight into the films Russians themselves watch (usually Hollywood blockbusters), with news of recent films and stars (in Russian only).

Journals

Iskusstvo kino
Serious monthly journal with emphasis on world cinema, but regular features on latest Russian releases and directors (website: www.kinoart.ru).

Kinovedcheskie zapiski

Irregular but serious publication with emphasis on Russian and Soviet cinematic history, usually with publication of original documents or archival materials (website: www.museikino.ru).

INDEX